Cast out of bronze and awarded for conspicuous gallantry, pre-eminent valour and acts of self-sacrifice under enemy fire, the Victoria Cross is the highest military decoration in the former British Empire and today's British Commonwealth. Fewer than 1400 VCs have been awarded in the past 150 years. The high eligibility threshold makes it extraordinarily difficult to win one.
To win two is almost unheard of.

Searching for
CHARLIE

In pursuit of the real
Charles Upham VC & Bar

TOM SCOTT

upstart press

A catalogue record for this book is available from the National Library of New Zealand

ISBN 978-1-988516-60-8

An Upstart Press Book
Published in 2020 by Upstart Press Ltd
Level 6, BDO Tower, 19–21 Como St, Takapuna
Auckland 0622, New Zealand

Designed by Nick Turzynski/Redinc. Book Design, www.redinc.co.nz
Cover illustration by Mardo El-Noor
Jacket and front endpaper photos: Charles Upham's VC & Bar and Group. Credit: National
Army Museum Te Mata Toa, Waiouru
Back endpaper photo: Charles Upham statue, Amberley, North Canterbury, New Zealand.
Credit: Tom Scott
Printed by Everbest Printing Co. Ltd, China

Contents

Author's note

I walked hill trails to Mt Everest, had afternoon tea with the Dalai Lama's spiritual advisor in a remote Nepalese monastery on the border with Tibet, interviewed Sir Edmund Hillary at the South Pole for a television documentary, traded emails with the first man on the moon, Neil Armstrong, about appearing in another documentary about Ed (they were friends and, after a lot of equivocation, he eventually declined to participate).

I attended the UN General Assembly with two New Zealand prime ministers, dined with Indira Gandhi at Hyderabad House in Delhi, and enjoyed hefty gin and tonics on the royal yacht *Britannia* and wrote this book solely because my father met a bunch of New Zealanders in a Munich bar after the war who were cut from the same cloth as Charlie Upham.

My father was in the Bavarian capital serving in the RAF as part of the Allied Forces of Occupation and remembered the New Zealand troops fondly. 'They were big raw-boned bastards who wore shorts in all sorts of weather and didn't lord it over the locals like some of the other occupation troops.' He was in a bar one night when a barman refused to serve a Maori soldier, saying that they didn't serve monkeys. Even fifteen years later, my father's Northern Irish brogue danced and his eyes lit up with delight recounting what happened next: 'He wanted to let it go, but his Pakeha mates took exception and tore the place apart — completely wrecked the joint — and when British Military Policemen came running to restore order in their distinctive helmets and white puttees, waving their long batons and blowing their whistles, the Kiwis kicked the snot out of them as well. Then, as casual as you like, they strolled next door and ordered another round. Jesus, it was impressive!'

It was straight out of the Charlie Upham playbook — bullying and bullies needed to be confronted and challenged head on. Intolerance would not be tolerated. Mad dogs needed to be shot!

The New Zealanders' egalitarian instincts, disgust with racism and casual disdain for authority appealed to my father. He wanted to be on that team. When his tour was over, he went to the New Zealand High Commission in London and enlisted in the Royal New Zealand Air Force.

Once the paperwork was finalised, he set sail for New Zealand and was posted to Ohakea Air Force Base in the Manawatu in New Zealand's lower North Island. A year later when our paperwork was sorted, my mother Joan, my twin sister Sue and I set sail to join him.

This book is dedicated to the New Zealand soldiers who so impressed my father. I did not grow up in Belfast, Bristol or Birmingham, and so was not denied the freedoms, privileges, advantages and opportunities that life in Aotearoa has afforded me. Thank you, Charlie, and every Kiwi soldier, sailor, airman, doctor, nurse and chaplain who journeyed from the bottom of the world to help rid the world of a monstrous evil.

Tom Scott
Wellington

Prologue

Wind beats heavy on the borderline between tussock and scree. Swirling snowflakes dance past two black circles. A dropping jaw reveals a flash of pink.

A newborn lamb bleats. Her dead mother is vanishing beneath a carpet of white. A rider is approaching, dogs begin to howl. Hat pulled low, pipe clenched upside between his teeth, he nudges his mare up a rocky slope, dismounting when it becomes too steep. Darting nimbly between boulder and tussock, he reaches the shivering lamb. Cleaning mucus from its nostrils, he tucks it inside his jacket. He whistles to his dogs and waiting mare. The ewe that he thought was dead gurgles. Pink bubbles blister her lips. He takes out the knife sheathed at his waist and with a single swift stroke cuts her throat. Arterial blood spurts across pristine snow. Taking off his hat, he nods his head, marvelling at the mysterious line between life and death that all living things fight furiously to avoid crossing.

As he heads back across a high saddle, the snow turns to stinging rain. Eagle-eyed, he spots a distressed ewe nuzzling a dead lamb. He dismounts, pulling his knife from his belt. Unhappy and agitated, the ewe circles as he deftly skins her lamb and fashions the bloody pelt into a woolly overcoat for the orphan wriggling inside his jacket. It fits snugly. The ewe sniffs the imposter cautiously. He'll stick around a bit to see if the fraud works.

He presses fresh tobacco into his pipe. His mare and dogs shelter from the storm in the lee of a large outcrop of rock and look on with idle curiosity. Maternal longing eventually overwhelms suspicion and the ewe lets the lamb suckle. His handsome face lights up in a smile. It's craggy like a sackful of chisels. He is not yet twenty-six but looks older. He is joined silently by his dogs. He is wet through to the skin, so saturated he could be swimming. He could sleep rough in these clothes if he had to. Caught too far from a hut after dark, sometimes he'd done just that. Besides, the rain had eased off. It was light rain now. Dry rain he called it. Not many understood the concept. Meteorologists didn't. But he'd had a blazing row or two in smoko rooms and public bars over this paradox. Only another shepherd or musterer understood the notion, and he suspected many of them only agreed with him for the sake of a quiet life. 'Stuff 'em!' he grins.

Back in the cobb hut, he lights the cast-iron stove. Thick walls made from a mixture of clay, tussock and manure provide excellent insulation. Every stockman, fencer and rabbiter in this neck of the woods will tell you these huts have good hats and dry feet. You can't ask for more than that. He throws dried peas, whole onions and curry powder into a pot of disgusting cold, grey, congealed mutton stew to freshen it. His dogs creep nearer in anticipation of leftovers. There will be plenty. All a man really needs is two feeds a day and a warm, dry place to sleep. This is his mantra. Not that he would call it that. He just says it often.

Overhead the skies clear. His guts rumble. He is busting for what a Maori shearer mate calls a cave-in. He won't be incorporating that into his vocabulary. His prim mother finds his new vernacular shocking enough as it is. He heads out to the long-drop under heavens milky with stars. A long trail of leaping flame turns his hurricane lamp into an Olympic torch. The glass globe went west yonks ago. Up here toilet paper comes in two brands: *Weekly News* and *The Press* nailed to the wall in thick wads. A headline dated 16 September 1935 catches his cobalt-blue eyes. In the gloom they blaze with a laser-like intensity:

NUREMBERG LAWS PASSED
GERMANY BANS MARRIAGE TO JEWS
The two Nuremberg Laws were unanimously passed by the Reichstag on 15 September 1935. The Law for the Protection of German Blood and German Honour prohibited marriages and extramarital intercourse between Jews and Germans, and forbade the employment of German females under 45 in Jewish households. Only those of German or related blood were eligible to be Reich citizens.

'Bastards! Filthy, bigoted sons of bitches!'

His voice carries surprisingly long distances, especially at night. Inside, his dogs prick up their ears then sink lower into the rammed-earth floor. They recognise this molten fury. You don't want to be on the receiving end of it. They creep closer to the fire and hope it will pass soon. It usually does.

Chapter 1

'You face difficulty here'

When I was in sixth form at Feilding Agricultural High School two books were passed hand to hand, from boy to boy, that year. They could not have been more different, yet they had much the same effect on adolescent males.

The books were read furtively at night, and the next morning eyes were bloodshot from lack of sleep. Some boys stammered, most were ashen. One of the books was *Memoirs of a Woman of Pleasure*, popularly known as *Fanny Hill*, by John Cleland, the other, *Mark of the Lion* by Ken Sandford. Both were impossible to put down. I can't recall the cover of the eighteenth-century erotic novel — it may have been removed for purposes of camouflage — but I remember the impact that the cover of *Mark of the Lion* made on me. It was burnt orange, black and grey, a striking combination well ahead of its time for a New Zealand publication in the 1960s when woodcuts of fern and watercolours of woolsheds were compulsory. On the top left in silhouette a Victoria Cross blazed like a supernova. A handsome man in a battle jacket dominated the rest of the cover. A steel helmet draped in camouflage netting cast shade over chiselled cheeks. Deep in shadow, his eyes were out of reach, but something — possibly amusement, possibly menace — gleamed within. His mouth was wide and sensual with a top lip shaped like

Michelangelo's *David*, reinforcing the impression that this face had been sculpted out of stone. It was the face of a hero from Central Casting. It belonged to Captain Charles Hazlitt Upham VC & Bar. The author was Ken Sandford, a Hamilton lawyer few people had heard of and writer of crime thrillers that few people read.

Mark of the Lion arrived at the height of my war-comic frenzy and I read it from cover to cover in one sitting, from dusk to dawn. It was visceral, moving and gripping. I was left awestruck, thunderstruck and dumbstruck all at once. Discovering that true stories could be more extraordinary than comic-book fiction was a revelation. Retracing Charlie's footsteps across North Africa, Greece and Europe, I carried a disintegrating copy of *Mark of the Lion* with me at all times, much like every driver of every battered cab I caught in Cairo carried a copy of the Koran in silk shawls on their dashboards. My holy book was tucked alongside my wallet and passport deep inside my R.M. Williams shoulder bag, which never left my side the whole time except when I was in the shower — even then with great reluctance and always in line of sight.

Despite this separation anxiety I have not treated the book with the respect it deserves. The cover is falling apart, every second page is smeared with yellow highlighter and I have scribbled copious notes in the margins. Few people would do that to their copies of the Koran, Torah, Gita, Bible, Book of Mormon or Donald Trump's *The Art of the Deal*.

In the 1950s books about the war began surfacing and selling in stupendous numbers. The story of the only combat soldier to win two VCs was a pot of gold at the end of the rainbow for some lucky author. Like it or not, with or without his permission, Charlie's untold story was going to be told. It was just a question of when and by whom. Sandford says the idea came to him when he was in London and met the Australian author Paul Brickhill, whose recently published *Reach for the Sky* about the legless RAF fighter-ace and war hero, Douglas Bader, was selling by the truckload. It got Sandford thinking that he should attempt a war story. Back home he gave it more thought: 'I searched for a while to find a suitable subject — then it belatedly dawned on me that the war's greatest hero, Charles Upham, was already here in New Zealand.'

He made enquiries and heard that other writers, including well-known authors, had approached Charlie and had been politely but firmly turned down. Sandford also heard that Charlie would do anything for Major General Sir Howard Kippenberger, one of his wartime commanders, so he travelled to Wellington to talk personally with the then editor-in-chief of the War History Branch of the Department of Internal Affairs, responsible for New Zealand's official war histories.

Kippenberger was frank:

> It would be a difficult book to write. Infantry fighting is a hard, brutal business. Still, if you think you can do it, I am willing to help. Your best chance would be to get material from the numerous people who knew him during the war, but most of them would give you very little help unless you had Upham's agreement. You face difficulty here.

Sandford asked how he could overcome this hurdle. Kippenberger replied that Charlie would do it if he asked him to. He would write to Charlie on Sandford's behalf. Leaving nothing to chance, Sandford wrote a deliberately vague letter to Charlie followed up by a long-distance phone call. Toll calls were a radical gesture in those days. If nothing else, it showed that Sandford was deadly serious. Charlie expressed disbelief that Sandford would want to travel 600 miles south to talk to him about 'some book'. When they met, Sandford was impressed with Charlie's friendly casualness, the interest Charlie took in him personally, his strong face, his mop of greying hair and the most striking eyes he had ever seen; 'Everyone talks of his eyes — they see right through you.'

After that first meeting, Sandford left Charlie mulling over the idea of a book about the New Zealand infantryman, with himself as the central character. 'He didn't like that last bit.' Meantime, as promised, Kippenberger wrote to Charlie as well: 'I have met this chap Sandford, who wants to write your biography and I think you can trust him to tell the story without exaggeration. I'd like you to agree.'

It clinched the deal. Sandford paid a second visit to the remote farm, where Charlie lived with his wife, Molly. The two men shook hands. Sandford was now Charlie's official biographer. News that Charlie had entrusted his biography to an obscure, dabbling writer of crime fiction came as a shock to established New Zealand writers who fancied their chances. One or two had boasted privately that the book was as good as theirs, and they had to lie down in darkened rooms.

Sandford stayed a week, helping in the woolshed and around the farm during the day, and poring over photos and letters and talking with Charlie late into the night. It was a thrilling but ultimately exasperating experience. Charlie would not countenance any conversation about himself. Instead he talked openly with pride and affection about the bravery of his men in battle and the ingenuity of his friends in various POW camps. Sandford jotted down their names. One evening, weary with deflecting questions about himself, Charlie told Sandford it would be best if he forgot the whole thing. Sandford pretended he hadn't heard.

On the last day, at the junction of Conway Flat Road and the main highway, just as the bus that would take Sandford to Christchurch was slowing to a halt, Charlie turned to him anxiously: 'When you write the book, if you put anything in about me, call me by some other name — like Jack Smith or Joe Doaks. Don't mention me!' Stepping onto the bus, Sandford replied, 'No, Charles. I can't do that. We can't have a true story with an imaginary central character.' As the bus pulled away, he waved to Charlie from a window. Standing by his Land Rover, the war hero looked stricken.

Armed with his list, Sandford made two tours over dusty roads around the South Island talking at length to members of Charlie's battalion. Inevitably, people remembered events in different ways. Months of correspondence began, comparing, checking and double-checking stories until a version of an event was drawn up that had the weight of evidence behind it. The trial lawyer was back in his element. Locked and loaded, Sandford returned to Conway Flat.

'By this time, I knew where he had been at various times during the war. For example, I'd say to him, "That night the battalion attacked at Maleme — what was your role?"'

Charlie had no choice but to help make the book as accurate as human memory would allow. The first draft of the finished manuscript was vetted by the War History Branch and corrected where deemed necessary. Sandford paid a final visit to the farm with this version. He stayed for a week in the guest room:

> We picnicked on the beach, travelled in his Land Rover to the nearest settlements, or to the local pictures in the school hall, and in office hours went through the manuscript page by page. 'This is what they tell me, Charles. Is it true or false?' He demanded my sources of information for this and that, and insisted that some passages be deleted. Which they were. I'm sure these sessions were a great trial to him, but Molly's tact helped us through. He was in a sense resigned to the inevitability of the book.

Sandford was not a historian, nor had he served any apprenticeship in journalism. He was a complete novice at this sort of writing, but he had confidence in his own ability and backed by Charlie, albeit reluctantly, he wrote a remarkable biography. He was prone to purple passages, fell short on historical context, was light on battlefield choreography, skirted over some parts of Charlie's life and made the odd glaring error — Charlie was not knighted, for example — but it mattered little in his robust, vivid telling.

It's a tribute to Sandford that no other biography of Charlie has been written. The lives of great heroes are seldom confined to a single tome. New Zealand's other great hero, Sir Edmund Hillary, has had three major biographies written about him, and he wrote multiple action-packed, muscular biographies about himself. In his autumn years he asked me to assist him with the final fly-past of his rich life, *View from the Summit*. My job was to insert the broken-glass moments that time had worn smooth in his memory. I relished writing the chapters covering his and Tenzing's historic first ascent of Everest. Ed was never boastful, but at the same time he knew down to the last Higgs boson particle exactly how much he had accomplished. When he downplayed his achievements, a degree of finely calibrated self-effacement was in play. Charlie in contrast was locked into a defiant, bewildered, almost pathological modesty. He didn't downplay his achievements so much as wish vehemently that they would go away.

§

Ken Sandford wore many hats, all of them at a rakish angle. In every photograph I've seen he is a snappy dresser with an impish smile. Slightly built like Charlie, handsome like Charlie, he looks cuddly and approachable — which is where the physical similarity ends. There was something about Charlie that made people keep their distance. A *Weekly News* profile of Charlie's biographer was headlined: 'Ken Sandford is a Man who Gets Things Done'. He was senior partner in a Hamilton law firm and a Crown Solicitor in the city for many years. He served as President of the New Zealand Cricket Council and took promising young cricketers on overseas tours.

Mark of the Lion was the result of a stern rebuke from his doctor. Suffering from stress and exhaustion, he was ordered to take up a relaxing hobby. 'Would writing another book do?' asked Sandford meekly. 'Certainly,' said his doctor, never imagining his patient would embark on a five-year odyssey involving extensive travel and countless hours pounding a typewriter.

Sandford's son Roger, a lawyer with several crime thrillers of his own under the mattress waiting to take the world by storm, had copies of his father's novels, *Dead Reckoning* and *Dead Secret*, along with cricketing scrapbooks, laid out on the dining room table for me when I arrived at his comfortable Cashmere Hills home overlooking Christchurch. Pleading a shot amidships by Admiral Alzheimer, he apologised for not being able to find a box containing the first draft of *Mark of the Lion*, assuring me that it would surface and be dispatched north. He was as good as his word.

§

Reading Charlie's letters, I noted that some included the Maori salutation 'Kia ora', a common enough nod at the time to being a New Zealander by those in the services abroad. But it is not what I expected from a farmer in deeply conservative rural New Zealand in the 1950s.

I should not have been surprised. Charlie loved the earthy humour and warrior spirit of the Maori Battalion. He wasn't alone. In his memoir *Regular Soldier*, Colonel Frank Rennie describes an early example of their enthusiasm:

> Halfway through training there was a long weekend leave
> to allow everyone to get home. It wasn't very sensible
> of us to have issued two battledresses to them before

they departed. I had a real problem when they returned because when I called the roll I had 160 instead of 146, all in battledress, all looking like soldiers. When I checked names and there was an overlap, I was told there was confusion over their Maori and Pakeha names. I was getting nowhere. I had the answer. There were only 146 beds, so I chased them off and told them to lie on the beds. I went over and I found 14 lying under the beds. It was clear what had happened. When the trainees arrived home older brothers and cousins wanted to be in so they'd drilled each other, dressed each other and turned up at Trentham.

Relatives and cousins deserted civilian life to smuggle themselves into the army. There is a beautiful boutique museum in Gisborne dedicated to C Company of Maori Battalion. Charlie's youngest daughter, Caroline, and her husband, Marty Reynolds, took me there. The letters on display are heartbreaking, like this distraught husband writing to his wife:

What a terrible thing war is. How miss-fitting in the scheme of God's Universe . . . In the midst of war we have no time to preach philosophy or for fine feelings . . . We must be ruthless. We must kill, we must shoot the Hun first or he'll get us. We must win the war and then talk of beautiful things . . .

It was addressed to 'Dearest sweetheart' and signed off 'Arohanui, ever yours always. Peter'. Arapeta ('Peter') Awatere. The decorated soldier, much admired city councillor and respected Maori elder who stabbed to death the lover of the woman with whom he'd been having an affair. In prison he started haka groups and taught young Maori their language, and introduced them to their culture, restoring his mana as he built theirs. Tragically, he died on the eve of his release.

One wall of the museum is dedicated to photographs of

East Coast meeting houses including Kaiuku Marae on the wild and remote Mahia Peninsula. Charlie loved recounting the time he and the military attaché at the British High Commission in Wellington were invited there as Anzac Day guests. After a few beers and a serving of meat pies, some of which went flying across the hall, the RAF officer in full military plumage, scrambled-egg spilling across his shoulders, a paint colour-chart spreading across his chest, a ceremonial sabre dangling from a sash at his waist, and quite possibly mince in his hair, rose and gave a tedious speech, closing gamely with, 'I don't know what else I can tell you gallant gentlemen. I'll take your questions?' A voice came from the back of the hall: 'Bro, what use is a fucken sword in a Spitfire?'

Charlie's affection for the Maori Battalion notwithstanding, the whole war was fuelled by racism. Nazi ideology divided the world into competing superior and inferior 'races'. Their hatred of Jews and Slavs led to the slaughter of innocent millions whose only crime was the wrong DNA. The Japanese considered themselves a master race and treated other Asians with abject cruelty and inhumanity. The prevailing social order meant US troops were largely segregated at home and abroad.

All sides demonised the enemy and resorted to racial stereotypes and epithets. Churchill referred to 'the dull, drilled, docile brutish masses of the Hun soldiers', otherwise known as 'Jerries', 'Fritz', 'Krauts' or 'Boxheads'; the Allies called Italians 'sleazy, yellow-livered Wops', and the Japanese were 'Nips' and 'slit-eyed yellow monkeys'. Even non-belligerents copped it. Egyptians were 'Gypos', while other Arabs were 'Wogs'. Dehumanising an enemy combatant made it easier to squeeze a trigger, hurl a grenade and thrust a bayonet.

Some of Charlie's best mates in POW camps were liberal South African lawyers opposed to the Afrikaner-dominated National Party whose leaders were imprisoned during the war for being openly sympathetic to Nazi Germany. After the war, these politicians came to power on a platform of racial segregation in which, with savage swiftness, bigotry and rank injustice were enshrined in apartheid law. In the winter of 1981, when South Africa still practised apartheid, the Springboks rugby team toured New Zealand, splitting the country down the middle. Rural New Zealand demanded angrily that it must proceed no matter the cost. Urban New Zealand protested vociferously that it wasn't worth the price the country was paying and should be cancelled. Charlie was opposed to the tour. I imagine that sensible people in pubs along his stretch of coast during that unhappy winter stared silently into their beer and kept their pro-tour opinions to themselves when Charlie was in earshot.

He wasn't New Zealand's only VC winner to feel strongly about apartheid-era South Africa. So did Keith Elliott, who became an Anglican minister after the war. As a sergeant in the Western Desert, his battle cry when capture loomed was: 'What'll it be boys, the laager or the bush!' Elliott showed phenomenal courage during the battle for Ruweisat Ridge. Despite being badly wounded, he was instrumental in subduing four enemy posts with bayonet charges, taking one single-handedly. In 1960, at an army reunion, Elliott refused to wear his VC as a protest against Maori players being excluded from the All Blacks team to tour South Africa. At an Anzac Day dawn service in Featherston later that year, he took his medals off and gave them away to the mayor.

I learnt this in a roadside café near Foxton Beach from Massey University military historian and author Professor Glyn Harper. I was en route to the National Army Museum in Waiouru to check out their photo files on Charlie. Glyn is co-author of the authoritative *In the Face of the Enemy: the complete history of the Victoria Cross and New Zealand*. He pointed me to some Upham files in the National Archives that I didn't know about and generously lent me some files of his own where I read an interview with Elliott's son, Doug. He said their father would not talk about his medals, though he remembers one night at home when Keith listened to a radio broadcast at two o'clock in the morning, with fellow VC winners Charles Upham and Jack Hinton, of the All Blacks playing overseas. 'That was the sort of time they would talk about it.' Ken Sandford would have dearly loved to have been a fly on the wall that night.

Roger Sandford has vivid memories of his father tapping away on an old Remington with raised keys before graduating to a semi-electric typewriter. A softer sound emanated from the purpose-built study separated from the family lounge by a curtain. After dinner he would retire to this room, which was lined with books by Hammond Innes, James Hadley Chase and Carter Brown — their adrenalin-drenched prose inspiring his own writing. The curtain would part again at 8.30 when he emerged for supper, consisting of a cup of tea and a gingernut. Then it was back to the keyboard where he worked off dozens of tape recordings made with Charlie. This went on for six years.

Roger remembers visiting his father's law offices shortly after publication and being led around the corner to Hamilton's main drag where his dad pointed shyly across the road to the Whitcombe and Tombs bookstore. A sea of burnt orange and grey filled the front window. It was taken up entirely with displays of *Mark of the Lion*, as if it were the only book for sale in New Zealand, and for a couple of months that was pretty much the case.

In his introduction to the book Sandford thanks Charlie and Molly for their hospitality and the many pleasant hours spent at their fireside 'where Charlie has revealed (perhaps unconsciously at times) the thoughts and feelings that accompanied the deeds of which he is so disinclined to speak'.

Inserted coyly in brackets those two words — 'perhaps unconsciously' — spoke volumes. Sandford had earnt Charlie's trust, no mean achievement, and while this trust was never abused Charlie said more than he intended to say, and once said it could not be unsaid. Charlie had second thoughts about sharing his thoughts and offered Sandford money to forget about writing the book. In a wry aside at the time of publication, Sandford said the only satisfaction Charlie got from the book was the news that the publishers wanted the manuscript reduced by 25 per cent to make it a more economic venture. 'I'm sure he would have been delighted if they had asked for it to be reduced by 100 per cent.'

The two men's intimacy did not extend beyond publication. On occasion Charlie wrote to Sandford: 'It was good to get that cheque.' But that was about it. There was no falling-out. They just went their separate ways and the relationship became polite and businesslike. I put this down to the fact that no one enjoys running into their marriage guidance counsellor at the supermarket; you get disapproving looks if you are with a new partner and even weirder ones if you are still with the old one. Over the years they remained in contact to discuss new editions of the book, possible movie projects and a possible television series. Modest option payments took ages to negotiate. Nothing ever eventuated. But not from want of trying. Tucked inside *Detour: the story of Oflag IVC*, a handsome collection of charcoal drawings and pieces by former Colditz Castle POWs, kindly lent to me by Caroline Upham, was a letter from Guy Nunn, an American film producer who was incarcerated in Colditz with Charlie, thanking her and her husband for their hospitality on a trip to New Zealand:

> No one can really budge Charlie's infantryman's mindset
> about anything, but if any of you can pry him into
> agreeing to production of a film or TV series based on
> MARK OF THE LION we would be extremely grateful.
> His reasons for ducking any further personal adulation
> or memorialisation are perfectly understandable but
> it seems to us, especially with Sam Neill's personal

interest, that there is a great opportunity here to tell
the world of the truly astonishing contributions to the
winning of WW2 of the New Zealand Division.

When it was published by Hutchinson in London in 1962, *Mark of the Lion* became a worldwide best-seller, shifting 5000 copies in America alone. In 1963 it appeared in paperback. Additional paperback editions have been published with different covers at regular intervals ever since. The pot of gold at the end of the rainbow turned into King Solomon's mines, helped in no small measure by glowing reviews. *The Times Literary Supplement* said it was as exciting as anyone could wish for. *The Edinburgh Evening News* said it was a magnificent story. *The Manchester Evening News* called it a stirring tale. *Book of the Month* said the full-blooded character of the man and his comrades exploded across the pages. Reviews at home were also generous, save for a handful of sour blasts. Writing in the *New Zealand Listener* on 30 November 1962, W.E. Murphy complained:

> Charles Upham is an authentic New Zealand hero. A
> biography of him is therefore an important literary event.
> This one is bitterly disappointing and he was ill advised
> to endorse it. I found this book entirely unworthy of its
> subject. Three actions for which Upham was decorated
> — Crete, Minqar Qaim and Ruweisat Ridge — have been
> reduced to cheap melodramas unrecognizable to anyone
> who knows the facts.

W.E. Murphy clearly saw himself as someone who did know the facts, who should have got the gig. The sportswriter and author T.P. McLean, who was also adjutant of 22nd Battalion, dismissed Sandford's best-seller as 'the blood and guts version' of Charlie's life and not what he would have written. *The Times* of London columnist Bernard Levin wearily observed of this school of criticism: 'Some people would criticise the miracle of the loaves and fishes on the grounds that Jesus did not provide slices of lemon and tartare sauce.'

Levin would have applauded the review published in the 8 September 1962 edition of the *New Zealand Herald*, which asked questions that are still relevant:

> The subject of courage holds endless fascination and has been studied in innumerable books. How can comparisons be made between timorous individuals who conquer trivial fears and the bold man unmoved by danger? Where is the boundary between bravery and foolhardiness, between shrewd judgement and good luck? The feats of Charlie Upham were not momentary and unthinking reactions — they extended over days and were repeated numerous times. The author has realised the wish of Charles Upham that the story should be read as a tribute to the men with whom he served. Yet the enigma of Charlie Upham and the qualities that set him so far apart from others remains.

The enigma of Charles Upham gripped me when I first read *Mark of the Lion* and it fascinates me still. Sometimes all you can do with an enigma is measure its dimensions and fix its position in space and time. Astronomers do this with black holes. Then you brighten the background to bring the silhouette into sharper focus. At the very least, this is what I would like to do for Charlie.

Until I read *Mark of the Lion*, my interest in the Second World War had been confined to War Picture Library comics. Commonwealth schoolboys in their millions could purchase four titles a month blissfully unaware that their heroes piloting Spitfires, leaping from Crusader tanks and firing Bren guns were the work of Italian and Spanish artists whose countries were on Nazi Germany's side during the war. When a shy migrant from Liverpool arrived at high school and whispered that his parents had allowed him to bring a trunk of War Picture Library comics with him, a rowdy bunch of us followed him home that afternoon like swarming bees. The trunk took up much of the sun porch that served as his bedroom. There were gasps when he lifted the lid. To us it was a moment akin to Howard Carter opening the coffin of Tutankhamun. With his mum looking on anxiously, he said we could borrow two at a time if we treated them with care.

My favourites were set in North Africa. The rendering of men, munitions and machines was superb. I enjoyed laconic, lantern-jawed Kiwi and Aussie Desert Rats in baggy shorts and wide-brimmed hats taking on the panzer tanks of the Desert Fox, Field Marshal Erwin Rommel. Many years later, the blunt, walking stick-whirling Member of Parliament for Southland, Norm Jones, wrote a terrific memoir about his experiences in North Africa, where he got a leg blown off. He asked me to illustrate the cover. Drawing Norm was easy, but when I tried matching the graphic skills of my war-comic heroes or capturing the spirit of New Zealand war artist Peter McIntyre's charcoal sketches, I fell woefully short.

After putting down *Mark of the Lion* I immediately began picking up other war histories like *Reach for the Sky*, the biography of Battle of Britain hero Douglas Bader. *The White Rabbit* is the biography of a British secret agent, Forest 'Tommy' Yeo-Thomas, who parachuted three times into enemy-occupied France before he was caught and tortured by the Gestapo. *Slaughterhouse-Five* by Kurt Vonnegut describes his experiences as a POW caught in the horrific fire-bombing of Dresden. The forensically detailed and searing *If This is a Man* was written by Auschwitz survivor Primo Levi; the encyclopaedic *Inside the Third Reich* by Hitler's Minister of Armaments and War Production, Albert Speer, who somehow escaped the noose at the Nuremberg war crime trials. Plus, everything published since by Antony Beevor and

Max Hastings. In one of his best short pieces, Woody Allen brilliantly parodied the never-ending tsunami of literature about the Third Reich, in particular the suspiciously detail-rich memoirs of top Nazis who were part of Hitler's inner circle yet claimed to have no knowledge of the Holocaust.

THE SCHMEEL MEMOIRS
The recollections of Hitler's Barber
In the spring of 1940, a large Mercedes pulled up in front of my barbershop at 127 Koenigstrasse, and Hitler walked in. 'I just want a light trim,' he said, 'and don't take too much off the top.' I have been asked if I was aware of the moral implications of what I was doing. As I told the tribunal at Nuremberg, I did not know Hitler was a Nazi. The truth is for years I thought he worked for the phone company. When I finally found out what a monster he was it was too late to do anything as I had made a down payment on some furniture. Once, towards the end of the war, I did contemplate loosening the Führer's neck-napkin and allowing some tiny hairs to get down his back but at the last minute my nerve failed me . . .

There are two war books I always purchase in second-hand bookshops when I happen across them, to give to friends and strangers: *Mark of the Lion* and *Explaining Hitler: the search for the origins of his evil*. The latter by Ron Rosenbaum is a superbly researched, brilliantly written masterpiece, shocking and searing. Rosenbaum:

Before Hitler, we thought we had sounded the depths of human nature. He showed us how much lower we could go, and that's what was so horrifying. It gets us wondering not just at the depths he showed, but whether there is worse to come.

A few years ago in the foyer of the Grand Hyatt in Melbourne, I was having a coffee with the late, great comic genius John Clarke, and I told him that Rosenbaum's book about searching for the origins of Hitler's evil had got me thinking that someone, not necessarily me, should write a book about searching for the origins of Charlie Upham's courage. John flashed his wry, knowing smile. 'You know about Upham's death notice, don't you?'

I didn't. Leaning forward keenly, John told me the Christchurch *Press* had published four death notices for Charlie: one, as you'd expect, from Molly and the girls in memory of a loving husband and devoted father, another from his old chums in the Second Expeditionary Force, a third from the Greek community extending their deepest sympathy, and a fourth from a most unlikely source. John paused for effect, his eyes bright and popping: 'The Germans! They must have known he was crook and they had someone monitoring the situation. Pretty flash, the Germans. I'll send it to you.' He did, and the obituary read:

UPHAM, Charles Hazlitt (VC and Bar)
One of the bravest and one of the best soldiers — in deep respect. Sympathy for family and friends on behalf of the Association of former Afrika Korps, Karl Heinz Boettger (Col. Ret'd), Hamburg. Germany.

Whoa! The Germans put a death notice in a New Zealand newspaper saluting a former foe? How extraordinary is that? It may be without precedent. According to Lieutenant Colonel (Retired) Christopher Pugsley, respected military historian and prolific author, the Afrika Korps and the Fallschirmjäger (Paratrooper) association formed links with Allied ex-servicemen groups at various commemorative reunions over the years, so it may well have happened for others. Exploring the forces responsible for a seemingly bottomless well of courage that even his enemies admired appealed to me.

What happened to Charlie after the war intrigued me as well. How did this painfully shy man manage the rest of his life under the crushing weight of unwanted attention and fame? A great deal about him is a matter of public record. A great deal is not. Clouding and obscuring his story are falsehoods and urban legends. Is it true, for example, that as an old man Charlie stalked the cliff-tops of his Conway Flat farm at night, like mad King Lear on the moor, armed with a .303 rifle and firing wildly out to sea at Japanese squid boats glowing on the horizon? Did he really fly into a rage and order people in German cars off his property? Wikipedia hedges its bets on the latter. Their entry on Charlie reads: 'He obtained a war rehabilitation loan and bought a farm on Conway Flat, Hundalee, North Canterbury. It is said that for the remainder of his life, Upham would allow no German-manufactured machinery or car onto his property.' I have met people over forty who believe this is gospel. I have met people under forty who have never heard of Charlie. This is blasphemy.

An updated adjudication on Charlie would not be such a bad thing. I knew his daughter Amanda would give me pointers and introduce me to the right people. Only a handful of the Second World War generation who served with her father were still alive. By default, any book I wrote would be based on archival sources. No problem. The bulk of the New Testament was written half a century after the crucifixion of Jesus.

§

When I resigned as a syndicated editorial cartoonist for Fairfax newspapers, with my work published daily in half the newspapers in New Zealand, friends my vintage who were finding regular employment of any sort hard to come by wondered to my face if I'd taken leave of my senses. Explaining that I had to get a book about Charlie Upham out

THANKS FOR HAVING ME AT YOUR PLACE FOR A THIRD OF A CENTURY. I'M OFF TO WRITE ABOUT SOME HEROES OF MINE – UNTIL WE MEET AGAIN BE KIND...

TOM SCOTT

My last cartoon for the *Dominion Post* before taking leave to research and write this book. Ripping off Peter McIntyre's evocative, brilliant charcoal sketch proved harder than I expected.

of my system confirmed this: 'You do realise, don't you, that Upham was a psychopath!'

I heard this more and more as I got further into my research. Based solely on hearsay, this forensic conclusion was reached by intelligent people who'd never met him. It was armchair psychiatry. Second-hand armchair psychiatry at that. They'd met someone at a wedding who had met someone on a plane who knew his neighbour. Not being a health professional was not a disqualification. They didn't need Charlie to interpret ink blobs for them or to have him lie down on a couch and pour his heart out. Nor would subjecting him to an MRI scan looking for frontal lobe lesions serve any useful purpose. Not when the proof was blindingly obvious. Upham was a serial killer. Everyone knew that.

True. But Charlie was fighting a war. That's what soldiers do. Kill the enemy. Preferably in large numbers. Furthermore, they argued, Charlie wasn't really brave because he knew no fear. Fearless people aren't brave because true courage involves overcoming fear. So, strictly speaking, he didn't deserve any medals. This is not true. Charlie was fearful many times. Mostly of the unknown. He preferred his risks to be calculated. When he knew the odds, his fear didn't magically vanish, it just seldom got the better of him. Not all the time — when the patient ahead of him in a filthy Italian field hospital in North Africa died in agony after having a mangled leg sliced off by guillotine without the benefit of anaesthetic, Charlie was terrified. Babbling, struggling and protesting loudly, he managed to stop them chopping off his mangled left arm. In doing so, there is no question he saved himself from dying of shock on the operating table.

§

I heard out my disapproving friends as calmly and patiently as I could. I didn't want my indignation to be as knee-jerk as their condemnation. I was pretty confident they were wrong. On and off, I have been researching Charlie's life since the mid-1990s when it first occurred to me, with monstrous presumption on my part, that I was the best person on Planet Earth to make a movie about the double VC hero.

After Charlie's death in 1994, a number of fevered and amateurish attempts to make a film about him failed. Which is a blessing. They would have been dreadful. More recently, more professional endeavours have been mounted. I was briefly involved in one of them. I wrote two drafts and got feverishly excited myself until the producers brought me back to earth with a thump when they hired the award-winning English screenwriter Jeff Pope to write subsequent drafts. They may yet be successful, and I will have to watch it in a lather of envy and resentment.

A German film company, who thought that Hardy Krüger resembled Charlie and could play him, once made tentative enquiries. I don't think this idea was run past Charlie, or if it was the person responsible is probably still running. Charlie's main concerns about any movie were romance and scandal.

He didn't want any of that nonsense, which of course is the heart and soul of most biopics. He wanted final say on every page of any screenplay, to which Hollywood would never have consented. Still, had he been an American or a Brit, a compromise would have been reached and a movie or two would have been shot by now. Chances are that any film made this long after his death will have enough heaving breast and thrusting buttock in it to kill him again.

I knew Ken Sandford's son-in-law, the late Bruce Wallace. He worked in the Parliamentary Press Gallery when I was writing a weekly column on politics for the *New Zealand Listener*. Bruce had assumed control of the Sandford estate. I would need to charm him to get the screen rights to *Mark of the Lion*. Years before, Bruce's first wife, Ken's daughter, died tragically when their baby daughter was tiny. Unable to cope, Bruce gave her up to her maternal grandparents to raise as their own. This may have contributed to the strangely detached, glacial zeal Bruce exuded. He was hard to warm to, and through no fault of his own he bore an uncanny physical resemblance to the Nazi Adolf Eichmann, one of the main organisers of the Holocaust. An unfortunate look for someone handling Charlie's biography.

I courted Bruce for months, buying him coffee and taking him to lunch in Wellington at his favourite cafés on The Terrace just up the road from the Reserve Bank, Treasury, Broadcasting House and Parliament, all of whom he seemed to have mysterious dealings with. He was playing a secretive game with me as well. He really wanted Peter Jackson to direct a movie about Charlie. Eventually, he got to the point and asked me to sound Peter out. But Charlie was a hero in the wrong war for Peter. His grand passion was the First World War, and back then his every waking moment was consumed with filming *The Lord of the Rings*. Peter didn't have time for an Upham project and in short order Bruce didn't have time for me. Everything lapsed and we never met for coffee again. Sadly, he died of cancer in 2007 at just fifty-nine.

Around that time, I laid the movie idea to rest.

Chapter 2

'I think I went around the bend a good bit'

When I talk to people who knew Charlie well, they rubbish the suggestion that he was a psychopath. Taking their assurances at face value just because they had met Charlie in person didn't feel like refutation enough.

It was armchair psychiatry in the reverse direction. More conclusive proof was required. I have a degree in physiology and I worked for a time in a psychiatric hospital as a student volunteer. I appreciated and understood that I needed a second opinion from a higher authority. I did the right thing. I consulted Dr Google and I read *The Psychopath Test* by the best-selling behavioural science writer Jon Ronson. It became very obvious very quickly that Charlie didn't remotely qualify as a psychopath.

Were it posthumously possible to subject Charlie to the gold-standard diagnostic screening test used worldwide to assess psychopathy, the Psychopathy Checklist–Revised, the PCL-R, he would tick a couple of boxes, no question. Most of us would tick some of them at some point in our lives. This doesn't mean the psychologist asking Charlie questions wouldn't be quietly shitting themselves — they would. He had that effect on people.

In his journey through the madness industry, Ronson

commented several times on the unnerving, icy stare of some of the psychopaths he interviewed in high-security prisons. Cold, piercing eyes, however, are not necessarily windows into a skull churning and broiling with murderous rage and, as a consequence, are not on the PCL-R checklist. This checklist, compiled and refined over many years by Robert D. Hare, a former Vancouver prison psychologist, is an inventory of twenty distinct traits that psychopaths typically exhibit. Points are awarded 0, 1 or 2 depending on the strength of the trait. A zero for complete absence. A score of 1 when the trait is present in a mild form, and scoring 2 when it honks like a car-alarm. A total score over 30 would be cause for concern. When the maximum score of 40 is achieved, the psychologist conducting the test is advised to make no sudden movements. Within easy reach on the wall of the prison or psychiatric hospital assessment room there should be a red panic button. This should be pressed as discreetly as possible as soon as is practicable, followed by silent prayer with the eyes held open.

The famous PCL-R checklist follows. I have added my thoughts and my estimated score for Charlie:

ITEM 1: Glibness/superficial charm
Charlie made little effort to be diplomatic. He was described by one neighbour as being the rudest man she had ever met. Dr Fred Moody, who was in Colditz with Charlie, remembers him taking a set against one hapless POW for no good reason, informing him bluntly: 'I don't like your bloody face. Keep away from me!' In the confined quarters of a medieval castle with only one small exercise yard, this was easier said than done. ZERO.

ITEM 2: Grandiose sense of self-worth
Charlie was reserved and hated being singled out for special attention. He had to be ordered by his superior

officers to participate in a radio interview after winning his first VC. The hand-lettered Upham name on the nondescript letterbox at his front gate is definitive proof. Nothing could be further removed from a neon sign. To the distress of his family, this letterbox was stolen within days of Charlie and Molly leaving the farm for the very last time. ZERO.

ITEM 3: Need for stimulation/proneness to boredom

Charlie loved repeating a quote he incorrectly attributed to his favourite author, Mark Twain. 'Sometimes I sits and thinks and sometimes I just sits.' No one needing stimulation or prone to boredom moves to a remote farm at the end of a long metal road on a lonely stretch of Kaikoura coast. ZERO.

ITEM 4: Pathological lying

Charlie was truthful to a fault. If he had been a little less candid, life would have been much easier for him and the people who knew him well. ZERO.

ITEM 5: Cunning/manipulative

Charlie was never devious and seldom scheming, except for when it came to plotting escapes from POW camps. ONE.

ITEM 6: Lack of remorse or guilt

Charlie was seemingly unbothered about the number of Germans he killed in battle, but he had deep regrets about his behaviour behind wire, admitting to Sandford (my emphasis):

I think I went around the bend a good bit when I was in that Italian cellar at Matruh and never really recovered until I had been back in England a few days. *I am not proud but ashamed* of most of my life as a POW. I never accomplished anything and must often have been a damn nuisance to my mates and no help to anyone. Looking back on it all dispassionately, I would never have taken from Jerry a quarter of the things they took from me.

Back in New Zealand after the war, moments of blinding rage continued to occur, but apart from terrifying people no harm was ever done. After calming down, Charlie would pay a visit to his next-door neighbour and close friend, Frank Wilding, to recount the exchanges over a beer or two and ruefully concede that he might have overstepped the mark. ONE.

ITEM 7: Shallow affect
Charlie was not unresponsive or emotionally inert. He was more than capable of showing anger, disgust, joy, sadness and surprise. Nor were his emotions superficial, as anyone who saw him lose his temper will confirm. As for immunity to surprise, Charlie hated being surprised. During the war, however, it's true he didn't show fear even when it was clearly the most mature, sensible and legitimate response to many of the situations in which he found himself. ONE.

ITEM 8: Callousness/lack of empathy
Charlie cared deeply about the safety and welfare of the men under his command. Once, when still just a sergeant, after dusty, energy-sapping desert manoeuvres he threatened to smash up a mobile canteen truck with a pickaxe handle if his platoon were not served hot tea along with their hard rations. He sobbed uncontrollably when he was evacuated from Crete and many good men were left behind to be taken prisoner. He wanted to stay with them but was denied permission. He shared

his water bottle with tied-up German prisoners in the middle of a desert battle under a blazing sun. Friends, neighbours and his children tell me that Charlie was kind and thoughtful, albeit sometimes veiled behind a brusque veneer. ZERO.

ITEM 9: Parasitic lifestyle
Charlie was proudly self-reliant and perfectly content to live a simple, modest life. He often said that all a man needed in life was two feeds a day and a warm, dry place to sleep. ZERO.

ITEM 10: Poor behavioural controls
On several occasions behind wire, Charlie completely lost his temper and physically assaulted German officers, which was absolutely *verboten*. He was extremely fortunate not to have been shot dead on the spot. 'Sometimes I got so bloody angry I didn't care what happened to me' was his sheepish explanation later. TWO.

ITEM 11: Promiscuous sexual behaviour
Charlie was prim, proper and almost Victorian in matters pertaining to the opposite sex. His language when talking to his troops was direct and earthy, except when it came to warning them of the dangers of unprotected sex in the fleshpots of Cairo. He coyly advised them to wear a condom if they felt they must have a 'naughty'. ZERO.

ITEM 12: Early behaviour problems
According to his nanny, young Charlie was a quiet, caring and thoughtful boy. ZERO.

ITEM 13: Lack of realistic long-term goals
Charlie survived the war as a POW in no small measure by planning the farm he wanted, the stock he would run

and the crops he would plant when he returned home.
ZERO.

ITEM 14: Impulsivity
Some of Charlie's escape attempts were spur-of-the-moment acts of near lunacy. He argued that desperate times sometimes call for desperate measures. In the heat of battle, actions that others considered wild and reckless Charlie considered carefully calibrated and finely judged. TWO.

ITEM 15: Irresponsibility
Apart from invariably appearing scruffy on parade, being insubordinate when he thought superior officers had issued orders he considered daft and dangerous, a couple of bouts of drunkenness and losing his pistol, a chargeable offence, Charlie performed his duties as a soldier in an otherwise exemplary fashion. ZERO.

ITEM 16: Failure to accept responsibility for his own actions
Charlie often berated himself for failings both real and imagined. But not always immediately. ONE.

ITEM 17: Many short-term marital relationships
Charlie was devoted to Molly during their long and happy marriage. ZERO.

ITEM 18: Juvenile delinquency
As a boarder at Christ's College in Christchurch, Charlie casually broke many rules, especially those he considered petty and pointless, but his behaviour never came close to delinquency. He didn't shoplift, vandalise property, convert cars, or physically assault or sexually molest people. ZERO.

ITEM 19: Revocation of conditional release
As a POW, Charlie was frequently punished with long spells in solitary confinement for insubordination and attempting to escape, but he never altered or tempered his behaviour in any way as a consequence. TWO.

ITEM 20: Criminal versatility
Charlie was never a criminal, let alone a versatile one. ZERO.

By my reckoning Charlie scores 10 points out of 40. Mother Teresa, the Queen Mother and Oprah would score higher. Charlie's only chance of qualifying as a psychopath would be to miss the test altogether and apply for an aegrotat.

During the war, many of Charlie's fellow soldiers referred to him as 'mad' or 'crazy', but this was after witnessing his fearless feats or insubordination. Charlie was 'mad', but only in the sense of being rash, reckless, impulsive, quick-tempered, rebellious and an irrational risk-taker and rule-breaker.

If Charlie wasn't a psychopath — and he most certainly wasn't — another explanation is needed for the source of his physical and moral courage. I have a theory that involves a relative who gave him a timepiece as a gift.

§

I got my first wristwatch in my late teens and treasured it for years until my Irish gravediggers' arms stretched the strap to breaking point and it dropped unnoticed to the ground, leaving me devastated when I discovered its absence. When the strap on my latest watch, which is solar-powered and will keep running in total darkness for a year, which is strangely comforting to know, snapped recently in Crete, I promptly got it repaired in a coastal village, figuring that locals tilling stony soil and repairing fishing nets would have brawny, powerful forearms. Less than a week later the leather broke when I was tightening it on a flight to Cairo. Worried I might lose it, I promptly tucked it into a zipped pocket inside my R.M. Williams bag for safekeeping.

§

Few things are more personal to a soldier than his watch. They are often a cherished present from a parent, an uncle or an aunt to mark some milestone in their lives. Passing exams, turning twenty-one, getting engaged, heading off to war. Along with identity tags and wedding rings, they rest against the skin. The wearer's blood pulses directly beneath them.

In his wonderful book *Gunner Inglorious*, New Zealander Jim Henderson describes sustaining hideous wounds in battle and being driven back across the Western Desert in a German ambulance by German Red Cross orderlies. He was in great pain. They drove as carefully as they could over the rough terrain so as not to jolt him. Throughout the long gruelling night, the driver stopped at regular intervals to open the rear doors and check on him with a torch. After taking Jim's pulse, he lifted a flask of coffee to his cracked lips, insisting softly that he needed to drink and assuring him that he would be all right. They eventually arrived at an assembly of tents in a dust storm. Sand whipped against Henderson's face as the driver and his assistant hastened him into the shelter. When the driver turned to go, Henderson offered him his only remaining thing of value: 'A prized wristlet-watch, the farewell gift of my mother. He refused. I indicated by signs I wanted him to take it as a present. Again, he shook his head, and, without a word, turned and disappeared into the storm outside.'

In *Mark of the Lion*, Beau Cottrell had the reverse experience when he was wounded and taken prisoner in North Africa. His watch, also a present from his mother, was unstrapped from his wrist by a young German. He did it gently, but the psychological wrench was still jarring. Beau wept as quietly as he could. He was lying in an Axis Powers' field hospital in El Daba, quite possibly the same tent city Jim Henderson fetched up in. It was after the disaster on Ruweisat Ridge, where Charlie was also wounded and taken prisoner. Charlie lay close by, his left elbow smashed. Earlier that day Italian soldiers on a looting spree got short shrift when they reached Charlie's cot. 'Fuck off!' he shouted, and they did.

Beau's suppressed sobs got to Charlie. They had been pupils at Christ's College together. Beau was a couple of years ahead of Charlie, a first-fifteen star and later an All Black. Charlie looked up to him. 'You okay, Beau?' he asked quietly. Beau's weeping got worse. 'Sorry, Charlie. It was a gift from my mother.' Upham swore under his breath and gingerly prised his watch off his throbbing arm. 'Have mine, Beau. Too fucking heavy for me now, anyway.' Beau was aghast. 'No, Charlie. I don't want your watch. You keep your watch. Please!' It was too late. Charlie had wrestled it clear. 'If you don't want the fucking thing, they're not gonna get it!' Charlie flung it at Beau and dropped back onto his cot, exhausted from his painful efforts. The watch landed in the sand beside Beau. 'Thanks, Charlie,' he whispered. There was no response. Charlie had already lapsed into unconsciousness. Beau wore it for the rest of the war, trying several times to return it to Charlie, who bluntly refused to accept it.

Back in New Zealand, Beau worked for a time as a barrister in the Auckland courts where he met and became friends with another young barrister, Ken Sandford. At the end of long, tiring days appearing before learned judges, they threw their horsehair wigs and black gowns onto pegs and raced downhill to pubs like The Occidental in Vulcan Lane for the six o'clock swill. The air was thick with shouting, laughter, cigarette smoke, Brylcreem and Old Spice. As a precaution against the revelry coming to an abrupt halt, tables were forested with full jugs of beer. It was here that Beau told Ken about his experiences behind wire with the most decorated Commonwealth soldier in the war and showed him the watch with the initials CHU on the back.

Learning how it came into Beau's possession was crowning confirmation for Ken that Charlie's story had to be told and that he was just the man to tell it. Roger Sandford believes his father asked Cottrell as well as Kippenberger to put in a good word for him with Charlie. It wouldn't have hurt.

§

Beau's daughter, Anna, a prolific, award-winning documentary filmmaker, who kindly sent me excerpts from her father's meticulously kept war diaries, says her father loved Charlie. Of the watch with CHU engraved on the back, there is no trace. Anna says the Cottrells had a house fire, and her father's memorabilia went up in smoke, a few months after her mother died.

Charlie wouldn't have lost any sleep over it as he demonstrated on his eleventh birthday when he was given a pocket watch by a relative who proudly informed him that it was 'boy proof'. Charlie waited until the adult visitors had gone then took his friends upstairs to witness him conduct a scientific experiment. Leaning out over a balcony, he tossed the watch into the air. Landing on the gravel driveway, it was disembowelled, bleeding cogs and springs. Surveying the entrails, Charlie scoffed at the claim that it was 'boy proof'.

I suppose you could argue, as some of my friends have, that the experiment proved that young Charlie was indifferent to material possessions. I don't buy that. Charlie's experiment proved only one thing to me: he was a spoilt little snot.

§

Charlie's parents lived in a stately, spreading, two-storey colonial home in central Christchurch, a stone's throw from Hagley Park, the Botanic Gardens, the Gothic revival splendour of Canterbury University, the Canterbury Museum and Christ's College. The Upham home was decorated Edwardian style with dark woodwork, high-backed sofas, heavy drapes, brocaded chintz and a tall grandfather clock. It reeked of decorum and gentility. Perfect for the daughter of the manse. Charlie's mum, Agatha, was the daughter of Canon Coates, a man of legendary piety and probity. Charlie's dad, John, wore a top hat at his daughters' weddings. The Uphams had four servants: a cook, maid, nanny and a gardener for the grounds. This was during the Great Depression when some men were reduced to wearing sugar bags and many New Zealanders went hungry. It was a far cry from the modest rehab-loan house on Conway Flat where Charlie would eventually happily raise his own family.

I have no proof, only a suspicion, that the pocket watch that met an untimely end most probably came from his uncle and namesake, Doctor Charles Hazlitt Upham, a much-loved Lyttelton general practitioner. To the end of his days, Uncle Charles dressed as an Edwardian gentleman with matching Edwardian views. He wore tweed jackets with voluminous sleeves over high-buttoned waistcoats with a fob-watch chain dangling across his trim midriff. He firmly believed that a woman's place was in the home. When Charlie and his sister came to stay in the school holidays they ate in the kitchen with his housekeeper while he ate alone in the formal dining room — no doubt regularly checking his fob watch to make sure his niece and nephew's bedtimes were strictly observed.

The gift of a pocket watch rather than a new-fangled wrist-watch sounds like Uncle Charles. If the wilfully destroyed timepiece was a present from his frugal relative, the dressing-down would have been blistering and salutary. Charlie loved and admired his eccentric uncle. Some in the

Upham clan believe the gruff, humble doctor, who relaxed at night by reading the Bible in Greek, had a huge influence on his nephew and was more responsible than anyone else for the powerful magnetic north in Charlie's moral compass.

Uncle Charles was born in Hampstead, London in 1863. He came from a well-to-do, well-connected family. He was a relative of the celebrated portrait painter John Hazlitt, and nephew of the widely quoted essayist, literary critic and social commentator William Hazlitt. His many aphorisms included: 'No really great man ever thought himself so'. Egalitarian principles and a sharp intelligence flowed in the sap of the Hazlitt family tree.

After studying at Christ's Hospital and further studies in France, Uncle Charles completed his training in medicine and surgery at St Bartholomew's Hospital in London, and at the tender age of twenty-three he entered the Royal Navy as a surgeon. At the time of his appointment, he was the youngest staff surgeon in the Navy and at five feet four most probably the shortest as well. Officers and ratings seeking medical treatment for the pox must have feared at first that they were being examined by the cabin boy.

When Charles met Ethel Norbury, the daughter of Sir Henry Norbury, Director General of the Medical Department of the Admiralty, he fell head over heels in love. It was reciprocal. They held hands everywhere, rare in those days, even in church, which was not approved of. In 1896, within months of meeting, they were married in Plymouth. Charles was thirty-two and Ethel was twenty-six.

When he returned to duty as a Royal Navy surgeon aboard the single-funnel, triple-masted sloop HMS *Torch*, they wrote to each other constantly. Charles looked forward to the collection of letters waiting for him at every port of call. One of those ports on the other side of the world was Lyttelton. Struck by the beauty and tranquillity of the harbour and surrounding hills, Charles decided he could settle here. Three winters earlier it might have been a different story. Climate change deniers might want to note that on 10 July 1895 the Port Hills were blanketed in deep snow that came down to the water's edge and the harbour was frozen over with a sheet of ice an inch thick. Think Anchorage, Alaska with more charm.

As luck would have it, the local GP wanted to retire so Charles bought the medical practice along with his house, furniture and medical instruments. Resigning from the Navy, he returned to England to fetch Ethel. As she was heavy with child, it was agreed she would follow him out once he had settled back in Lyttelton. En route, a devastating blow awaited him in Sydney — a letter from Ethel flatly refusing to join him in New Zealand. As far as she was concerned, the marriage was over. Charles never disclosed her reasons and he never met Reginald, the son he fathered. Stumbling despairingly down Sydney streets contemplating taking his own life, he was drawn through the open doors of a church by a hymn, 'Souls of Men, Why Will You Scatter Like a Crowd of Frightened Sheep?' Never previously especially devout, some sort of spiritual catharsis overwhelmed him. He emerged determined to strictly observe the teachings of Christ and dedicate his life to his patients.

Charles was lonely and homesick in Lyttelton at first, until his recently widowed sister, Edith McKenzie, and her young son, David, came out from Scotland to join him. Charles bought the house next door for them and treated David as his own boy. His brother John migrated to New Zealand as well, to practise law in Christchurch. Every Sunday, John walked over the Port Hills to dine with his brother and sister and attend the Anglican Holy Trinity Church. It was here that John met the canon's attractive daughter, Agatha — his future wife and Charlie's mum.

Everyone in Lyttelton referred to Charlie's uncle as the 'Little Doctor', a term of endearment until Hitler's diminutive Propaganda Minister, Joseph Goebbels, who had a doctorate in philology, came along and ruined it. Lyttelton's little doctor was famously crotchety and famously generous. He sent patients only one bill. If they didn't pay, he never sent another because it meant they couldn't, and he wasn't going to add to their burden. Nuns, clergy and Bible class students were seen free of charge. He survived on his wages as Port Health Officer, even though these duties made up a small percentage of his practice. On several occasions, his sister went upstairs in the morning to make his bed to discover he had given away his blankets. He came home from one house call in his socks, having given away his shoes. In *Mark of the Lion*, Neville Holmes, who was a prisoner in Weinsberg Camp with the Little Doctor's nephew, describes a man who sounds uncannily similar:

> In appearance he was slight with a magnificent head and he was astonishingly wiry and strong. He hated sham. I never knew a more generous nature. For example, it was always a great day for a POW when a clothing parcel arrived from home. But when this happened Charlie would promptly empty the contents on the table, pick out one or two items he needed urgently, then call out: 'Anyone need a shirt? Who wants socks? Anyone short of blades?'

Apart from the collapse of his marriage, the biggest tragedy of the Little Doctor's life was the death of his son, the son he never saw but never forgot, Lieutenant Reginald Upham, a Royal Marine who died in action at Beaucourt, France in 1916, and the death of Sergeant David McKenzie, his sister's boy who became like a son to him, who died in action at Passchendaele thirteen months later. Bewildered, broken-hearted and weighed down by grief, the Little Doctor for some years afterwards would ask parents of newborn boys to name them David in memory of his adored nephew.

Charlie helped fill the aching void in his uncle's life.

He accompanied his uncle on launch trips to tend to nine lepers kept in isolation on Quail Island in the middle of Lyttelton Harbour. Charlie's uncle did this weekly for fifteen years, and such was his dedication that if the lepers needed hospital treatment he took the train into Christchurch every Wednesday afternoon to check that they were being given the right care and to keep them company when everyone else was giving them a wide berth. To the Little Doctor they were God's children and Jesus himself had cured lepers by washing their feet. It's tempting to think that the seeds of Charlie's fierce egalitarian spirit were sown at his uncle's elbow.

Uncle Charles lived frugally, which allowed him to be generous. When the grateful community bought him a car, he refused to drive it and continued making house calls on foot, sometimes many miles distant, accompanied by his spaniel, George. When there was an emergency, he prevailed upon the vicar or took a taxi. Long before it was fashionable, his carbon footprint was minimal. In 1945 he turned down a knighthood.

On Monday, 31 July 1950, while sitting in a chair in his home in the presence of a visitor, he pulled out his pocket watch, checked the dial and calmly nominated the time of his death. It was his last diagnosis. He was out by a few hours.

On the day of his burial, all flags in Lyttelton flew at half-mast. Shops and businesses closed. Watersiders stopped work. Over a thousand mourners turned out to pay their last respects. *The Christchurch Star* said it was probably the biggest funeral ever held in Lyttelton. Three years later, a 30-foot clock tower commemorating his fifty years of service to the town was dedicated. Built from local stone with four faces, it stands on a knoll overlooking the port. Representing the Upham family at the dedication service, Charlie thanked Lyttelton for the honour paid to his uncle and recalled fondly the holidays he and his sister had spent with him.

It wasn't just generosity bordering on insanity that uncle

and nephew had in common. Charlie also turned down a knighthood. Charlie turned down the money the people of Canterbury raised to buy him a farm. And when Charlie died, over five thousand people lined the streets to pay their last respects as his flag-draped coffin passed by on a gun carriage. There are rest homes, streets, playing fields, school buildings, postage stamps and a statue in a small North Canterbury town honouring Charlie's memory.

I have seen it stated as absolute fact in newspaper profiles and some obituaries that Charlie went to war consumed with a raging hatred of Germans and that specifically he wanted to avenge the death of his first cousins and settle scores for his uncle. His wife Molly said in a 1989 interview that she thought that her husband's hatred of Germans had arisen from the fact he had lost two uncles in the Great War. They were his cousins in fact, and this doesn't square with the last words his uncle, the Little Doctor who had more cause for anger and vengeance to burn in his chest, said to Charlie before he went overseas: 'I do hope you don't have to kill a German.'

By the time Charlie was a POW in Germany, however, he had witnessed enough to have a fearsome hatred of Nazis and Nazi Germany, which drove his insubordination and defiance. Those feelings were compounded once he saw the horrors of their concentration camps at first hand.

Chapter 3

'Conspicuous gallantry ... in the presence of the enemy'

The other trait the Little Doctor shared with his nephew was courage. As Port Health Officer, he was obliged to inspect incoming ships. At the age of eighty he was still climbing up the sides of swaying vessels in heavy swells on swinging rope ladders. Was Charlie's courage inspired by example or woven into his DNA? Or did inspiration and predisposition join forces like Marvel Comic heroes — and if so where?

'But screw your courage to the sticking-place, and we'll not fail,' implored Lady Macbeth when her husband had second thoughts about murdering King Duncan. The hunt for the wellspring of courage looks as if it could be over. Like Victorian explorers searching for the headwaters of the Nile, neuroscientists mapping dense synaptic jungles deep inside our central nervous systems believe they have discovered the source and the sticking-place: the subgenual anterior cingulate cortex (sgACC) in the brainstem, which plays an important role in regulating emotion.

When people are exposed to images that frighten them, the sgACC system lights up like Guy Fawkes Night. Then it goes into overdrive suppressing the psychological and physiological responses to fear. It's this suppression that allows people to act more courageously. Fear doesn't vanish, but the indecision and paralysis that can accompany it subside to manageable proportions. If you are retreating at high speed from danger, heading for 'the very thin of the fray' as Spike Milligan's famous coward in *The Goon Show*, Major Denis Bloodnok, used to put it, your sgACC system allows you to make a handbrake turn and head straight back into harm's way.

Until such time that MRI scanners can be miniaturised and be fitted inside soldiers' helmets and their sgACC activity recorded in real time in real battlefield situations, we are stuck with measuring bravery by its external manifestation. Precisely because this is an imprecise science reliant on subjective assessment, medals for courage are awarded only when rigorous criteria have been satisfied and after painstaking deliberation. For that reason, as the Commonwealth and Great Britain's highest award for conspicuous gallantry, the benchmark and hallmark of supreme valour, the Victoria Cross is almost impossible to win. Only three people have won it twice; along with Charlie the other two were Noel Chavasse and Arthur Martin-Leake, both doctors in the Royal Army Medical Corps earlier in the century, awarded for rescuing wounded under fire. Charlie probably deserved to win it another six times. Don't take my word for it. This is what Major General Sir Howard Kippenberger had to say in a 1949 edition of *The Legionary*, the Canadian war veterans' association newsletter, when describing the feats of the man who served under him during the Crete disaster:

> On arrival in Egypt I was ordered to put in citations.
> I started to write a M.C. citation for Upham then it
> became clear this was a V.C. case. We made most

careful inquiries and got numerous signed and sworn
statements. What resulted was an epic series of valiant
actions, rating a dozen Military Crosses or three VCs.

Charlie's sgACC centre didn't go into a well-earned hibernation after this — far from it. In his 2004 book, *Supreme
Courage: heroic stories from 150 years of the Victoria Cross*,
General Sir Peter de la Billière, in a chapter devoted to
Charlie, said this about his subsequent exploits in North
Africa: 'Once again, over a period of more than two weeks
he displayed the most outstanding gallantry. Over these two
and a half weeks he performed no fewer than five acts of
conspicuous gallantry.'

In 1999, when New Zealand instituted the 'Victoria Cross
for New Zealand', the criteria were identical to that of the
British VC with the wording changed ever so slightly. The
person recommended for a VC had to have demonstrated
'conspicuous gallantry' or some daring or pre-eminent act
of valour or self-sacrifice or extreme devotion to duty in the
presence of the enemy or belligerents.

Using this definition, Charlie earnt five VCs in North Africa
on top of the three VCs Kippenberger felt he rated on Crete.
At a bare minimum, he deserved a Bar to his VC for his feats
at Minqar Qaim where the Second New Zealand Division were
surrounded by Rommel's Afrika Korps. His superior officers
thought so. And there is no question he deserved another bar
to his VC for his feats at Ruweisat Ridge where New Zealand
troops led a night-time assault on enemy-held higher ground.
Again, everyone thought so, but at the time a war was being
waged and the pinning of crimson ribbon on khaki fabric
was not a high priority. Paperwork involving citations was
shelved but not forgotten.

When the time came to consider these matters again, his
commanding officers were never going to nominate Charlie
for five more VCs. The British would never have accepted it.

And why would they? On the face of it no man could ever be that brave. It defied common sense. It just wasn't humanly possible. Had Charlie been three separate people fighting on Crete and five separate people fighting in Egypt their task would have been easier but still difficult. In the end their discretion got the better part of Charlie's valour. Two weeks' worth of sustained fury and extraordinary courage at Minqar Qaim and Ruweisat Ridge were treated as a single action and only one recommendation was forwarded to His Majesty, King George VI for consideration.

§

Vietnam was the world's first 'living-room war'. Graphic footage of hilltop jungle and rice-paddy fire-fights was beamed nightly into millions of homes by CBS News, anchored by the most trusted man in America, Walter Cronkite. When he told viewers that America was never going to win in Vietnam and should seek a negotiated peace, such was his standing President Johnson announced within days that he would not be seeking re-election.

The Crimean conflict of 1853–56 was the world's first 'drawing-room, scullery and public tavern war'. Thanks to increasing literacy, the surge in popularity of the popular press and the invention of the telegraph, eminent Victorians upstairs, parlour maids downstairs, and butchers, bakers and candlestick makers in alehouses could read about a bungled military campaign in a foreign land very soon after it had occurred.

William Howard Russell, *The Times* correspondent, was print journalism's first superstar. His accounts of common foot soldiers being led to slaughter by arrogant, foolhardy commanders shocked readers. Previously the heroic deeds of lower ranks had been drowned out in the drum roll and trumpet blast of generals conferring honours on each other. In December 1854, tapping into a groundswell of public opinion, Captain G.T. Scobell MP moved in the House of Commons that Her Majesty institute an 'Order of Merit' to be bestowed for distinguished gallantry in war, open to all ranks in the Army or Navy, from the highest to the lowest. It would be an award for field marshals as well as the bloke next door, as Jeremy Clarkson put it in a 2003 BBC documentary on the Victoria Cross.

The Queen's husband, Prince Albert, embraced the concept. Ruling out membership of an ancient order, he suggested a small cross, unlimited in number, accompanied with modest annuity, named after his missus. On 29 January 1856 Queen Victoria signed a warrant to that effect. She requested a number of changes to the final design, the most significant being amending the wording from 'the reward for bravery' to the simpler 'for valour' — altogether more elegant and no longer implying that any soldier who hadn't won a Victoria Cross hadn't been brave.

Just over a hundred medals were cast in the initial batch and half of these were presented to recipients in a ceremony in Hyde Park on 26 June 1857 by Queen Victoria herself, appearing in public on horseback for the first time. She had been monarch for twenty years but still regarded this as a grand and glorious occasion, as her journal entry attests:

A thick heavy morning — full of agitation for coming great event of the day, viz: the distribution of 'Victoria Cross'. Breakfast early. We went down and mounted our horses. I in my full uniform riding 'Sunset'. The road all along was kept clear & there was no pushing or squeezing. Constant cheering & noise of every kind, but the horses went beautifully. The sight in Hyde Park was very fine — the tribunes and stands full of spectators, the Royal one in the centre. After riding down the Line the ceremony of giving medals began. I remained on horseback fastening crosses . . .

This can't have been physically easy and would have been fraught with risk for Her Majesty. According to legend, with her arms stretched wide, the distance fingertip to fingertip was less than the circumference of her hips — an achievement thought anatomically impossible. It was a consequence of her diminutive stature (she was barely five-foot high), multiple pregnancies where she never got her figure back between births, that and her gargantuan, eye-watering appetite for cake. She came to bear an uncanny physical resemblance to the orb she holds in the palm of her left hand in thousands of statues spread across Great Britain and her former dominions.

As if sitting side-saddle on Sunset were not unstable enough, essentially a ball bearing resting on top of a barrel, Her Majesty then had to lean out beyond her own girth to pin small crosses onto tunics. Maybe the soldiers were exceptionally tall or she was riding a Shetland pony. Her diary is silent on this.

Over time, the warrants regarding the awarding of VCs were modified. Eligibility was extended to include acts of conspicuous courage in peacetime as well as in war, and extended to include civilians as well as soldiers and the catchment widened to include citizens of Commonwealth countries and, in rare cases, citizens of foreign countries serving with Commonwealth forces. It was also agreed that it could be awarded posthumously and could be revoked for high crimes and treason. King George V took issue with this in a forceful letter to his private secretary in July 1920:

> The King feels strongly that no matter what the crime committed by anyone on whom the VC has been conferred the decoration should not be forfeited. Even were a VC to be sentenced to be hanged for murder, he should be allowed to wear the VC on the scaffold.

To my knowledge no VC holder has yet taken advantage of

this generous provision, though Charlie might have been tempted on occasion. Once asked by a reporter on the Christchurch *Press* who he hated most, the news media or the Germans, Charlie growled that it was six of one and a half dozen of the other.

The concept of the VC was born in the muck and heartbreak of the Crimean War, and fittingly the bronze for the medals comes from captured cannons, possibly from the Russians at the siege of Sevastopol or from the Chinese during the first Opium War. While research has shown that the current metal is of Chinese origin, there is debate over when this metal was first used, and where it came from. However, what is known is that the metal is sourced from the cascabels, the bulbous knobs projecting from the rear of muzzle-loading cannons familiar to anyone who has remained awake during *Pirates of the Caribbean*. The practice of capturing enemy weapons of war is as old as war itself. Retreating soldiers are instructed to disable vehicles and weapons rather than let them fall into enemy hands. Disabling a bronze cannon wouldn't be easy.

Today, the last remaining portion of cascabel, a chunk of madeira cake-coloured bronze weighing 10 kilograms, enough for eighty-five more medals, is held in a padlocked wooden box, inside a safe inside a vault with its own alarm system. This vault is housed in a colossal concrete warehouse with thirty-two aisles of shelving stacked ten shelves high. There are twenty such buildings at the Royal Logistic Corps Army supply base in Donnington, storing all manner of weapons and munitions, as well as nuclear, chemical and biological warfare suits. Security is so tight that only Jeremy Clarkson and a BBC film crew have ever penetrated it. Watching Clarkson walk away from camera down an endless aisle was like watching the very last scene from *Raiders of the Lost Ark*.

It won't happen again. When metal is required it is sliced from the cascabel under watchful eyes and taken under armed escort to a jewellery shop in plush Burlington Arcade in Mayfair: Hancocks of London, established in 1849. The metal is too brittle to be pressed into shape. Hancocks heat it to 940 degrees Celsius and molten bronze is then poured into sand moulds. Below the shop, seven unmarked medals awaiting recipients are stored in a vault that would give Fort Knox a run for its money.

§

Knowing my chances of getting into Donnington were less than zero, I thought I'd pop into Hancocks to see if I could see their medals. Staff in pinstripe suits and immaculately knotted ties informed me politely that they were stocktaking and the director was away. I returned two days later and was greeted by Guy Burton, a handsome young man in a cobalt-blue suit, tan shoes and open-necked, button-down-collar white shirt: the funky banker looked all the rage in London that spring. He was so stylishly casual and casually stylish you knew immediately he was the boss. I told him I had come all the way from New Zealand. I was writing a book about Captain Charles Upham, the only man to ever win the Victoria Cross twice in combat. Could I pop down to their vault and have a quick squiz at the unmarked medals? Guy flashed me a charming smile and shook his head. He was afraid not. Even his access was limited. He was happy to answer any emails. 'Yeah — right!' I thought to myself, while thanking him warmly.

Stepping back into the arcade, I saw a sale sign directly opposite in the window of a shop selling vintage Rolex watches — 20 per cent off. A square Rolex from 1940 priced at £18,425 was knocked down to £14,900. A steal! Context is everything. The seven unmarked crosses that I was not allowed to see were worth about two quid each as pieces of jewellery. Once engraved on the back with the winner's name, rank, number and unit, their value raced past that of the Rolexes across the tiles.

Most military decorations are tiny solar flares erupting on soldiers' chests. The VC is more moth than butterfly. When it was unveiled for the first time its design was heavily criticised. 'Poor looking in the extreme' snorted one newspaper. 'It looks like it was designed by a person who once designed a hat!' fumed another. Despite being modest and withdrawn in appearance, it acts like a homing beacon at any regal or military gathering, drawing all eyes. Such is the status of the Victoria Cross, there is a special wing devoted to it at the Imperial War Museum in central London — the Lord Ashcroft Gallery — which also pays homage to winners of the George Cross awarded for acts of gallantry carried out in peacetime or away from the heat of battle. I felt I should pay homage myself.

To reach it from Lambeth North tube station I had to cross a no-man's-land of exposed streets in a freezing downpour and arrived drenched to the skin and chilled to the bone. Even head down, running with my R.M. Williams bag over my head, it was impossible to miss. Two giant naval guns capable of hurling 800-kilogram high-explosive shells or a score of circus midgets 30 kilometres reared up in front of a grand building with a six-pillared entrance topped by a tower with an impressive copper dome. Sodden grass and paving covered in sheets of water further reinforced the impression that a battleship from some gilded age had been scuttled in a mudflat. I headed straight upstairs for the Ashcroft Gallery. If I was going to die from hypothermia, I wanted it to be there. The gallery's collection is grouped into seven categories of courage:

Boldness — dash, daring and quick thinking
Aggression — using speed and sheer force in the uproar
of battle to carry the day

Leadership — taking command of a difficult situation and inspiring belief, hope and confidence in your comrades

Skill — keeping your head under pressure and harnessing your skills, resources and technical knowledge to greatest effect

Sacrifice — offering up your life to save others

Initiative — not just following orders but seeing what needs to be done and doing it

Endurance — not just being brave on the spur of the moment but sustaining it in the full knowledge of the price you might have to pay

Charlie satisfied these categories in full measure, apart from sacrifice, which is a miracle in itself. It wasn't from lack of trying on his part. There were numerous occasions where he risked his life to save the lives of others. Maybe it was damp clothing and physical discomfort that soured my mood. I went from VC winner to VC winner noting their extraordinary exploits and thinking ungraciously to myself that Charlie did that sort of thing before smoko most mornings. I was guilty of the chauvinism that Charlie despised. Growing disgusted with myself, I left. I got soaked again walking back to the tube station, which was no less than I deserved.

The Victoria Cross is always the first award to be presented at an investiture — even before knighthoods. The Victoria Cross is the first decoration worn in a row of medals. The letters VC are first in line when honours and titles are listed after a person's name. For example, were the current head of the Catholic Church ever to win the Victoria Cross he would become Pope Francis VC, Bishop of Rome, Vicar of Jesus Christ, Successor of the Prince of the Apostles, Supreme Pontiff, so on and so forth. Were he to win it twice like Charlie, he would be Pope Francis VC & Bar, so on and so forth. Although there is no statutory requirement in the official Warrant of the VC, and none in the Queen's Regulations and Orders, it is not uncommon for all ranks to salute a bearer of a Victoria Cross. An Admiral of the Fleet dripping chandeliers and draped in gold braid will typically feel duty bound to snap to attention and salute an intoxicated rating wearing a VC who has just been violently sick on his shoes. Those who go forth into battle and those who have been subjected to enemy fire know what this drab cross represents.

A recommendation for the VC is normally issued by an officer at regimental level, or equivalent, and has to be supported by three witnesses, although this has been waived on occasion. The recommendation is then passed up the military hierarchy until it reaches the UK's Secretary of State for Defence. The recommendation is then laid before the monarch who approves the award with his or her signature.

Even with strict procedures in place, the winning of a VC is a lottery. There may be no eyewitnesses to an incredible act of gallantry, or the eyewitness may be inarticulate and lack credibility. Two Victoria Crosses have been awarded posthumously on the testimony of enemy combatants who clearly had no reason to lie or exaggerate. It helps hugely if the regimental officer making the recommendation is a passionate and persuasive advocate. Many in the New Zealand Division joked that if you had Kippenberger drafting your citation you were halfway there. It also helps if not too many medals have been handed out for a particular battle or won by a particular unit. In a crowded field many worthy contenders miss out.

All that can be said with absolute certainty is that anyone winning a Victoria Cross thoroughly deserved it. In his BBC documentary, Jeremy Clarkson has no hesitation declaring the Victoria Cross the world's highest award for valour. One of his guests, General Sir Peter de la Billière, formerly of the British Army, ringingly insists that of all the awards for valour the Victoria Cross is the mostly highly regarded. An editorial in the December 1949 edition of *The Legionary* doesn't hold back either: 'No decoration or award ever devised by man has acquired the prestige, significance and respect that the Victoria Cross has gained.'

To better appreciate just how high the bar is set for winning a VC, you need look no further than the number of medals other nations awarded for gallantry in the Second World War. Gallantry is impossible to quantify yet instantly recognisable the world over. It is bravery that beggars belief, courage that catches in the throat. Comparing individual acts of gallantry is ungallant, but when comparisons are made there is no comparison — the Victoria Cross stands alone. It has no equivalent. The numbers speak for themselves.

Japan's primary award for combat heroism, The Order of the Golden Kite, established in 1890 and abolished by the Supreme Commander of the Allied Powers after Japan's surrender, has been awarded a total of 1,067,492 times — the great bulk of those during the Second World War. The French, jokingly labelled 'cheese-eating surrender monkeys' in an episode of *The Simpsons* because of their refusal to take part in the fraudulent, disastrous American-led invasion of Iraq in 1999, have been awarding The Order of Légion d'Honneur for valour since 1802 when it was established by Napoleon Bonaparte. It's not courage the French lack but decent bookkeeping. Complete lists don't exist of how many have been handed out — possibly a million, including 3000 recipients of Grand Crosses in the Second World War. Nor was courage in short supply in the Soviet Union. Their highest award for civilians and soldiers was simply called Hero of the Soviet Union. During the war, it was awarded to 12,755 recipients. The highest award for battlefield courage in the Third Reich was the Knight's Cross of the Iron Cross. It was awarded to 7321 recipients. The United States' supreme medal for valour, the Medal of Honor, was awarded to 472 recipients. The Victoria Cross was awarded just 182 times to

181 recipients — Charlie winning it twice.

If that looks asymmetrical, imagine how out of kilter it would look if it had been awarded 188 times to 181 recipients — Charlie winning it eight times. He would have taken home nearly 4 per cent of all the Victoria Crosses awarded in the Second World War. Not only mind-boggling but greedy. It's pub-quiz trivia and academic now.

Chapter 4

'There's only one thing you can do with a mad dog'

It was another time and another place. Soon there will be no eyewitnesses left and the Second World War will be lost to living memory.

The past is a foreign country; they do things differently there. Or so claimed L.P. Hartley in a famous opening sentence to a novel that no one can remember. Which means we will soon be strangers in a strange land when we visit the places where events occurred. Were *Lonely Planet* to ever publish a travel guide to the Second World War, their editorial offices would reverberate with heated debate just deciding on where to start. Historians disagree over when it began, where it began, when it ended and where it ended. Some scholars contend that the Second World War was just a continuation of the First World War with a very long intermission. Others say it began with the Russian Revolution in 1917 and dribbled to a halt with the fall of communism in 1989 and the break-up of the Soviet Union. Some say it began in 1936 with the Spanish Civil War, Hitler lending succour and comfort to Generalissimo Franco's Fascist forces because it was the perfect dress rehearsal for his own black opera.

It depends on where you live. Lithuanians say it began as the ink was drying on the Molotov–Ribbentrop non-aggression pact signed in Moscow on 23 August 1939. That pact publicly trumpeted trade cooperation between Hitler's Fascist Germany and its sworn ideological enemy, Stalin's Bolshevik USSR, while privately dividing Eastern Europe into spheres of influence — spelling out who would get what spoils of war when war came. Barely eight days later, Germany attacked Poland, inviting Lithuania to join in. Lithuania declined, declaring neutrality and giving refuge to thousands of Polish soldiers. Sixteen days after that, as secretly agreed, Stalin's armies swarmed in to take their allotted share of Poland, swallowing up Lithuania and the other Baltic states in the process — with barely a word of protest from the West. To this day Russians get prickly and change the subject when this inconvenient truth is brought up.

Lithuanians are also very particular about when the Second World War ended. For them it was 31 August 1993, the day the last Russian troop transporters belching diesel exhaust fumes trundled across the border. It almost didn't happen. The Russians were broke and had run out of vodka. The chairman of the Lithuanian Parliament ordered the purchase of several cases and it was handed over to the Russians on the strict understanding that they drank it at the wheel. They agreed and departed blind drunk.

Historians in East and South East Asia insist the Second World War began in 1931 with the Japanese invasion of Manchuria. Don't expect to find confirmation of this in any Japanese war museum or Japanese textbooks. Unlike Germany, which has been scrupulously honest about its role as the precipitating aggressor and willing participant in Hitler's cynical carnage, Japan has smothered her territorial aggression and atrocities in euphemism, evasion and distortion. So much so that my smart, witty and sophisticated Japanese daughter-in-law, Sanae Hayashi, on a flying visit to

Wellington, came downstairs one morning ashen-faced to ask if her country did shameful things during the war. I nodded and quickly resorted to euphemism, evasion and distortion of my own. After all, it was hardly this lovely girl's fault.

What is beyond argument is the Second World War's standing as the most devastating war of all time. Only the Third World War, which looks increasingly possible, has any chance of overtaking it. Its reach was truly global. South America and Antarctica were the only continents to be spared, although naval actions took place in their waters. Conspiracy buffs have also posted incontrovertible proof on the Internet that Hitler was spirited away by U-boat to a hideout in Argentina, and that the Nazis built a vast bunker complex under the ice in Antarctica.

The war stretched from Norwegian fiords to Saharan sands, from the Bering Sea to the Timor Sea, from the banks of the Mersey in Liverpool to the banks of the Volga in Stalingrad. Previously estimated at forty million, the death toll keeps rising as secret files are declassified and construction sites on the Russian and Chinese fronts uncover mass graves. It is expected eventually to reach over sixty million. On average 27,000 people died every day for six years. That's the equivalent of one September 11, nine times a day, for six years, and America is only now recovering from the terror that came out of the clear blue skies that crisp autumn morning in 2001.

§

Chairman Mao, once asked what he thought of the French Revolution, replied, 'It's too early to judge.' Good line, neat sidestep, except the story is apocryphal. The Great Helmsman, in practice a grotesque monster whose criminally lunatic agrarian reforms are estimated to have led to the deaths of millions of people, said no such thing. The answer that never was nevertheless applies to the Second World

War. Its wheels are still in spin. Like background radiation from the Big Bang at the birth of the universe, the after-effects of the most foul chapter in human history continue to ripple outwards, spreading from generation to generation. In faraway New Zealand my own family are part of this ever-expanding force field.

Will and Sanae have a son called Yamato. One Japanese grandfather had such poor eyesight it kept him out of the armed forces. He spent the war as a telegraph operator, tapping out messages in Morse in a small town just outside of Tokyo. When wave after wave of American B-29 Superfortress bombers dropped 1600 tons of jellied gasoline and white phosphorus on the Japanese capital on the night of 9 March 1945, incinerating an estimated 100,000 people, he couldn't see a thing but he could taste the cinders on his lips for weeks afterwards.

My daughter Rosie and Max's little boy, Freddie, has a paternal grandfather, Nikolas Olijnyk, who was twelve years old when the Germans invaded the Ukraine. His father, a chemical engineer, was required to work for the occupiers. When the Germans retreated the family were forced at gunpoint to go with them, working in a Third Reich factory making electrical generators. After the German surrender, facing possible execution for assisting the enemy, the Olijnyks could not go home. Stateless, running from the Russians, but not accepted as legitimate refugees, the family scrambled for food and shelter until they were accommodated in a Polish transit camp. Nikolas's father travelled long distances by train collecting stinking buckets of fat from farmers, which he made into cakes of soap and sold. He made vodka from an illegal homemade still and sold that as well — anything to keep his family of six together until they were accepted as refugees by Australia and were able to set sail for Adelaide in 1949. The war left Freddie's great-grandfather paranoid and distrustful of all institutions. For years he hoarded tiny amounts of gold, encasing it in concrete and burying it deep in the backyard, which his family dug up frantically after his death.

My son Sam and Jessica's two boys, Gus and Ralph, have a paternal great-grandfather from Northern Ireland who was part of the Allied Forces of Occupation in Munich after the war and a maternal great-grandfather who served as a dental surgeon in the New Zealand Medical Corps in North Africa, reconstructing jaws and mouths shattered in battle.

My grandson Oliver, son of Shaun and Vilma, has a maternal great-grandmother living in Lithuania. She was a small girl when the Germans invaded in June 1941 and has no memory of them forcing the Russian occupiers out. The Germans were welcomed as liberators but soon became brutal overlords themselves. Partisan bands hiding in Lithuania's thick forests tormented the Germans until they retreated in January 1945 in the face of the Russian advance.

The Soviets picked up the repression, torture, executions and deportations where the Germans had left off. When she was twelve years old, the great-grandmother's father sheltered an anti-Soviet partisan in a secret hiding place under flagstones in their kitchen. She returned home after school one day to find the Soviet secret police had tossed a hand grenade into this cubbyhole and taken her father away. They heard nothing until word came through that he was buried in a fresh grave on the edge of a wood. Under cover of darkness, relatives armed with shovels took a horse and cart to the clearing and dug him up. He was naked and frozen stiff in a crouching pose, his knees drawn up under his chin.

A favourite NKVD (People's Commissariat for Internal Affairs) practice was to strip prisoners and put them in a small indoor pool filled ankle-deep with freezing water with a small circular pad in the centre to stand on. They maintained their balance and lived a little longer if they squatted like a frog on a lily pad. I saw this room in the Museum of Occupations and Freedom Fights (previously the Museum of Genocide Victims) in downtown Vilnius, Lithuania's capital. This grim edifice had served first as the KGB headquarters, then the Gestapo headquarters and then the KGB headquarters again — all of them making good use of the ice-water paddling pool. Oliver's great-great-grandfather's scrunched-up corpse was about to be heaved onto the cart when his relatives were terrified by coughing and hacking sounds: Russian soldiers were camped in pines nearby. Dropping the body, they fled into the night at full gallop.

§

When I was in Europe, researching this book, Vilma Pakenyte and my son Shaun took me on a side-trip to Vilnius — a city so awash in cemeteries and mass graves cynics call it the most necro-friendly place in Europe. In the absence of anything resembling a road, Lithuania's glacially flat landscape of damp forest and lake was for centuries impassable in winter — as Napoleon's Grande Armée discovered in 1812 on their retreat from Moscow. Expiring from typhus, frostbite and starvation, their bodies piled up in the snow outside the city gates.

It's best to fly into Vilnius. The international arrivals hall is one of the few buildings the Russians got right. Built like a tzar's summer palace, it is painted a soft apricot with a white trim. It has patterned marble floors. Pillars rising two levels support grand, colonnaded balconies. A gigantic chandelier is suspended from an ornate ceiling. Hammer and sickle motifs have been chiselled off, but delicate plaster wreaths of bay leaves and flowers remain. It's a sumptuous contrast to the blunt and functional Stansted Airport forty-seven minutes north-west of London by train, the base of Ryanair. I had a window seat with no window. I missed out on Germany and Poland gliding serenely beneath us in late-afternoon sunshine. There was no view in Vilnius either. We arrived after sunset and bumped over rough tarseal through a dimly lit city to the historic old quarter where crooked, cobbled streets teemed with young lovers, inviting bars and baroque churches spotlit like film sets.

Night-time is the right time to arrive in a new city. You glimpse a tantalising world that defies deciphering. You experience it again in daylight and the two experiences seldom match. Under a clear, chill spring sky, the medieval centre of Vilnius was more beautiful than I could have imagined. We were guests in an eccentric boutique hotel tucked inside a potholed, gated courtyard across the street from the glorious baroque Church of Saint Casimir. Construction by the Jesuits began in 1604 and it has survived centuries of war, plague, pestilence and fire. It was badly damaged in the Second World War, but the Russians repaired it lovingly. A sputnik satellite was suspended from the ceiling and it reopened as the Museum of Atheism. Congregations of non-believers never eventuated, but devout Poles on pilgrimage kept arriving by the busload, and in 1991 it was returned to the Jesuits.

Just a block away the Great Synagogue, a muscular columned monolith, was almost completely destroyed by the Nazis. Sixty years after the firebombing which reduced their beautiful city to rubble, the citizens of Dresden completed the reconstruction of their cathedral from less — a single scorched arch. In Vilnius the Russians made certain that wouldn't happen by demolishing what remained of the ruins, carting away what they could and burying the rest so thoroughly that only recently have archaeologists managed to uncover from deep underground the altar stone from which the Torah was read. A shabby school, decaying and abandoned, sits where the synagogue once stood. I couldn't summon children's laughter when I closed my eyes, just wind sighing in bare trees lining a rancid playground.

Vilnius was once a spiritual and intellectual magnet for central European Jews, its cosy streets home to schools, libraries, publishing houses, concert halls and theatres. Over a hundred synagogues teemed with worshippers. Today only one functioning synagogue exists, not well marked in my guidebook; I walked straight past 39 Pylimo Street twice. Some singing would have helped but the Taharat Ha-Kodesh Choral Synagogue was as silent as a tomb. Grand in a muted way, the building refuses to draw attention to itself, which might explain why it is still there. No one came in or out, apart from the white-haired old lady from the Vilna Gaon State Jewish Holocaust Museum who sold me the guidebook, *Sites of Jewish Memory*, listing 104 places where Jews once lived, loved, learnt and prayed. All that remains in narrow alleys and broad boulevards are brass plaques fixed to walls inscribed in Hebrew and English.

Bob Dylan's maternal grandparents were Litvaks — Lithuanian Jews who migrated to America to escape the anti-Semitic pogroms that periodically swept through Europe. Walking through the aching, heavy stillness of the old Jewish quarter, it occurred to me that these silent cobbled lanes could be the 'ancient empty streets too dead for dreaming' that Bob Dylan sang about on 'Mr. Tambourine Man'.

Despite the impressive name, the Vilna Gaon State Jewish Holocaust Museum is little more than a weatherboard house painted sea-green with shuttered windows. Tucked at the end of a cul-de-sac, it could be a Boy Scouts hut. The innocent exterior hides the stuff of nightmares. Around the walls are photographs of people and places that were wiped off the face of the earth, but the real horror lies within the black ring-binders placed on desks in each of the small rooms — first-hand accounts of the Lithuanian Shoah beginning with descriptions of Jews being rounded up and herded into the Vilnius Ghetto:

On Kwaszelna Street, Lithuanian Snatchers are leading a group of Jews. One of them is an old man, the rabbi of Kwaszelna. His face and snow-white beard are bloodied. Just the sight of him, without a hat and with red blood marring his majestic appearance, would make the stones scream. The rabbi falls down. Several young people in the group pick up the old man and try to carry him, but the hooligans won't let them. He has to walk by himself. Everyone is padded; they wear several coats, they drag packs, they take things on baby carriages. People push wheelbarrows. The picture is awful. Christians come to help friends. Others come to buy for almost nothing; others come like jackals — already waiting for Jewish belongings . . .

When the Germans occupied Vilnius in 1941, they took note of the unfinished fuel tank farm next to the Paneriai railway station. The Russians had dug deep circular pits, and if you arranged the condemned like fruit in a flan, they were tailor-made for mass extermination. Jews were transported here on trucks and trains from all over Lithuania:

A young German officer addressed us: 'In spite of all the ridiculous rumours, you're going to be transported to working camps in the east. You will shower and then be issued working clothes. Undress and leave your clothing here.' He spoke in civil tones, and in spite of all we knew about this death factory he almost sounded convincing. Whatever spark of hope we felt was extinguished when we heard a long burst of machine-gun fire and distant screams. The Germans heard it too, for they raised their guns and pointed them at us. 'Quickly, you Jews! Undress and into the showers! You're just hearing the backfire of some trucks.' They wanted to dispatch us at maximum speed and efficiency but no one moved, no one seemed able to move a muscle. The officer calmly walked up to an elderly man who was standing near the front, drew his Luger and shot him in the face. When he fell to the ground his head opened up and his brains poured out into the mud. Suddenly everyone was undressing. When you're about to die, even a few minutes seem precious, as if another second might bring a reprieve . . .

Lithuanian men participated in the slaughter. Thick forest muffled the gunfire and hid the bestial pits from unwanted attention, but peasant farmers working adjacent fields knew what was happening. Most shrugged. Others downed tools, bared their heads and wept at the rolling thunder. Somehow a handful of Jews survived to bear witness:

> How long I lay there like that I don't know. Human blood flowed over my body. It must have lasted about four or five hours because it began to get dark. I looked around and didn't see anybody; I tried to get up, to get away from the pyramid of bodies. I saw the Lithuanian murderers still standing and dividing up the remaining clothes. But they stood with their backs to our grave and were absorbed in what they were doing. I crawled out of the grave. I was naked and covered with red blood spots, but I wiped myself off with snow and crawled along the ground. Later I stood up and ran as I never had before . . .

On the wall above one of the ring-binder tables was a photo of Archbishop Juozsapas Skvireckas. His vestments and the massive crucifix on his chest proclaimed loudly that he was a man of God. Alongside his photograph was an entry from his diary dated 25 June 1941:

> The fight against the Jews is continuing. All the houses are being searched and groups of criminals are being led to be shot. Hitler is not the only enemy of the Jews, but his thinking is also very right since there is plenty of information about the massacres perpetrated by the Bolsheviks and the Jews.

Winston Churchill and New Zealand-born Fleet Street cartoonist David Lowe could see the gathering storm and issued warnings that fell on deaf ears. The world had just emerged from the horror of the Great War — the so-called 'war to end all wars'— a conflagration on a scale so vast and ghastly everyone assumed lightning of that dimension couldn't possibly strike twice. Human beings had learnt important lessons and would never allow it to happen again. The Anglo-Irish poet William Butler Yeats saw this reasoning as a dangerous illusion. In his 1919 masterwork 'The Second Coming', he issues a prophetic warning of stark and terrible beauty. Written in the wake of the brutal chaos of the Russian Revolution and heart-breaking nationalist turmoil in his native Ireland, Yeats despairs that the centre cannot hold, the best lack all conviction, while the worst are filled with a passionate intensity. He ends asking the question:

And what rough beast, its hour come round at last,
Slouches towards Bethlehem to be born?

Charlie knew.

§

Heavy rain lashes the windscreen of Charlie's jalopy. The canvas roof had folded back on itself an hour earlier and was flapping like a broken spinnaker, but it didn't bother him. It happens a lot and he drove wearing oilskins for occasions such as these. The water sloshing back and forth across the windscreen bothered him more. It was like driving underwater behind a giant squid leaking ink. He could hardly see a thing. The night was almost as dark as his mood. Timaru and his warm bed were at least an hour away. Calling it a bed was an exaggeration. It was a sleeping bag on the floor inside a pup tent erected in the corner of the living room to give him some privacy in the miserable two-bedroom cottage the three farm valuers shared.

Approaching a rural crossroads, the windscreen strobes with blinding light. In the middle of nowhere, well after midnight, a two-storey, double-verandah colonial pub is still open for business. Cars and trucks nestle against its flanks like suckling piglets. It's fair to say that six o'clock closing introduced as a wartime efficiency measure in 1917 never really caught on out here.

'Jesus Christ, what hour do you call this?' grins the local constable, making an elaborate pretence of checking his watch when Charlie enters. 'It's almost opening time!' This earns a round of loud laughter and applause. The banter fades quickly when they see that Charlie is in no mood for jokes. 'Have you heard the news? Bob Semple — the gutless, grovelling bastard — has apologised for calling Hitler and Mussolini mad dogs!' No one is quite sure how to respond. They know Charlie. You sure as shit don't want to piss him off when he's in this sort of mood.

Putting down his beer and straightening his jacket, the constable breaks the uncomfortable silence. 'With all due respect, Charlie, I don't think it behoves a Minister of the Crown to insult the leaders of Germany and Italy when we are trying to avert another war in Europe.' Locals, some of them veterans of Gallipoli and the Somme, nod in silent agreement. This incenses Charlie even more. 'If you think sweet talk and reason are going to work with Hitler and Mussolini, you're fucking dreaming! Look at Abyssinia! Look at the Rhineland! Look at Austria! Look what happened to Czechoslovakia! If these bastards are not stopped soon, there'll be no stopping them. Semple was right the first time! Hitler and Mussolini are mad dogs!'

Heading out into the night, Charlie pauses at the door to address the shocked gathering. 'I've owned mad dogs. There's only one thing you can do with a mad dog and that's shoot the fucking thing!'

§

In the unpublished Sandford manuscript, it is the Honourable Robert Semple, New Zealand's Minister of Works, who issued a retraction and apology to Hitler and Mussolini. I went to the Parliamentary Library in Wellington to check this out. The neo-Gothic library building attached to Parliament's main building has been lovingly restored. It now sits on base isolators. When the tectonic plates beneath Wellington roll over in their sleep it will remain an oasis of gentility amid burst water mains, sparking power cables and smoking rubble. News rooms will be disabled, Civil Defence emergency radio operating out of a bunker deep beneath Parliament will have Manuel and The Music of the Mountains on high rotate — but if it's yesterday's papers you want, the Turnbull will be open for business.

The story I wanted was from 9 November 1938. The hushed reading room was filled with chocolate-brown leather Chesterfield couches, western saloon chairs and gleaming kauri tables. Salmon-pink walls rose to a high-vaulted ceiling dripping chandeliers. A staff member brought me a large folio of straw-coloured newsprint bound with green ribbon inside a heavy cover. Stylistically, it had more in common with the Gutenberg Bible than today's digitally generated newsprint. The headline I wanted leapt out:

APOLOGY MADE --
MR. SEMPLE'S WORDS ---
HITLER AND MUSSOLINI ---
PROTESTS TO GOVERNMENT
Strong protests against a statement by the Minister of Public Works, the Hon. R. Semple, in which he referred to Herr Hitler and Signor Mussolini as 'mad dogs' have been received from the German Consul-General Herr E. Ramm, and the Consul of Italy, Dr. B. D'Acunzo, by the Prime Minister, Mr. Savage. The Prime Minister has apologised

on behalf of the Government.

'I have to express on behalf of the New Zealand Government my extreme regret that such a comment should have been made and to inform you that the New Zealand Government entirely dissociate themselves from such statements.'

Mr. Semple's remarks were made during a recent address to railway workers at Oaro, in which he stated that the menace of war and the necessity of the Dominion providing for its own defence could not be ignored when 'mad dogs like Hitler and Mussolini were running loose'.

I could find no apology from the Honourable Bob Semple. Two columns across on the very same page there appeared this story:

JEWS' TERROR ---
COMING REPRISALS ---
DR. VOM RATH DIES ---
VIOLENT NAZI CROWDS

The death of Dr. vom Rath, a secretary at the German Embassy in Paris, who was shot by a young Polish Jew, occurred yesterday. The French Government is deeply shocked, and the President, M. Lebrun, the Prime Minister, M. Daladier, and the Foreign Minister. M. Bonnet immediately expressed their sorrow to the German Ambassador, Count von Welczeck. The French Chargé d'Affaires in Berlin repeated his Government's regret. Jews are crowding synagogues in Paris praying for the safety of their co-religionists in Germany who it is feared will suffer terrible reprisals.

Anti-Jewish disturbances broke out in Munich early this morning. The windows of Jewish shops were smashed and a number were set on fire. The demonstrators set fire

to a synagogue, and the fire brigade is trying to prevent
it spreading to the adjacent buildings. The windows of
every Jewish shop in the Friedrichstrasse were smashed.
Herr Hitler's 'Old Fighters' wearing their 1923 uniforms
instigated the disturbances. Several of the shops were
looted, and the wrecks watched by enthusiastic crowds.

One month earlier, on 18 October 1938, on Hitler's orders
more than 12,000 Jews were expelled overnight from Nazi
Germany. They were Polish born and had been living in
Germany legally for many years. Ordered from their homes,
they were taken at gunpoint to railway stations and put on
trains to the Polish border.

One expelled couple had a seventeen-year-old son, Herschel
Grynszpan, living in Paris. From the border his sister sent him
an anguished postcard: 'We haven't a penny. Could you send
us something?' Enraged by his family's treatment, Grynszpan
purchased a pistol and walked into the German Embassy in
Paris saying he had a message for the ambassador. He was
sent instead to a junior diplomat, Dr Ernst vom Rath, who,
as it happened, was no fan of the Nazi regime and was under
investigation by the Gestapo, but for the purposes of what was
about to follow he was a patriot and martyr. Five shots were
fired, two struck him. He was grievously wounded, and Hitler
ordered his personal physician to fly to Paris to assist. Vom
Rath took three days to die.

German newspapers denounced Jewish people as mur-
derers. When news reached Berlin that vom Rath had died,
German radio stations observed two minutes' silence. On
the city's fashionable Unter den Linden boulevard, a mob
stormed a French tourist office where Jews were waiting to
collect travel documents, chanting, 'Down with Jews! They
are going to Paris to join the murderer!'

Hitler learnt of vom Rath's death when he was in Munich at
a gathering of Nazi party leaders and SA troops — Nazi Party

paramilitary — for the annual celebration of the failed Beer Hall Putsch of 1923. He felt the death needed to be exploited to the fullest possible extent. His Minister of Propaganda, Dr Goebbels, informed him that violence against Jews had already broken out in some German cities. Goebbels noted jubilantly in his diary:

> Hitler decided that this should be allowed to continue, I immediately gave the necessary instructions to the police and to the party then I spoke briefly in that vein to the party leadership. Stormy Applause. All are instantly at the phones. Now people will act!

Reprisals across Germany, Austria and the Sudetenland were ordered, with the caveat that they had to appear spontaneous. Over the night of 9–10 November, as instructed, policemen and firemen looked the other away as hundreds of Jews were murdered, synagogues were torched, Jewish shops, homes, hospitals and schools were vandalised and Jewish cemeteries desecrated in a forty-eight-hour orgy of violence which became known as *Kristallnacht* — Crystal Night: the night of broken glass. Some 30,000 Jews were arrested and put into concentration camps. Those who weren't incarcerated were forced to clear the rubble-strewn streets.

Two days later at the Air Ministry, Hermann Göring chaired a meeting to find a way to make the Jews bear the cost of the damage. Insurance company representatives pointed out that the cost of replacing broken windows alone came to five million Reichsmark (roughly $US2 million) and many of the trashed Jewish shops and factories were owned by Aryan landlords. Göring was incensed. He shouted that it would have been better to kill 200 Jews than to destroy so much valuable property.

Michael Joseph Savage's apology was cringe-worthy enough, but it paled in comparison to a story appearing in

London papers the same day that took wishful thinking to new and dizzying heights:

MR. CHAMBERLAIN'S WISH FOR QUIETER TIMES AHEAD

'I wish this Government to be a "go-getter" for peace.' This statement was the keynote of the speech made by the Prime Minister, Mr. Neville Chamberlain, at the Lord Mayor's banquet at the Guildhall. 'This does not mean that we undertake the role of policeman for the world,' he added, 'but if we see peace is threatened we shall use our influence to save it, and if war breaks out we shall seek to stop it. Munich demonstrated the four Great Powers were able to agree on the main outlines of settlement of one of the most dangerous problems of our time.'

After the war, blithely unaware that he'd once sent Charlie into a rage, Bob Semple wrote him a letter. Long before dyslexia was recognised, his missive is littered with grammatical errors, spelling mistakes and poor sentence construction but is redeemed by heartfelt sincerity. He expresses his admiration for Charlie's principled views and thanks him for his service and the moral example he set the nation. He felt strongly that Charlie should offer himself for election to Parliament. He stressed it was immaterial what party he stood for, though he would prefer it were for Labour. The country needed young men with his courage and determination to deal with the post-war problems that were looming.

There is no record of Charlie's response. If he had done so, it would probably be unprintable, which is a shame. They were in agreement. They could both see the rough beast whose hour had come. Another war was coming and Charlie's privileged childhood prepared him perfectly for it.

Chapter 5

'You'll never make a civil servant'

The motto of Waihi School, 'Thou shalt therefore bear hardship', was taken to heart by the founders of the Anglican preparatory school for boys, especially in the early days.

It was established in 1907 on bare, exposed South Canterbury plains just out of Winchester at a time when there were few shelterbelts blunting the ceaseless nor'westerlies and freezing southerlies jetting up from the Ross Ice Shelf. It shared the same ethos and wind-chill factor as Gordonstoun School on the bleak North Sea coast of Scotland, which has nothing between it and the Arctic Circle save for the Shetland Islands and a few oil rigs. Prince Charles went there when conditions were famously spartan. Interviewed by a film crew prior to the arrival of the future king, the headmaster declared proudly that the purpose of the school was to immunise children of the rich against the terrible virus of privilege. Maybe this is what Charlie's parents intended when they sent him to Waihi in 1918 aged nine, reserved and small for his age. Macrocarpa hedges, a tree-lined drive, an orchard and flower beds made it slightly more hospitable by the time he arrived, but it was still grim and a long way from home.

Charlie's nickname was 'Pug'. Legend has it the moniker

resulted from his performances in boxing. It was short for 'pugnacious', which he needed to be both inside and outside the ring. Summer and winter, first thing every morning the boys had to have cold showers in a bathroom that had a lead floor — sometimes jagged and slippery with ice. Once a week there was a tepid bath shared by up to eight grubby boys, two at a time, the last two sharing what was by then chowder.

In summer the shower was replaced by a compulsory swim in the green, untreated pool. Before breakfast they had to exercise outdoors with dumbbells for half an hour. In winter the dumbbells were often so cold if felt as though the metal was burning their skin. They would then stand on forms in the big hall while the headmaster inspected their shoes, after which they knelt on the hard floor in prayer while he paced and read aloud from the Old Testament. Classes followed in rooms heated with smouldering stoves hopelessly unequal to the task. With up to fifty filthy boys packed into a single dormitory, colds, mumps and flu swept through the school like the Black Death. Only boys who felt terminally ill placed their fate in the hands of the stern, unsmiling matron, the headmaster's sister, who looked and behaved like a witch with a humourless cackle to match.

If that weren't punishment enough, a long-handled wooden jam spoon that made a loud whack when it hit a backside was used by the headmaster for minor breaches of discipline. For more serious offences he used a hockey stick with the 'hook' sawn off. The masters used straps. Prefects, boys barely into their teens, were allowed to use the cane on bare skin. For minor transgressions, a prefect could order a boy to 'walk the dorm'. This involved traversing the long room in pyjamas and being subjected to a beating with slippers by all those present. This was William Golding's 1954 novel *Lord of the Flies* set in raw provincial New Zealand. Years later Charlie confided to his wife, Molly, that his buttocks were often black and blue from beatings. Molly shared this secret with her appalled girls. You don't have to be Sigmund Freud to figure out where Charlie's lifelong loathing of bullies and bullying came from.

Another punishment was 'Stones'. Boys had to collect rocks that peppered the alluvial gravel plains which served as playing fields. Today those rough paddocks are billiard-table perfect thanks to generations of errant schoolboys. Had they been required to split the rocks with picks, they would have officially qualified as convicts. Oliver Riddell's *Behind the Hedge*, a fascinating and candid account of the first hundred years of Waihi School, describes a typical Sunday afternoon from Charlie's era:

> The school would divide into two sides, picked by prefects, and roam the countryside. The side that won the toss would choose some suitable place to defend, and five to ten minutes later the attacking side would set out in search. A couple of scouts would be sent out and the main body would follow them. Once they had located the defending side the scouts would report back and plans were made for the attack. The side that killed off all its opponents won. The procedure was then reversed with the former attackers going off in search of a place to defend, and so on for the rest of the afternoon. All sorts of tricks and deceptions including ambushes were employed. There were no umpires and disputes had to be settled amicably. Any breach of the rules meant the offender had to go dead. Players could have flax daggers as well as swords, but they could be used as a means of defence only.

Small wonder then in basic training at the outbreak of the war that Charlie excelled in flanking manoeuvres and ambush when he led his platoon in mock battles in the Port Hills behind the town of Tai Tapu. He learnt how to do this when he was nine. These tactical skills also served him well when it came to placing his men advantageously on training exercises in Syria and Egypt, and later in real battlefields where it really counted.

While hardly loquacious, little Charlie was not afraid to publicly challenge teachers and question authority when he considered something silly, unfair or incorrect. A former pupil, John Rolleston, remembers Charlie's outspokenness:

> When the headmaster came up behind Charlie and placed his hands over his eyes, in his most blistering tones Charlie remarked: 'I don't know who you are, but your hands smell worse than Dad Uden's!' The headmaster was delighted.

Uden was the school gardener who spread manure, crutched the sheep, fed the pigs and without fail ate a cheese and raw onion sandwich every day for lunch. He also cut the boys' hair. You would never forget that combination of odours assaulting your nostrils at close quarters.

Charlie holidayed with classmates from farming families and fell in love with country life, the big wide skies, the rolling hills the colour of lions' hide and the towering snow-capped Southern Alps filling the western horizon. A popular boyhood pastime on farms was tossing dry cow pats into rushing rivers and blasting them to smithereens with rifles. More rehearsal for war.

Charlie's nephew, Dr Robert Wynn-Williams, the second son of Charlie's favourite sister Agatha, went to Waihi in the early 1950s. He remembers it as both a great and dreadful place. He loved the freedom they enjoyed in weekends. Completely unsupervised, boys swam, fly-fished for trout, went eeling, snared wildfowl and generally fooled in and around the Waihi River to their hearts' content. No one drowned or went missing. Climbing trees was popular. Some trees had no lower branches so they scoured the main trunk railway line just outside the boundary fence for loose rail spikes, which they prised out of sleepers and drove into trunks to make ladders. By some miracle no locomotive ever derailed and slithered over the grass into the school.

The food was appalling. There was never quite enough of it for ravenous pre-pubescent boys — whose sex education consisted of a brief lecture in small groups from the red-faced, flustered headmaster in his living room. (Hens and roosters were mentioned fleetingly, and they were advised they needed to contain unspecified feelings in the presence of girls.) Containing nausea at the dining table was the more pressing issue. Porridge came in two options: watery to the point of translucence and ferro-concrete. Sausages were coated thickly in marmalade to give them flavour. New Zealand schoolboys in rural South Canterbury invented fusion cuisine long before the rest of world.

Fist fighting was permissible as long as some semblance of Marquess of Queensberry rules was observed. Ideally gloves were worn and the bouts took place in a thatched-roof playhouse with a prefect present. In an elegant and touching memoir prepared for his grandchildren, Robert writes wistfully that he knew Waihi boys and his teachers better than his own family. He was put on a Road Services bus in Christchurch with a small suitcase at the age of eight and often did not see any family until he returned by bus at the end of the term. He loved Waihi but resolved to never send any of his children to a boarding school because of the inevitable family disconnects that occur.

§

Robert Wynn-Williams lives in retirement on a pretty, leafy property with his wife Beth, just north of Lincoln where he conducted research studies into lucerne at the DSIR. His directions were so thorough and so precise Stevie

Wonder could have driven there without difficulty. Allowing myself plenty of time to get hopelessly lost, I arrived way too early and they insisted on sharing their takeaway sushi lunch with me. Takeaway sushi? What is rural New Zealand coming to? Fit and hyperkinetic, Robert was constantly springing up from the table to fetch file boxes of newspaper clippings and bulging envelopes of photos, postcards and letters. That done, he leapt to his feet again and took me to visit Charlie's gravestone in St Paul's Anglican Church Cemetery in Papanui. Parking on the opposite side of a busy road, the tennis-playing pensioner sprang nimbly from his car and without pause dashed through speeding traffic like Nadal approaching the net for an overhead smash. I joined him five minutes later pale and shaking, feeling I had just witnessed echoes of his uncle running straight at a German machine-gun nest.

There are two memorials in the family plot for Charlie: a small plaque on a shared plinth and behind it a large Jabba the Hutt-shaped rock with a red RSA poppy embedded in it. The beautiful wooden church with its witch's-hat steeple reminded me of churches dotting the countryside around Colditz Castle, which I had just visited. The sun-dappled railway line running between trees beside the Upham graves could have borne the carriage Charlie jumped from en route to the famous prison. It was the perfect setting for slipping the surly bonds of earth and touching the face of God — not that Charlie or many in the once ferociously devout Upham family were remotely ecclesiastical any longer. Chapel every morning at Christ's College successfully drummed that out of Charlie and Robert, who followed his uncle there.

Despite my pointing out that I'd toured his old high school earlier, Robert insisted I pay another visit. 'Did you see the painting of Charlie?' I had to admit I hadn't. 'I can't believe you missed it. You have to see the painting of Charlie!'

'The Battle of Waterloo was won on the playing fields

of Eton' is often ascribed to the Iron Duke, the Duke of Wellington, an Eton old boy. A more compelling case can be Christ's College's involvement in the battle for Crete. Here is Denis Glover writing in *Register*, the Christ's College newsletter: 'In the dark night of Crete a cry went up, "Sch-o-o-l!", and from a not seen dig-in came back on the desperate dark air, "Coll-ege!"'

Christ's College is set in park-like grounds and its buildings' magnificent grey stones look as though they have been transplanted from Kent, which was the intention. Charlie was a pupil here from 1923 to 1927, boarding at Flower's House, an unlovely, red-brick block destroyed in a fire and replaced with a modern three-storey building that compares dismally with the glorious architecture across Rolleston Road. Flower's House is adjacent to the former Upham residence at No. 32 Gloucester Street.

Robert's family lived in rural Waipara well north of Christchurch. When his parents elected to send him to Christ's, becoming a boarder was the only option. When I asked Robert why Charlie's parents thought it necessary to enrol their only son in a boarding school that with a little effort they could reach out and touch, he replied with a cryptic smile that it was to give his sisters, Esther, Agatha and Monica, some respite.

Robert's guided tour was my second that day. The forest of white crosses on the central lawn commemorating Anzac Day looked even more melancholy in the late-afternoon sun. Robert whisked me straight past them, striding purposefully towards the majestic dining hall to show me the painting I had somehow overlooked. Kitchen staff laying out cutlery for dinner let us wander around. Robert noted immediately that the refectory tables now ran longitudinally down the hall rather than latitudinally as in his day. The heritage-listed school was badly damaged but survived the 2011 earthquake only because it had been seismically strengthened twice in its recent past. In a quake, liquefaction works much like a coffee plunger — underground water rises when the land falls. The heavy stone walls of the hall sank and the floor between them rose like a surfacing whale, scattering furniture like doll's-house toys. The bow in the floor could not be completely eliminated, necessitating the change in the axis of the tables. To my relief, Robert couldn't find the painting either. I wasn't going blind. It had been shifted somewhere for safekeeping during the repairs and no one could tell us where.

Robert has two abiding memories of his uncle. One is specific. Driving in opposite directions, the Upham and Wynn-Williams families met in the middle of the long bridge that spans the braided Ashley River as it nears the sea. Not content with a cheery wave, the two vehicles stopped, engines were switched off, windows were wound down and a long natter ensued, oblivious to the fact that they were blocking a state highway. The other memory is more diffuse. It is of a kind, unassuming man, staring intently at the ground while speaking softly, his views on most matters black and white.

There is a rough-hewn, post-modern bronze bust vaguely resembling Charlie in the visitors' reception area at Christ's. There is a quadrangle named after him. There is an impressive painting of him hidden somewhere in a cupboard. His name pops up in all manner of school publications where they keep elevating him to a Knight of the Realm. He won prizes in divinity, which was inevitable given his extended exposure to high levels of piety growing up. He won no sporting trophies. He is remembered as a dogged, determined rugby player. He stood out more when it came to barracking support from the sidelines. The decibel level was out of all proportion to his small frame. It was a gift he would employ when urging his troops forward on battlefields.

My chum Joe Bennett, brilliant award-winning columnist and best-selling author, was formerly a housemaster at Christ's. When I told him I was writing a book on Charlie, he snorted like a racehorse and informed me loudly that in the staffroom Charlie was only ever mentioned disparagingly in dispatches. I did the maths. They must have had centurions or even double-centurions on the staff in Joe's day. I gently quizzed him on this possibility and he came clean:

> 'There was no one at Christ's when I arrived in 1987 who could possibly have taught him. I do vaguely remember hearing a few suggestions that he wasn't universally loved, but I cannot remember who made those suggestions, nor any details of what was said. They cannot have been based on first-hand knowledge. Such was his fame they may well have been the carpings of the small and envious. I once met Upham. He was not the smartest or necessarily the nicest cookie in the box. I even attended his funeral, in the sense of lining up on Rolleston Avenue with 600 Christ's College kids who bowed their heads as the coffin passed.'

Charlie shone at school where it counted most — with other boys. Another mate of mine, the comedian and broadcaster Leigh Hart, who was taught by and remains a friend of Joe's, boarded at Flower's House some fifty years after Charlie had left the building. He says his spirit and memory loomed large precisely because he was average like everyone else, except for his off-the-charts fearlessness, which made him the stuff of legend even before he went to war. Apparently, he used to rig his bed at night to fool patrolling masters then shimmy down drainpipes to visit a girlfriend. Penalties for being caught would have been a severe caning or expulsion. On other occasions, he snuck down the fire escape with a pillowcase and returned from the pie-cart in the square with it bulging with hot pies for upwards of twenty boys. There was fierce competition to get a pie from as close to the top as possible as the bottom third tended to disintegrate into hot mince and pastry shrapnel. It was another portent of things to come. During the war Charlie's weapon of choice was a bulging bag of grenades which he would employ with even more scalding results.

Charlie had rigid views on what he thought was right and wrong and responded badly when he considered those in authority had overstepped the mark. Given detention once, unjustly in his view, he was writing out lines with other boys serving time in a small downstairs study next to the library. Across the foyer and stairwell was the housemaster's office with the door open. He sat at his desk in a black gown marking papers, looking up from time to time to check on the miscreants and make sure there was no talking. Outside, late-afternoon sun cast long shadows across Hagley Park where boys playing sports made joyous sounds. Other boys in straw boaters cycled past nearby, chatting and laughing. It was intolerable. Pressing a finger to his lips, Charlie darted to the window and disappeared from view up a drainpipe. In the second-storey ablution block adjacent to the stairs, he put plugs in all the baths and hand basins and turned the taps on full. He was back downstairs and through the window in seconds. It began at first with a few drops plopping on the housemaster's desk, then quickly became a deluge, with water coursing down the stairs like a hydro dam spillway. Charlie feigned concern when he joined the housemaster who, trousers rolled up and barefoot, was slipping and sliding in shock. 'Are you all right, sir?'

Bullying was rife in Flower's House. Fagging made it permissible for older boys to demand that younger boys perform all sorts of tedious and vile chores for them. Charlie was a new boy, tucked out of sight in a toilet cubicle, quite possibly smoking, when older boys dragged another third former, the pudgy, overweight and weeping David Clarkson, into the dunnies with the intention of putting his head into a lavatory bowl and flushing it. Charlie stepped out of his cubicle in a cold fury. Calling them pigs, he demanded they leave Clarkson alone. He was outnumbered and the shortest person there. For years afterwards, still awestruck by what happened next, Clarkson would tell the story again and again; something in Charlie's blazing cobalt-blue eyes spooked them. They let go of him and fled.

When Charlie was ailing, close to the end of his life, Clarkson made a special visit from the West Coast to pay his last respects, thanking him not just for standing up for him, but also for being an amusing mate who never told the same joke twice.

§

It's hard looking at photos of Charlie's barrister and solicitor father, John, and imagining a joke ever leaving his soft, delicate lips. He has a permanent sepia air about him. His looks were deceiving. The pint-sized, courtly, quietly spoken Clark Kent in chambers became Superman in court — a steely resolve coupled to an elephantine recall of statute made him a formidable figure. He wanted his son to follow him into law, but seeing how much Charlie loved the land, he reluctantly agreed to him enrolling at Canterbury Agricultural College (later known as Lincoln College then Lincoln University) where farming theory and practice were taught to university level. For the first time in his life Charlie was a fully engaged, enthusiastic scholar, gaining firsts in agriculture, veterinary science and economics, as well as becoming the college's most astute judge of livestock values at the Addington Saleyards. He enjoyed his time at the college even though it meant boarding again.

At the war's end, after six years in the army, three of them behind wire, all told it meant Charlie had spent nearly two thirds of his life sleeping in dormitories and accommodation of one kind or another with other men. Small wonder, then, that, living at Conway Flat with his adored wife and cherished daughters, Charlie felt he had gone to heaven.

A model student in most respects, Charlie showed glimpses of the prickly POW he would later become in his dealings with authority. When a bossy new lecturer insisted on rigidly enforcing a long-ignored rule that no gramophone could be played between 7 and 10 p.m., Charlie arranged for every student to lock their study doors on the inside and at an appointed hour play their gramophones at full blast. Cometh the hour, the college rattled and shook to popular show tunes, swelling symphonies and jaunty ragtime jazz in cacophonous discordant competition. Incensed, the lecturer ran down corridors screaming and shouting through locked doors to no avail. Apoplectic with frustration, he returned to his own study only to be greeted by screeching cockerels erupting out of his wardrobe and discover burrowing weaner piglets soiling his bed linen.

At Canterbury Agricultural College, Charlie developed a reputation as a droll raconteur and wag. Students helped cart sacks of coal from the railway station to the college bunkers and nothing was said if a sack or two was purloined for the fire grates in their studies. During one particularly cold snap, the raiding got out of hand and the boilerhouse coal bunkers were left almost bare. Miffed and disappointed, the principal was obliged to address the college on fair play. Although it was forbidden to burn coal in their studies, he had turned a blind eye to students helping themselves to a sack or two on occasion, but this time they had gone too far. His kindness had been abused. He went on in this vein for some time. Charlie rose when he sat. 'Sir, on behalf of the students, I wish to lodge a complaint. The quality of the coal in this last shipment is well below standard . . .' Even the principal joined in the laughter.

Early in his incarceration at least, Charlie's sense of humour was still intact. Crossing the Mediterranean on a hospital ship, Charlie was more than a match for his German captors, who gloated in perfect English that New Zealand's top commanders came from German stock. General Freyberg was really General von Freyberg. Colonel Kippenberger was really Colonel von Kippenberger. New Zealand was discovered by a German, Abel Tasman, who was really Abel von Tasman. The Bard of Avon was German. William Shakespeare was really Wilhelm von Shakespeare. All the world's great people had German ancestry. Charlie listened patiently then growled that they had left one famous person out: 'Jesus von Christ!'

The provocation continued at Weinsberg Camp. Pacing the perimeter fence while exaggeratedly counting his steps and scribbling in a notebook attracted the attention of sentries in watchtowers, as Charlie knew it would. In short order a phalanx of guards and an officer came flying across the compound demanding to see what he had written. Charlie resisted, pleading that it was personal and private. When they became agitated and cocked their rifles, he handed it over with a show of great reluctance. There were no numbers. Just a drawing of a desert island with a palm tree and an 'X' marking the spot of buried treasure.

§

After graduating from Canterbury Agricultural College in 1930, Charlie headed for the backblocks of North Canterbury, working at Island Hills, Glynn Wye, Rafa Downs and St Helen's sheep stations, mastering every job from farm manager and head musterer to fencing, shooting rabbits and hunting pigs. He lived through hot dry summers, parching nor'westerlies, freezing snow-bound winters and sodden springs. He learnt how to read the lie of the land in all its moods, how to read the sky and stars, how to ford flooded rivers, how to break in horses, how to shoe horses, how to train dogs, how to slaughter sheep and dress their carcases, how to fend for himself in remote musterers' huts, building uncanny strength and prodigious stamina into his wiry frame. He judged people on deeds and character rather than title or appearance. He became dismissive of pretence, airs and graces. Fiercely egalitarian, he was better than no bastard and no bastard was better than him. His grooming, apparel and vernacular became as rough as guts. Visiting the family home in Christchurch lank-haired, rough-shaven, badly in need of a bath, two dogs in tow, with a drover's tongue to keep them in check, he shocked his mother. He made an effort and scrubbed up for Christchurch race meetings — which is just as well.

In 1935 at Riccarton Park one Saturday he met a petite, pretty, extremely elegant brunette, Mary Eileen 'Molly' McTamney, a dietician at Christchurch Hospital who wouldn't have given him a second glance otherwise. Charlie was instantly smitten. They went dancing that evening. He was waiting for her with red roses when she came off duty the next day and proposed marriage. She refused, but this was by no means the end of their relationship.

The marked improvement in his wardrobe can be traced back to this afternoon. He became a snappy dresser when the occasion demanded, especially when Molly was doing the demanding. She was a gifted, classically trained musician. At high school she won a piano scholarship to Trinity College, Cambridge. Her family were Catholic and poor. Raising four kids on a widow's benefit, her mother could not afford the passage fare. Molly didn't take it up and went nursing instead. She would not have destroyed the gift of a pocket watch. There was no piano in the Conway Flat home, even though they could afford one. Molly didn't need reminding of dreams she had to abandon.

In 1937 Charlie came in from the cold and joined the Valuation Department as an assistant district valuer in Timaru. He was conscientious, industrious and good at his job, but his rough appearance, coarse language and blunt manner of expression did not endear him to the Valuer General when he paid a visit to the Timaru branch. After interviewing their raw recruit, he not unkindly commented, 'Upham, you will never make a civil servant!' As accolades go, they don't come much higher, but Charlie didn't see it that way at the time.

The job made it easier for him to see more of Molly. He never tired of chugging north and standing alongside his old rattle-bang motor vehicle, red roses in hand, waiting for her when she came out the main doors. The canvas roof which flipped back in strong winds obliged them to drive everywhere in oilskins if the weather looked risky. This didn't prevent her saying yes when Charlie popped the question a second time. Early in 1938 she set sail for Singapore to stay with her sister then continued on to England in 1939 to take up a nursing position, with Charlie's engagement ring on her finger. Charlie was worried about developments in Europe, but Molly was not going to be denied a second time.

His High-Church Anglican mother wasn't thrilled at the prospect of her son marrying a Roman Catholic and even less impressed when her daughter Esther converted to her husband's religion and raised her children as Catholics. When Charlie and Molly had daughters, they didn't go to his mother's old school. Charlie's clipped explanation that the girls would go where Molly wanted them to go led to muttering in the Upham sisterhood that she had too much control over him. It led to a certain coolness in the family. Amanda Upham believes her dad started losing faith in organised religion around that time.

To advance his career and keep himself busy while Molly was away, Charlie took leave from the Valuation Department in March 1939 and returned to Canterbury Agricultural College to take a course in valuation and farm management. Drawing on his wide farming experience, he excelled in the classroom, and with his rich fund of riotous yarns and his readiness to help colleagues who struggled in practical subjects he was a popular figure on campus. He obtained a Diploma in Valuation and Farm Management. The 1941 college magazine records that he was an outstanding student regarded as a certainty for Honours and the likely winner of the gold medal for the course. However, a radio broadcast from London made him close his books, pack his bags and depart the hallowed halls before sitting his final exam in Agricultural Law.

After the war Kippenberger was staggered when Charlie told him that he cancelled his wedding planned for February so he could get overseas good and early. He could have taken an officer training course and walked down the aisle as Second Lieutenant Upham and left for Egypt with the main force like everyone else, but he decided that his nuptials could wait but the war couldn't. Molly could wait but not Hitler.

Chapter 6
'Correct way to hold a camel'

In the autumn of 1939 a group of Nazi SS men faked an attack on a German customs post.

Prisoners from Sachsenhausen concentration camp, which had been operating since 1936, were drugged and dressed in Polish uniforms, then taken to the customs post and shot, their bodies left strewn as 'proof' of Polish aggression. Using this grotesque burlesque as his excuse, Hitler's forces stormed across the Polish border. Honouring commitments to Poland, Great Britain formally requested that the Germans leave and set a deadline. A scornful Hitler ignored the ultimatum. At 11.15 a.m., British Summer Time, on the morning of Sunday, 3 September 1939, Prime Minister Neville Chamberlain, dressed appropriately for the occasion in a stiff high-collar shirt, bow tie and tuxedo, made a live broadcast to Great Britain in a thin, weary voice:

> 'I am speaking to you from the Cabinet room at 10 Downing Street. This morning the British Ambassador in Berlin handed the German Government a final note stating that unless we heard by 11 o'clock that they were prepared at once to withdraw their troops from Poland, a state of war would exist between us. I have to tell you now that no such undertaking has been received and

consequently this country is at war with Germany . . .'

Within minutes air-raid sirens began howling in London. It was a false alarm. But there was genuine alarm on the other side of the world. It was approaching midnight in Wellington. Cabinet ministers who had been Christian Pacifists in the last war, officials and service heads huddled around a crackling short-wave radio in Parliament listening to Chamberlain's announcement in confusion and consternation. What had he said exactly? They prudently waited a few hours before responding. As Gerald Hensley observed wryly in *Beyond the Battlefield*, it would have been awkward if it turned out New Zealand had gone to war on a burst of static. Admiralty messages in Morse putting the British Fleet on a war footing provided confirmation.

In the wee small hours of the morning, New Zealand officially declared war on Germany. The proclamation pledged support for justice, freedom and democracy. It was signed by the Governor General and backdated to coincide with Chamberlain's announcement. There was no sabre rattling — just the knocking of knees. Standing in for Prime Minister Michael Joseph Savage, who was terminally ill, Peter Fraser made the announcement on radio. From his sickbed Savage decided he needed to get in on the act — it would be his last act as well. Savage's feeble voice and heartfelt words are what most New Zealanders from that time remember about the outbreak of war: 'Both with gratitude for the past and with confidence in the future, we range ourselves without fear beside Britain. Where she goes, we go; where she stands, we stand.'

In his courtly fashion, Savage was conceding that the only thing you could do with a mad dog was 'shoot the fucking thing'.

When Howard Kippenberger heard the broadcast, he turned to his wife, who had gone white, and said, 'That's the end of the old pleasant days.' A soldier in the last war and a part-time officer in the First Canterbury Territorial Battalion, he promptly enlisted. He passed a medical examination and prayed hard for a command. He hoped that, at forty-two, he wasn't too old. His prayers were answered and three weeks later he was in command of the 20th Battalion based at Burnham Camp, a military depot and ordnance store set in stony fields surrounded by belts of blue gums in the midst of the bare Canterbury Plains. According to Kippenberger, it was an unlovely spot. Hundreds of workmen were busy building huts, cookhouses, ablution blocks, dining halls and classrooms, excavating drains, laying cables, bulldozing roads and laying tarseal. It was noisy, dusty and dirty. Kippenberger and his team were tasked with selecting officers and NCOs from volunteers arriving by the busload. One of the first through the gates was Charlie.

§

Charlie's Canterbury Agricultural College principal, Professor Eric Hudson, who had served overseas in the Great War with distinction, wrote an extraordinary letter to the army on his former student's behalf. Hundreds of fine young men passed through the college during Hudson's tenure, but this was the only such letter he sent. It was succinct and uncannily prescient:

> Canterbury Agricultural College, Lincoln
> The Commanding Officer,
> Burnham Military Camp,
> Burnham.
>
> Dear sir,
> A young man by the name of Upham has left college to join your unit. I commend him to your notice, as, unless I am greatly mistaken, he should be an outstanding soldier.
> Yours faithfully,
> E. Hudson

Charlie did not entirely abandon college activities while in camp. He borrowed a bike and cycled to Lincoln at full speed to run in the Old Boys race at the College Sports and won. Leaping back on the bike, he cycled furiously to Burnham Camp, hoping his absence hadn't been noticed. It hadn't been. Nor had a push-bike been reported as missing.

§

Standing at the window, Lieutenant Colonel Howard Kippenberger surveys recruits in their new uniforms marching past battalion headquarters in ragged, unruly formation. He sighs unhappily. 'This is a dreadful shambles, Frank. We need to select some temporary NCOs pretty smartly. Any thoughts?'

His adjutant, Captain Frank Davis, has all the volunteers' details on index cards in cardboard boxes in front of him. 'Can I suggest, sir, that we look at the chaps who went to boarding school first. Most of those schools have cadet training and military drill.' There is a knock on the open door. Regimental Sergeant Major Steele enters. 'Sorry to interrupt, sir. A new recruit outside insists on seeing you in person.' Irritation flickers across Kippenberger's lean features. 'I'm pretty busy right now, Sar' Major.'

'That's what I told him, sir. He won't take no for an answer, stubborn bugger, pardon my French!'

'What's his problem?'

'He wants leave this weekend!'

'That's completely out of the question.'

'That's what I told him, sir. He's not leaving until he hears it from you, sir!'

Kippenberger smiles. 'In that case you'd better send him in. What's his name?'

'Upham, sir. Charles Hazlitt Upham.'

Kippenberger turns to Davis. 'Look him up, Frank.'

Davis is rifling through an index box when Charlie, scruffy

and coiled like a spring, steps into the room and stands rigidly at attention.

'At ease. Are you in some sort of trouble?'

'Not me, sir. Someone else. Big trouble. Owes me twelve quid, ten shillings on a car I sold him. If he won't pay, I need to give him a hiding.'

Kippenberger suppresses laughter. 'You know where this man is?'

'The Grosvenor Hotel in Timaru. It won't take me long.' Kippenberger is quietly impressed. 'I see. Debts should be honoured. Leave is granted. Make sure you are back in camp by eighteen hundred hours on Sunday.'

'Thank you, sir.' Charlie turns and heads for the door. When the coast is clear Davis waves a card aloft in triumph. Kippenberger smiles. 'Spit it out, Frank. What boarding school did he go to?'

'Christ's College!'

§

Charlie never got his money. The chap got a hiding. Kippenberger got a temporary Lance Corporal. Older than his fellow recruits, of wiry build and not tall, nevertheless Charlie stood out. It was something to do with his piercing blue eyes, his intensity, his practical attention to weapon-handling, his superior fieldcraft and tactics — everything apart from parade-ground drills where he was prone to shouting 'Whoa!' instead of 'Halt!' and 'Up a bit!' instead of 'Dressing from the right!'

One day on parade Kippenberger read out the names of men chosen for officer training at Trentham Military Camp north of Wellington. Charlie's name was on the list. Kippenberger explained that a train would be leaving that Friday night. If any man wasn't interested, they needed to fall out. Charlie's hand shot up like a pensioner with a bladder infection asking permission to go to the toilet — he wanted to know if officer training would delay his departure overseas. Told that it might, Charlie insisted that he be taken off the list.

On 4 December 1939 he was overjoyed when he was selected with ten other Burnham boys for the fifty-strong advance group to precede the First Echelon bound for Egypt. He was sent on final leave. In Christchurch he said goodbye to his parents and sisters then went over the hill to say goodbye to his uncle, the Little Doctor, who hoped he wouldn't have to take a human life. He was promoted to sergeant just before departure. Molly was returning to New Zealand in a few days' time, too late to say goodbye.

He took a Bren-gun manual to study en route, determined to become an expert despite never having seen one, let alone held one or fired one. Everyone had to give a lecture on the voyage. Charlie drew diagrams and gave an impressive lecture on the Bren gun. He stood out even then as no ordinary soldier.

§

Charlie also took a camera with him. His daughter Caroline entrusted me with two precious photograph albums that were showing their age. Filled with petite black-and-white snaps of the life at sea, a group photo of the advance party assembled on the deck, Sri Lankan women picking tea, glorious colonial architecture in Bombay, snake charmers in teeming streets, ancient ruins in Syria, ancient ruins in Athens, orange groves in Lebanon, the Wailing Wall and the Dome of the Rock and Church of the Holy Sepulchre in Jerusalem, elegant cafés in Alexandria, Kiwis playing rugby on burning sand, burnt-out tanks in an empty desert, the Commander of the Second New Zealand Expeditionary Force General Bernard Freyberg VC in leotard togs poised on the diving board at Maadi Camp south of Cairo, and Cairo throbbing and pulsing with life. Charlie handed his Box Brownie to a mate if there was an animal to pat. There is a photo of him squeezing a camel on the bridge of the nose with one hand and holding the halter firmly with the other. Ever the stockman, he has scribbled on the back: 'Correct way to hold a camel to stop it biting you.' On the reverse of another photo of a flock of sheep and shepherd, he has diligently made note of the salient features: 'Fat tailed sheep crossing an irrigation canal near Cairo'. The Pyramids of Giza dominating the horizon go unmentioned.

There is a photograph of him standing in front of the Great Pyramid at dusk and another shot of him, back to the camera, sitting on the top of the Great Pyramid with Cairo below vanishing in the evening haze. There are no photos from Crete where the stay was short and bitter. He starts taking snaps again in Egypt, Syria and Palestine. In May 1942, Charlie's photographic record and letters come to an abrupt stop.

Curiously, there is no mention of the pyramids in Sandford's book or in any of Charlie's letters that I have read. Other New Zealanders writing home or compiling memoirs were fixated on them. Corporal John Broad in his eloquent book *Poor People — Poor Us* writes lyrically about his visit to Giza:

As soon as we could obtain leave, two sappers and I engaged a Dragoman to take us on a personally conducted tour. By the aid of magnesium flares we ascended a sloping passage in the Great Pyramid which terminated in a hall twenty feet high. We followed a horizontal passage 109 feet long to the Queen's chamber. We continued to ascend to the King's chamber. This chamber contained a red granite sarcophagus without a lid. It was empty and has neither sculpture nor inscription of any kind. I thought I would lie at full length in the sarcophagus. The sepulchral atmosphere and feeling of desecration combined to unsteel my heart. Reclining in the midst of this affecting memorial of a Pharaoh whose earthly course

was terminated thousands of years ago I had a psychic
premonition of impending doom.

Well, you would, wouldn't you? The feng shui was hardly
conducive to feelings of deep calm and well-being. The sappers
who took turns after him experienced a similar awareness of
disaster about to happen. At Ruweisat Ridge they were both
blown to smithereens when the Luftwaffe scored a direct hit on
a truck of land mines on which they were riding. Nothing was
found except the handle of a penknife and the heel of a boot. In
the same battle, Broad was badly wounded and taken prisoner.

In *Jonesy*, ex-Member of Parliament Norm Jones, describing
his war experiences, is unsentimental about the pyramids,
moaning that he lost less sweat clambering to the top of
one than he did haggling with guides and souvenir vendors
and brushing away ragged urchins poking dirty postcards
under his nose. He wasn't impressed with Cairo either,
complaining sourly about the heady amalgam of heat, flies,
camel dung, donkey piss, horse manure and human faeces.
The last thing anyone needs when they travel is delicate nasal
epithelium. American comedian Bob Hope on a concert tour
to American troops stationed overseas landed in one Asian
capital and, exiting the plane, was sent reeling backwards
by something especially foul in the hot equatorial night.

'Jesus Christ, what's that smell?'

'It's shit, Bob.'

'I know, but what have they done to it?'

§

I was reminded of this when my cab arrived at Giza. The
olfactory assault lasted until I caught my first glimpse of the
pyramids close up, then jaw-dropping awe overwhelmed
everything. He took some work, but I finally convinced my
guide that I was flying out later that night and couldn't take the

extended horse trek tour or accept any of the other bargain tours he was offering me. He settled for standing me in one spot holding my hands just so. Borrowing my cellphone, he scrambled around in a half circle, taking pictures of me suspending the Sphinx and the pyramids from my fingertips.

It was the off-season. There were few foreign tourists about but scores of smiling locals dressed in their very best and parties of excited school children, many sipping soft drinks, everyone giddy with understandable pride. I walked back to my cab, delighting in their delight. Noor was waiting for me, sucking on a cigarette, holding a pack of light local beer in plastic bottles for me. I'd given him some Egyptian pounds. He refused point-blank to keep the change. I swigged two bottles in rapid succession on the motorway heading back into the city. Noor reached for the empties, saying he would take care of them for me. I assumed he had a recycling bag in the back. He tossed them out the window where they bounced down the road.

Traffic in Cairo races two, three and even four lanes thick in places, bumper to bumper, until it comes to a complete stop without warning. Drivers require the reflexes of a Grand Prix driver, a neurosurgeon's ability to judge microscopic distances, the courage of a bomb disposal expert and the patience of Job. Pedestrians were equally amazing. I saw an elegant man in a three-piece suit calmly thread his way through three lanes of streaming traffic as if he were crossing a drawing room. I saw a teenage boy dribbling a soccer ball dart in and around thundering trucks and buses. This has to be where Egypt and Liverpool superstar Moh Salah learnt his sublime skills. I scribbled in my notebook: 'Cairo is the calm centre of its own storm.'

I loved my time in the Egyptian capital. It helps when you are staying in a hotel on the Corniche in a stately garden suburb and beneath your balcony the Nile, wide and handsome, changes from bronze to liquid silver as night falls and the Cairo Tower, latticed like a vintage soda syphon, glows blue, pink and green against a deep purple sky. It wasn't intentional, but the giant soda syphon is a salute of sorts to the original Shepheard's Hotel which stood on these banks.

With its Persian carpets, stained-glass windows, lush gardens, potted palms and ferns, ornate terraces and granite pillars resembling Ancient Egyptian temples, Shepheard's was much admired for its grandeur and opulence. There were nightly dances for men in military uniform and women in evening gowns. Crown princes, merchants, diplomats, Greek governments in exile, Indiana Jones types, soldiers of fortune, seductresses and spies of every stripe crowded into the famous American Bar, also known as The Long Bar due to the interminable wait to get a gin and bitters, or the house speciality, The Suffering Bastard, a cocktail concocted to cure crippling hangovers. In the dark days of 1942, the waiting time was so bad and the fear so real that Rommel's Afrika Korps might sweep into Cairo at any minute — which a good many Egyptians were looking forward to — that Kiwi and Aussie servicemen used to joke, 'Wait until Rommel gets to Shepheard's, that'll slow the bastard down!'

Shepheard's exalted reputation was such that when the Germans were advancing rapidly across the Western Desert in the spring of 1942, Rommel allowed himself a rare boast, telling senior officers, 'I'll be drinking champagne in the master suite at Shepheard's soon.' The symbol of former colonial rule and reminder of Britain's sense of entitlement was destroyed during anti-British riots in 1952. No attempt was made to restore it, which is a great shame. The new Shepheard's is a poor substitute. The old building was an architectural treat equal to Raffles in Singapore. The jewel in the crown of English privilege would have become a jewel in the crown of an independent Egypt.

Chapter 7

'The war is going wonderfully here'

Under armed escort, the first New Zealand and Australian troopships arrived at the Egyptian port of Tewfik at the Red Sea entrance of the Suez Canal in February 1940.

Despite fears about Japan's future intentions — it had already invaded and was brutally occupying Korea, Manchuria and vast tracts of China — the New Zealand Government decided that our forces should be deployed to Egypt for training before moving on to France for operational service. That training would take place in Maadi Camp 15 kilometres south of Cairo on the eastern bank of the Nile. Backing onto a shady, pleasant town, Maadi Camp somehow managed to be neither. Hot and dusty by day, it could be bitterly cold at night. It became home to parade grounds, a tent city, an ice-cream factory, a meat pie factory, a small brewery, admin blocks, warehouses, workshops, garages, chapels, cinemas, a library, a swimming pool and an infirmary. Apart from the smallest of commemorative plaques, no trace of it remains today. It has been swallowed up in the ever-expanding megalopolis of Cairo and is now a swanky suburb of palatial homes, lush gardens and a riot of purple jacaranda and flame trees. As the Egyptians themselves have ably demonstrated, if you want to be remembered 5000 years hence you need to start with limestone blocks weighing 2.3 tonnes stacked one on top of the other to a height of at least 100 metres. Anything less and you are just kidding yourself.

§

Charlie disliked camp routine, parade drill and route marches. He resented every second not spent learning how to defeat the Germans, who were busy defeating everyone — Denmark and Norway fell in April 1940, then Holland, Belgium, Luxembourg and France in May and June. Chamberlain resigned and Churchill became Prime Minister. British Expeditionary Forces sent to bolster the borders of France and Belgium had to retreat to the beaches of Dunkirk and be evacuated by the Royal Navy and a makeshift armada of civilian boats, leaving behind heavy weapons, vehicles and equipment.

The humiliating fall of Europe in the face of lightning-fast German armour lent a new urgency to training exercises in the Helwan Desert south of Maadi. A fired-up Charlie quickly distinguished himself as someone not afraid to mix it with officers when he thought they were wrong. His bluntness was eye-watering. Having studied a Bren-gun manual endlessly on the troopship on the way over and finally getting to cradle one on a weapons course, Charlie's knowledge of how it operated appeared to be second only to Václav Holek, the Czech who designed it.

He was instructing a private on how to correct a stoppage when a supervising infantry officer intervened to tell him that he was doing it wrong. Charlie bristled silently as the officer demonstrated his preferred, laboured method.

'There you go, Sergeant. Teach it the way I have just shown you.'

Charlie jutted his jaw and responded crisply and calmly, 'I'm not doing that. Your way is wrong. I was showing him the right way!'

It was the officer's turn to bristle.

'You will teach it the way I have just shown you!'

'Who's giving this lesson?' snapped, Charlie. 'You or me? If you want to teach the squad, go ahead, knock yourself out.'

The officer digested this a moment, then turned and walked away.

Charlie's platoon, who had been holding their breath the whole time, exhaled in relief. Charlie scowled at the departing figure. 'Forget what that dipstick said. We'll take a short break. Smoke if you have them.'

It happened again a few weeks later in another sandy gully. Sergeant Upham placed his platoon sections in defensive positions to hold off an imaginary attack. A supervising officer arrived and roundly condemned the placement, curtly ordering Charlie to shift them. Charlie was having none of it. 'It would be bloody stupid to move those sections to where you suggest, sir. My boys are safer where they are. I'll take orders on where the whole platoon goes. After that it's my job to place the sections to best protect my men while putting the enemy at maximum disadvantage. I'm not shifting them.'

The officer swallowed, blinking rapidly. 'If you don't do as you are ordered, Sergeant, I'll have you placed under arrest and have you removed.' A tense silence followed while Charlie scanned the desert landscape, north, south-east and west. He hadn't just been reading Bren-gun manuals, he'd been brushing up on military procedure as well. 'Have me arrested? I don't think so. I have a right to two non-commissioned officers of equal rank to escort me. We're in the middle of a desert. There aren't two other sergeants within five miles of here. Don't take my word for it. Look it up!' He took Charlie's word for it and headed off.

When he was out of earshot, Charlie turned to his disbelieving men. 'Wouldn't know sheep shit from dried dates!'

§

Mussolini waited until 10 June 1940, when France had fallen and it looked as though the war in Europe was coming to an end, before throwing his tasselled fez into the ring. The war artist Peter McIntyre was sitting in a dark cinema at Maadi Camp watching Charles Boyer and Hedy Lamarr make love in the Casbah when the film stopped, lights came up and an officer stepped in front of the screen to state: 'Italy has declared war on us.' The entire audience rose and cheered. The elation subsided when people remembered that the Italian Army stationed in their Libyan colony outnumbered them ten to one. Mad panic ensued.

In the dead of night, it was decided to confuse the Italian Air Force, so tents that had been placed in neat rows needed to be uplifted and moved 100 yards sideways and staggered in neighbouring dunes in pits surrounded by sandbags. No lights were to be used. In the ensuing chaos, trucks crashed about in the dark snapping tent poles and crushing kit bags. Men cursed. One soldier was arrested for lighting a cigarette on the grounds he could have inadvertently guided the entire Italian Air Force onto them.

Some locals would have been thrilled. While never a British colony, the Kingdom of Egypt was effectively under British control. The British acted like Egypt's parents and were deeply resented for it. Tripoli was more than a thousand miles from Cairo, but as Rommel would later demonstrate, with no natural barriers in the way, no civilian populations to consider, save for Bedouins on camels who knew how to make themselves scarce, and with sufficient petrol, grease and water, a panzer division could cover that distance in next to no time.

Mussolini's private boast that he had declared war without actually having to wage it didn't last very long. In September 1940 an Italian offensive managed to occupy Nice just over the border from Italy, suffering colossal losses in the process for incremental territorial gain. They fared better in North

Africa. Italian and Libyan forces advanced 50 miles into Egypt before halting their offensive at Sidi Barrani. Outnumbered British troops retreated along the coast to Mersa Matruh, prompting Mussolini to brag, 'The loss of Egypt will be the *coup de grâce* for Britain!'

His celebrations were premature. In Operation Compass which followed, Allied troops drove the Italian 10th Army back deep into Libya, taking and garrisoning the strategically important port city of Tobruk. Italian troops surrendered in vast numbers. A frustrated and enraged Mussolini expressed the view privately that Italians were a degenerate race capable only of eating ice cream and singing. An English officer, asked over the radio to provide an estimate of the number of prisoners taken, replied laconically, 'Several acres I should think.' This was not the news the German High Command wanted to hear when General Erwin Rommel and the advance party of the Afrika Korps arrived in the Libyan capital of Tripoli less than a week later.

The Afrika Korps' arrival in North Africa didn't overly bother Charlie if his letters home are anything to go by. In his early letters Charlie is chatty, conversational and affectionate, referring to family members by pet names, rendering them incomprehensible unless you know the code. Deciphering these would give Enigma a run for its money, but his tone and intention are always clear. He is fine and they are not to worry about him; instead, they need to take care of each other. The topics are wide ranging. He covers geopolitics and is gung-ho about his first battle but less sanguine about events unfolding in South East Asia and the Pacific.

How are you all? I hope you are well. It is about 5-6 weeks now since I have had a letter. I hope you have been getting all of mine. If you don't get them regularly, it is only because of the hold ups etc . . . The news about the Japs is very disturbing & makes me worry a lot, but

I am quite certain of this that they will never attempt to tackle NZ or Australia. Italy will soon be done for & will never be a 1/3 rate power again, she will be a second Portugal, if it were not for our troops in Libya; the natives there would cut all the Italians' throats . . . I spent the day visiting a lot of my friends in the various hospitals, some of my friends are dead but not many, it takes a lot to kill anyone, & the medical stuff is very good now. We captured some excellent stuff from the Italians . . . There is a NZ Club in Cairo now. It is in the main European quarter, & is the old 'Fascist Club' closed up when Italy declared war. It is quite a good place & prices are very reasonable. There are thousands of NZ troops about now, they are everywhere. I meet so many old friends. They were the blokes I was with at Mersa Matruh . . . this Egypt seems to be the meeting place of 'em all. It is very easy to have an argument here.

Germany is flooding the Balkans & Italy with troops but we are not afraid of 'em now, we have weapons just as good & our boys are just as well trained & with much bigger hearts, the Germans have not seen our real army yet, & take my word, they'll get a shock. They'll never put anything across the shrewd old Turk either, all those people living round the N. Eastern end of the Mediterranean are good fighters, we are sitting pretty here & you'll soon hear of us away up in Europe, then it will be the time for Japan. When this war is over there won't be any more Red Terrors, Yellow Perils, margarine, saccharin tablets, slums, doles, wharfies ruling the roost any more than there will be millionaires. There is going to be a real clean up this time.

The boys of the 1st echelon are very bitter about the way people in NZ papers especially MPs call them 'wife beaters & tax avoiders'. It is pretty good when I think of so many in NZ who owe me money. The first echelon are always known as, & call themselves 'the wife beaters'. The second echelon are known here as the 'Glamour Boys' because of the hits they made with English girls & the awful fuss made of 'em. The 3rd echelon & the poor old reinforcements are all known as 'the conscripts', though they aren't really.

I think you had better take the £20 for my car, unless someone wants a car now. It is better than nothing. I hope Frame is getting his walks & you are not working too hard. Hope Paul is quite better & Pum has an easy time. You could call Pum's new one 'Garth, Darina, Mattia, Barrani, Winghargi Ben-sidi-Williams'. It is no worse than the numerous Kimberley Jones & Mafeking Brownes of 40 years ago. Tons of love to you all.

Your loving Chas

In August 1940, after several months training in the Western Desert, Sergeant Charlie was removed from his flock and sent with a bunch of other three-stripers to the Middle East Officer Cadet Training Unit (OCTU) in Cairo. Instruction took place at Kasr-el-Nil British Barracks adjacent to Cairo Zoo, the oldest zoo in the Middle East. Inspired by the architectural splendours of the Indian Raj, the zoo was obviously wondrous once. It has a decaying elegance now and an even richer olfactory smorgasbord than the necropolis of Cheops. The morning I visited not even scores of family groups enjoying picnics and running, laughing kids licking popsicles could disguise the melancholy. Doubly depressing were the signs on cages reminding visitors that many of the species being held in captivity here faced extinction in the wild. At one enclosure a cheerful keeper with even fewer teeth than the hippopotamus he was feeding insisted that I thrust a sheath of grass through the iron railings. The huge jaw snapped shut with the finality of a guillotine. I shuddered at the thought of Kiwi officer cadets running amuck here in 1940 and letting hippos, rhinos and monkeys out of their pens.

Their stay began innocently enough. General Freyberg paid a visit to Kasr-el-Nil Barracks to see how his boys were faring — all Kiwi soldiers were Freyberg's 'boys' and the affection and ownership was mutual and the burly, towering general was inevitably dubbed 'Tiny', just as every bald man was 'Curly' and less obviously all Clarks or Clarkes were 'Nobby'. Freyberg informed the uptight British commandant that when he was a schoolboy and a visiting VIP requested it, pupils were given the next day off in his honour. The commandant demurred, saying there was a war going on. Freyberg interrupted him to say the New Zealand officer cadets looked tired and they were to be granted leave next day and that was an order. He departed to ringing cheers.

Not happy, the commandant said that half the students — men with surnames beginning A to M — could have the morning off. Surnames beginning N to Z would remain in class and await their turn in the afternoon. Charlie, in the second group, was champing at the bit. Stella Brewery next door had invited the students to look over their plant and sample some of their product, which substituted onions for hops in the brewing process, giving their beer a strange pickle aftertaste. Refusing to be put off, students A to M sampled unstintingly. When Stella finally managed to get them off the premises, they reeled over the road to the zoo practically embalmed, singing at the top of their lungs. Years later, on fishing trips with his mates to the Marlborough Sounds and at battalion reunions, bent double with laughter, Charlie would recount what happened next.

'Within five bloody minutes all the bloody monkeys were out of the bloody cages swinging through the trees, and all of the bloody keepers were inside! A poor bloody RAP military policeman on traffic duty outside the zoo gates couldn't believe his eyes when a bloody hippo charged

onto the street heading for the Nile with a pissed
sergeant on its back prodding it with a bayonet!'

In other tellings, it was *two* sergeants astride a charging
rhino. In the scattering of pedestrians, destruction of
street stalls and mêlée, it's understandable that eyewitness
accounts varied. Charlie would finish the story in a frenzy of
faux outrage. 'And we never got our bloody afternoon off!'

Maybe this rhino, or this hippo — take your pick — was
the inspiration behind the trapped New Zealand Division's
famous midnight breakout at Minqar Qaim. Charlie hated the
spit and polish of the OCTU course and couldn't see the point
of studying First World War battlefield tactics and clashed
frequently with his instructors, who he dismissed as British
twits. Unsurprisingly, Second Lieutenant Upham graduated
bottom of his intake. Charlie disputed this. He claimed the
names were listed alphabetically, punishing him a second time.

It did him a favour of sorts. Graduating officers were not
supposed to return to their former battalions. Kippenberger put
in a special request to the Secretary of War to get Charlie back.
The request was declined then granted when Kippenberger
persisted. Charlie's bottom placing meant he wasn't in great
demand, so Second Lieutenant Upham was posted back to the
20th Battalion who were stationed at Baggush in the Western
Desert with the rest of the New Zealand Division.

§

On the outside, Alexandria Railway Station could pass for
a palace. Inside it's a different story. Kiwi reinforcements
in baggy shorts, socks down around their boots, helmets,
hats and caps on at casual angles, compete for space on the
crowded platform with screeching hawkers in smocks and
fez hats selling fruit and fake artefacts. Steam billows from
an ancient engine. Incomprehensible timetable information

blares from overhead speakers. A sergeant major bellows and points to carriages. Soldiers surge forward. Charlie, self-conscious in his new uniform, has two large kit bags at his feet and is clutching a knobbly musterer's stick. He lets everyone else board first before clambering into a stuffy, standing-room-only carriage.

Huffing and puffing, an ancient steam locomotive similar to the leviathans that Lawrence of Arabia famously used to dynamite and derail in the First World War chugs asthmatically west, hauling a long line of creaking carriages along the northern coast of Egypt. The blue Mediterranean is glimpsed between dunes, too distant to provide any useful breeze. A small man with cunning, darting eyes complains loudly to everyone and no one in particular. 'How much longer are we gonna be cooped up in this shit hole?' From his hard wooden seat, he spots Charlie, who is standing. 'Oi, squire! Mush! These carriages are not fit for pigs. There's not enough air. It's an outrage!'

Charlie smiles. 'Gidday, son. What's your name?'

'Le Gros, Leggy Le Gros. What's yours?'

'Upham.'

'Well, Second Lieutenant Upham, you're an officer, what are you going to do about it?'

Charlie grins, impressed with the impertinence.

'If you like, I'll stop the train and you can hail a camel.'

Soldiers smirk. Le Gros is silenced. Hours later they pull into a desert station. Someone reads a wind-blasted, sun-bleached sign. 'Baggush!'

This isn't the end of the journey. They have a long march ahead of them. Charlie, who has a large amount of kit including his musterer's stick, notices that Le Gros has a small, light pack.

He asks Le Gros, 'Couldn't give us a hand, could you?'

'Christ, we're all soldiers, aren't we? What's wrong with you?'

'Never mind,' replies Charlie curtly. 'Forget it!'

Le Gros dashes forward. 'Relax, boss, I'll take it.'

They join the long column of soldiers trekking towards the setting sun. It is dark when they reach a tent city in the sands. New Zealand flags flutter in the glow of lamps and campfires. A sergeant escorts Charlie to an officer's tent. Inside there is a camp bed, folded blankets, a steel cabinet, a hurricane lamp and a folding chair — into which Le Gros sags after he has dumped his load. Charlie unpacks while Le Gros groans, his eyes closed.

'You okay, Leggy?'

'Give me a minute. Don't speak.'

Charlie waits a few seconds.

'I need a batman, Leggy.'

Le Gros sighs.

'Would you be keen at all?'

'I don't do guard duty. I'm not much of a cook. And laundry is not my strong suit.'

'Fair enough. I reckon a cup of tea would be just the ticket.'

Le Gros nods in agreement, his eyes still shut. 'Wouldn't it just? My feet are killing me.'

'How do you take it, Leggy?'

'Two sugars. And strong. Can't stand hot water in a dirty cup.'

§

Kippenberger fretted about Charlie's first command. His platoon was made up almost entirely of West Coasters — rough-as-guts coalminers, fishermen, farmers and bushwhackers, hard men who had broken the spirit of two previous platoon officers. Kippenberger even took some of them aside and pleaded with them to go easy on their new second lieutenant. He needn't have worried. Pipe in mouth, Charlie leant on his musterer's stick and surveyed them silently for a bit then calmly told them they looked like a tough mob, a lot of boozers who weren't fit, which was true. He abandoned route marches, which he considered a waste of time and effort. Instead he got them leaping on and off trucks and digging in quickly as if under attack and drilled them relentlessly on how to use, maintain and repair their weapons. He demanded better meals from his cooks. He got them more water for drinking and washing. Most importantly, he talked their language. His language might even have been rougher than theirs. He was reprimanded twice for swearing at them on parade. They didn't mind. They called him boss rather than sir. He didn't mind.

Kippenberger need not have worried about Charlie. As this (abridged) letter home written on a train to Cairo shows, the newly minted officer is chatty and affectionate. Every family member has a nickname. He is optimistic about the war. The contrast with his monosyllabic letters from POW camps later in the war could not be more stark:

2/Lt C H Upham C Coy
20th BN.
NZEF Middle East Forces
Friday 11 Jan 41

Dear Hon and Frame,
I hope you are all quite well, it is some weeks now since I have had a letter from you, but had one from Pum about 2 weeks ago. At present you will be surprised to know I am in Alexandria. I got my leave at last. I came down from Desert on Mon. & go away tomorrow. When ever you go in a train here you get in at an early hour, I reached Sidi Gaber a suburb of Alex at 3AM & by the time I had arranged board for 44 NCOs & men also on leave, it was 5 AM when I reached this pub, so slept in 'til noon. I reach Cairo at about 1 AM. The war is going wonderfully

here. I was up as far as the outside of Bardia just before it fell, but now we are well into Libya, about 30 thousand more prisoners at Bardia, making a total over a fortnight or so of 70 thousand prisoners + 10 thousand dead 'uns, about 1/3 of the Libyan Army. Wavell & his generals are wonderfully good, because we lost so few. Of course the Navy & Air Force helped a lot, but there was never as much as 100 men of ours engaged in it. The Italians were not so much cowards as fools, & their officers hopeless, many of their regiments especially the gunners & Libyans fought very bravely, but their position in spite of much superior numbers was hopeless. I can understand easily now how Germany did so well, we were the same here, lightning fast tank attacks, & it is all over, especially if the defenders have been located & were machine gunned systematically from the air for days without chance of even 1 hours rest & sleep for days at a time. I don't know how this war will go, but it looks as if Italy is done, the poor fools don't know how to fight a campaign, & are often childishly simple & feeble, yet their engineering feats here are wonderful. Enclosed is an Italian rosette.

Alex here is very interesting, very full of Greeks (civilians only) who are very cock-a-hoop & no wonder. It is a pretty city full of the most cosmopolitan population in the world. The waterfront & naval shipping are very interesting too. I am staying at a pub called the Eden Hotel, & it is right on the sea about 8 miles out of town at a place called Stanley Bay near Sidi Gaber, only a few yards from a good sandy beach & hundreds of bathing sheds, but the sea is too cold. There are a lot of French & Greek restaurants cabarets theatres etc. I like the Greeks much better than the French, now I have met some of them. The French soldiers are quite decent, I came down in train with a Free French Captain, spoke good English. But the Poles are wonderful fighters & the most excellent, tough

looking, quiet, modest soldiers I've seen. They have mostly
already fought on 3 fronts (Poland, Finland & Norway &
France & Belgium) & also fought their way out to Syria into
Palestine. They & the NZers missed the last push. I am sure
the Polish Brigade will make a great name for themselves
yet, so will we. This is my last sheet of paper, I will write
again when I get down. Tons of love to all.
Chas.

Charlie was clearly homesick, with plenty of time on his
hands, and a week later he wrote another long letter, which I
have abridged.

2/Lt. C H Upham
'C' Coy 20th BN.
4th Inf. Bde. NZEF
Middle East Forces
Thursday 16/1/41

Darling & Frame
How are you all? I hope you are quite well, & had a good
Xmas & New Year. I have not had a letter for some time
but am looking forward to one any day now. Thank you
very much for your parcel Hon with all the things in it.
I hope you all got my Xmas presents & I sent some cigs
from Alex, 3 boxes in one parcel.
    I had a corker time on leave in Alex, 5 whole days, &
had some lovely feeds, tomato soup & rump steak, with
no sand etc or grease. I often think of the corker meals
I would be having at home if I was there. Alex is much
cleaner & more modern & Europeanised & generally
civilized than Cairo, the waterfront is very pretty, & I had
a good day looking at the shipping & had lunch on board
a Naval ship. The air-raid defences at Alex give one an
idea of what the English ports must be like.

The country all the way down from Alex is first rate there is no land as fertile anywhere else in the world, it seemed such a contrast to where we had been. We are now at Helwan Camp, similar but bigger than Maadi & a little further out. It is a rotten camp in my opinion, at least the camp is all right but it is a windy hole. It all seems so formal & boring after being up above, where we could wear anything etc., a platoon commander (i.e. me) was someone up there but down here even Colonels are thick as lice on a Gypo's shirt. Did I tell you I caught a plague of fleas from the Italian trenches. At present I am writing this from our orderly room, I am Bn. orderly officer to-day (same thing as officer of the watch on a ship) & have to sit here on duty till mid night; all sorts of imbeciles from different places in the Base keep ringing up about what one calls trifles.

I am enclosing some snaps, actually of course cameras were not allowed up there. It is much warmer down here & it is a relief to get away from the cold bitter winds. I expect the weather in Chch is pretty good now, & I hope the garden is looking well. I hope you all had a good Xmas, & Daddie got plenty of walks. Don't work too hard sewing etc for the grandchildren.

Tons of love to all
Your loving Chas.

Charlie's nonchalance and optimism about the war was soon to be sorely tested.

Chapter 8

'Our duty to intervene'

Desperate to show that he belonged at the dictators' table, in the early hours of Monday, 28 October 1940, Mussolini ordered his forces to make an unprovoked attack on Greece from bases in Albania. It was another disaster.

The Greek dictator Ioannis Metaxas's contempt for Mussolini outweighed his fondness for Hitler. A fierce Greek counter-attack drove the Italians back deep into Albania. When Italy had invaded Albania two years earlier, Great Britain had pledged to support Greece in any hour of need. That hour had come. It was a question of honour — and cynical expediency according to New Zealand historian Tony Simpson: Churchill desperately needed to demonstrate to President Franklin Roosevelt and America that Great Britain was a reliable ally that kept its word.

General Metaxas accepted help large enough to assist in his fight against the Italians but not so large as to provoke German intervention in Albania or to justify a German invasion of Greece itself. Metaxas died of throat cancer in January 1941 and his successor as prime minister, Alexandros Koryzis, a former banker with no military experience, was more amenable. He agreed to the dispatch of an Australian Division, the New Zealand Division and a British armoured brigade. After the humiliation of Dunkirk, this British Expeditionary Force would drop the tainted 'Expeditionary' label and call itself W Force.

In February 1941 the United Kingdom Cabinet cabled the New Zealand Prime Minister:

> We have taken full cognisance of the risks involved in the despatch to Greece of a large proportion of the troops in the Middle East, but failure to help this small nation putting up a gallant fight against one aggressor and willing to defy another, would have a grave effect on public opinion throughout the world.

The New Zealand Government agreed to join W Force but not without misgivings. Even Churchill had reservations — and it was his idea. He cautioned Anthony Eden, who was leading the British delegation in talks with the Greek Government: 'Do not consider yourself obligated to the Greek Enterprise if in your heart you feel it will only be another Norwegian Fiasco.'

W Force assembled on the Alexandria docks in pith helmets and voluminous tropical shorts called Bombay Bloomers, hoping to give the impression to both the men on board and spies on the dock that the troopships and the accompanying destroyers would be making a sharp left turn out in the turquoise Mediterranean and steaming towards Allied-occupied Tobruk or a hard right turn to the Suez Canal and East Africa, but few were fooled. Indeed, planners in Cairo were already working on detailed evacuation procedures from various Greek ports and southern beaches if need be, and all but the hopelessly deluded knew that they would be.

Back in England, writing in the July 1941 edition of *Partisan Review*, George Orwell admitted:

> No one expected the Greek campaign to be anything but a disaster. I could find no one of whatever kind who believed that the expedition would be successful: on

the other hand, nearly everyone felt it was our duty to intervene.

In short, a futile gesture was deemed morally essential. Greece was at war with Italy but not yet at war with Germany. A swastika fluttered atop the German Embassy in the Greek capital. W Force came ashore at Port Piraeus near Athens under the watchful gaze of German Embassy staff making a careful note of the men, munitions and machines being unloaded. Allied soldiers had strict instructions not to tear down Nazi flags, deface Nazi emblems or insult anyone wearing a German uniform. It could have been galling, but it didn't seem to cramp their style unduly. Charlie's photograph albums show the New Zealand Division enjoying 'eat, drink and be merry' times in Athens, clambering over the Acropolis like tourists. Clarence Furey, a sapper with 19 Army Troops Company, of course checked out the brothels and the dance scene, admitting later: 'The Greeks are good people. We picked up a couple of sheilas who took us into a dive where they throw girls around.'

It was a brief respite before moving 300 miles north to take up defensive positions near the Aliakmon River, west of Albania and south of Yugoslavia — which was hoping and praying to stay out of any fight — and south-east of Bulgaria which was bulging at the seams with Germans waiting to sweep across the border. Charlie's platoon ended up in a Greek hamlet called Riakia, where they stayed for seventeen days, furiously digging in, erecting wire and camouflaging their defences. Camouflage was something Charlie prided himself on. Their job was not made any easier by their line running close to a local church and through graves which had to be disturbed and Greek burial customs respectfully observed.

Charlie's vocal batman Leggy Le Gros was not convinced these customs served any useful purpose. In many respects, Leggy was to Charlie what Baldrick was to Rowan Atkinson's television scoundrel Blackadder. Unwisely, Leggy was put in charge of disinterring bones, shifting them to new graves and burying them again with due reverence. Getting confused, he literally lost the plot. Some skeletons ended up with three legs, others with two skulls, and worse. Perhaps in compensation, the padre of the 20th Battalion gave away sixty bars of chocolate to wide-eyed local children, who clutched them tightly in their grubby fists and raced home with them unopened. If the Greek gods were offended by this desecration, they punished the wrong man. Charlie, who had been a bad-tempered, tightly coiled spring, driving his men hard and himself even harder, was struck with debilitating dysentery which left him thin and weak. His boys found him a donkey to ride and foraged for fresh milk for him. His bowels would continue to plague him for some time.

On 6 April 1941, Germany attacked Yugoslavia and Greece with more than 29 divisions and over a thousand planes. The ill-equipped and poorly prepared Yugoslav Army collapsed, and Belgrade was bombed relentlessly then taken over in less than a week. Houses of cards have shown more tensile strength. Yugoslavia put up little fight. Completely unimpeded, German forces raced south, crossing the mountainous Greek border below the Allied defensive line, threatening to cut them off. New Zealand Prime Minister Fraser cabled Whitehall:

> The operation, which had always been regarded as highly dangerous and speculative, is now obviously much more hazardous. Pressure by the Germans might lead to a rapid collapse of the Greeks which would leave the British force in the air.

Prime Minister Koryzis advised the Allies to get out while the going was good. Excusing himself politely from a tense Cabinet meeting, he went into an adjacent room and shot himself. Not the best role model under the circumstances. Over the next three weeks, across exposed plains and over tortuous alpine passes, Commonwealth forces staged a ragged withdrawal and dogged rearguard action against the advancing Germans. Antony Beevor in his magisterial book *The Second World War* describes tearful, apologetic Allied troops destroying bridges and railways as they withdrew but being treated with great forgiveness and friendship by the locals. Orthodox priests blessed their vehicles and village women gave them bread. It was the same in Athens where they were hugged and had flowers, oranges and cigarettes tossed into their trucks.

Near Mt Olympus Charlie's platoon were posted to defend a vital crossroad clogged with streams of refugees and retreating Greek troops. With no British aircraft to be seen, German planes owned the skies. South of Larissa, a long convoy of trucks, nose to tail on a road raised about 3 metres above the surrounding land, watched helplessly as an enemy plane approached flying low, barely above the telephone lines. To make the point that the New Zealanders were in deep shit, the grinning gunner in the Dornier pulled the turret back and tossed out rolls of toilet paper.

Charlie ignored high-flying observation planes, paying them no heed, and his men followed his lead, until Kippenberger reprimanded him sharply. 'When the real thing comes, Upham, you'll find your men will be too slow. They'll think it's another snooper. You'll have casualties.' Charlie was more cautious after that, apart from the time he grabbed a Bren gun off a sergeant and stepped out into the open to fire a sustained burst at an enemy plane as it howled down on a long strafing run. It passed overhead unstruck. Underneath, by some miracle also unstruck, was Charlie. Others were not so fortunate. In his Waiouru oral history interview, Clarence Furey tells a shocking story. An old mate who'd been in Greece with him was on his deathbed and asked to see him.

'There was something he wanted to tell me. He'd never told anyone about it. It was the most terrible sight he'd seen in his life. It was on Mt Olympus. They were driving a British half-ton truck and they were hit by a sniper. The truck slewed into a bank. He and another bloke jumped out and started running. There was an air raid. A plane on a strafing run cut the other bloke clean in half through the navel. His upper body fell to the ground and his legs were still running down the road . . .'

According to General Sir Peter de la Billière's account in *Supreme Courage*, the frenzied retreat was punctuated with moments of light relief. One story has it that Charlie's convoy of trucks driving through a deserted town spotted a bank with two huge beautiful wooden doors and screeched to a stop. Charlie was persuaded to delay the column while they checked it out. He gave them six minutes and waited impatiently in his jeep. The doors were duly blown off their hinges and scavenging men rushed in, grabbing armfuls of drachmas from drawers, tills and open safes. A grateful soldier, probably Leggy, brought Charlie two great wads of notes, which Charlie stuffed in his trouser pockets.

Later, as they went out to the destroyer which had come to evacuate them, Charlie fell asleep in the tender. From his days as a high-country shepherd, he could pretty much sleep anywhere, strapped to the speakers at a heavy metal concert if necessary. When he woke up, he found he was the sole passenger heading back to the Greek harbour with the crew. The helmsman was most reluctant to turn around. Charlie was able to reach into his pockets and offer him a substantial bribe. The ill-gotten gains did the trick. The boat turned around and Charlie only just made it. They were hauling up the scramble nets as the tender pulled back alongside.

The Greek tragedy played out in two acts: the first in April on the mainland, the second act in May on the island of Crete,

500 kilometres south, where most of the Commonwealth troops were deposited so the Royal Navy could make more rescue runs. There was limited space on board and all manner of things had to be left behind. A wind-up gramophone and records were smashed on the sands. Even bagpipes were disabled lest they fall into enemy hands, as were rifles, machine guns, artillery pieces, tanks, jeeps and trucks.

Everything was in short supply on Crete, and as the Luftwaffe on low strafing runs there did not toss rolls of toilet paper out of the cockpit, Charlie's booty served yet another, higher purpose never envisioned by the Greek Mint.

Chapter 9

'They're dead on time'

The thing that most surprised me about Crete was the size and scale of it. I don't know what I was expecting when I emerged from the arrivals hall at Heraklion International Airport, but it wasn't high mountains running east to west as far as the eye could see covered in fresh snow.

It was high noon and cool, which again I wasn't expecting in the middle of the day in the middle of the Mediterranean. Suddenly, it seemed appropriate that Crete should be the birthplace of Zeus, the Greek god of the sky, lightning and thunder.

I picked up my economy VW Polo from ACE Rent a Car with less trepidation than picking up my rental in Berlin a week earlier. I was getting used to manual transmission again and driving on the right-hand side of the road was becoming less nerve-wracking. I hired a Sat Nav to make my life easier, but the nice lady in the yard couldn't programme it. Nor could I. It was in Greek. She insisted that I had nothing to worry about. If I drove west on the national highway, the beach resort of Georgioupolis would be on my right. I couldn't miss it.

As it happens I could. *Twice.* An English archaeologist and classics scholar once described Crete's roads as having gone artistically to ruin. True, but that wasn't the biggest problem. While no autobahn, the main highway was perfectly fine. The problem lay with Google Maps on my phone and the guidebook they had given me at ACE Rent a Car that stated place names in English when, on the ground, they were printed in Greek, which is derived from ancient Phoenician where they scratched lines in clay tablets to make letters — some looked like the footprints of wading birds, others looked like atomic symbols that bore scant resemblance to their English translation. I drove through a landscape defined by the periodic table in which every second town, turn-off and hamlet was a conglomeration of rare earth metal.

The mountains, olive groves, orchards, mulled mulberry trees, rocky coast and sweeping beaches were magnificent, but I was too anxious to fully appreciate them. The dipping, weaving road didn't help. Crete is only 260 kilometres long, but it's still a six-hour drive from one end to the other. Small wonder in the dead of night over a narrow winding metal road that the Australians, setting out from Georgioupolis, were late getting to the start line for a counter-attack on Maleme airfield on the first night of the German airborne invasion on 21 May 1941.

Night was falling when I finally got to Georgioupolis, having overshot it several times. The first time I was driving west to Chania then doubling back when I realised my mistake, only to overshoot it again when driving east. I was ready to scream and fully resigned to sleeping in my car, when I finally found the picturesque river-mouth resort just in time to see in the last rays of the sinking sun a slim causeway jutting out into the darkening sea. At the end sat the white chapel of the Orthodox Greek Church of Nikolaos, turning a gorgeous, soft phosphorescent pink — the perfect place to end any pilgrimage, but my pilgrimage wasn't done.

My hotel took some finding. It was modest to the point of austere. There was no signage, no place to park, and inside there was no reception desk and no receptionist. Just marble stairs splotched with stains the colour of milky tea leading to a gloomy second floor. The dismay on my face must have been obvious to the plump girl in a black T-shirt and black leotards who came puffing up behind me. 'You are going to stay?' she asked anxiously. When I told her I had pre-paid for four nights, she visibly relaxed and showed me to my room. Handing me the keys, she said I had better be quick because the supermarket downstairs was closing soon. My perplexed expression gave me away, again. 'For toilet paper and soap,' she explained. There was a small room off the small bedroom with a small blue couch facing a kitchen bench and a microwave oven attached to the wall in pride of place as if it were a flat-screen television.

The rooms were freezing. I slept fully dressed. During the night I had a repeat of the nosebleed I had on an autobahn in Germany and woke up in a room smelling like uncooked black pudding. As is my habit, I made my bed neatly in the morning, folding back a triangle of duvet so the cleaning staff could see the bloodstained sheets and pillow slip. Staying single nights in most of my stopovers in Weinsberg, Leipzig, Modena, Florence and Athens, I had fallen behind in my laundry. I used the kitchen sink to wash socks, underpants and two shirts and hung them out on the minuscule balcony overlooking a small square with sorry coloured lights and a feeble fountain and went off exploring battlefields.

I returned at dusk. The bed hadn't been changed and my clothes were still sodden. It was the same story the next day. The bloodstains were turning rusty. The shirts were dry, but the socks and underpants were damp. I dried them in the microwave and discovered that it is possible to overcook a sock. Who knew? They coagulate and shrink to half their normal size. Heading out to a taverna for a beer and a colossal unsatisfactory moussaka, I met the only other guest on the dim staircase. A massive, wild-eyed, bushy-bearded man in heavy boots, military-style camouflage pants and a black puffer jacket, he looked like a member of the Chechen Mafia on the run from a War Crimes Tribunal. He glowered at me on the milk, tea and urine-coloured landing. I reminded myself quickly: don't stare and no sudden movements!

I shifted out next day to a hotel around the corner with Wi-Fi, room service, soap *and* toilet paper and a flat-screen TV on the wall. Call me old-fashioned, but I felt pampered and spoiled, acutely mindful that on this stretch of coast most of W Force slept under the stars with temperatures dropping sharply after sunset.

§

Obliged to abandon their entrenching tools, picks and spades in Greece, Charlie's 20th Battalion dug slit trenches with their bayonets among olive trees. Having lizards drop onto their faces when at the bottom of trenches was disconcerting so everyone slept above ground. Digging any sort of trench was impossibly hard work, striking rocks and roots all the time. Thanks to the New Zealanders' excellent camouflage skills, German bombers and fighters had no idea they were tucked away in the grove, and they were left alone during air raids.

Cold nights and the hard ground made sleeping difficult. Lying on a thin ground sheet, trying to cover as much of themselves as possible, Charlie and Leggy engaged in an endless tug of war while sharing their one army blanket. The back and forth got more aggressive as the nights dragged on, their bones ached and their teeth chattered. 'For shit's sake, Leggy. I'm freezing my arse off here. You have to share!'

'You can talk, boss!'

'Fuck it! I've had a gutsful! I'm cutting the bloody thing in half!'

'You can't do that!'

'I can. It's my blanket. You sold yours, remember? Can I borrow your bayonet, or have you sold that as well?'

They stood and folded the blanket between them like

two housewives taking in washing, Leggy checking carefully to make absolutely sure that the fold was exactly down the middle. Charlie shook his head. 'For fuck's sake. Satisfied?' Leggy nodded. Surgery completed, they lay down with their separate rectangles of wool providing even less comfort than previously.

'Well done, boss. This was a really stupid idea.'

'Stop grizzling. It's fair.'

They were not alone in their discomfort. A ghostly figure rose from the ground mist nearby, slapping his arms across his chest and stamping his feet, gazing about as if in search of something in the gloom. 'What's wrong?' a voice asked.

'I'm looking for a warmer tree.'

§

Everyone in W Force assumed Crete was a temporary staging post on their exodus to Egypt where they were sorely needed. Having landed in Tripoli a few weeks earlier, Rommel's Afrika Korps were laying siege to Tobruk and subjecting the Australian garrison to a relentless bombing and artillery barrage. Freyberg was keen to get back to Maadi and Helwan camps south of Cairo as soon as possible to rebuild and re-equip his bruised and battered division, but a secret meeting in a small villa between Chania and Maleme put paid to all that. General Archibald Wavell, Commander in Chief Middle East, flew in from Cairo in a light aircraft with grim news. Crete was about to be attacked. After the retreat from Greece and the Dunkirk debacle, Whitehall were desperate for runs on the board. Churchill didn't want any more retreats. The island had to be held no matter what — and Freyberg would head the defence. News of an imminent attack came as no real surprise to Freyberg. What staggered him was the level of detail in the German invasion plans which the Germans had code-named 'Operation Mercury'.

Working in great secrecy at Bletchley Park, a rambling mansion set in rural Buckinghamshire north-west of London, home to the Government Code and Cypher School, after much trial and error and some eureka moments of pure genius from mathematician Alan Turing, a team of boffins had devised a machine half Heath Robinson contraption, half computer, capable of cracking the Axis Powers' previously impregnable Enigma and Lorenz codes. This allowed the Allies to eavesdrop on communications in which Operation Mercury figured prominently.

The brainchild of General Kurt Student, the invasion plan for Crete didn't impress Hitler. He didn't want anything to delay Operation Barbarossa — the massive attack on Russia scheduled to take place on multiple fronts in a few weeks' time. Student argued that taking Crete was a complementary exercise. Occupying Crete would deny British long-range bombers airfields from which to threaten the Rumanian oil refineries, upon which the German war effort depended. Conversely, occupying Crete would provide the Axis Powers with airfields and a naval base with which to threaten the Suez Canal and British interests in the Eastern Mediterranean.

On his special train thundering through the glorious Semmering Pass in Austria, Hitler finally consented to the attack. The initial blitz would capture all three airfields on the northern coast — Maleme, Rethymno and Heraklion — along with the capital, Chania, and the deep-water port at Suda Bay. From these toeholds German forces would fan out and occupy the whole island.

Ultra, the name given to intelligence obtained from breaking the German codes, gave the Allies a priceless advantage. Every book written on the battle for Crete makes the case that it was an advantage of which Wavell and Freyberg didn't take full advantage. Most authors attribute this reluctance to fears that using this information would draw attention to the fact that they had it and thus compromise its secrecy. This catch-22 is debunked by historian Chris Pugsley: Freyberg knew *precisely when* and *precisely where* the Germans would concentrate their attack. Artillery was placed, men were positioned, barbed wire was unfurled and mines were laid to best meet that threat. Unfortunately, the threat kept escalating while Freyberg's resources remained static. When he learnt via Ultra that the German invasion force had swollen to 35,000 men, including 12,000 parachutists, 150 long-range bombers and 100 fighter aircraft, Freyberg sent a jittery cable to Wavell:

> The forces at my disposal are totally inadequate. Unless the number of fighter aircraft is greatly increased and naval forces are made available to deal with the seaborne attack I cannot hope to hold out with land forces alone, which as a result of the campaign in Greece are now devoid of any artillery, have insufficient tools for digging, very little transport and inadequate reserves of equipment and ammunition. If these cannot be made available I urge that the question of holding Crete should be reconsidered.

Wavell's reply the next day was almost sunny: 'The difficulties and dangers of your situation are fully realised, but I am confident that you and the magnificent troops at your disposal will be equal to the task.' He didn't end with 'Toodle pip!' but he might just as well have. When junior officers sought permission to disable Maleme runway by mining it, digging trenches and blowing up a nearby bridge servicing the airfield, Freyberg consulted Wavell and permission was denied. Freyberg was told that the RAF, who had all but vanished from the sky, wanted the runway to remain operational as they might need it at a future date. So did the Germans, but much sooner.

Even without Ultra, the fact that the Luftwaffe spent three

weeks bombing towns and harbours, targeting gun batteries and strafing Allied defensive positions while taking great care not to destroy any of the airfields was a massive giveaway. A full-page Axis Powers ad in the Allied newspaper for the troops, *Crete News*, outlining their plans couldn't have made them any plainer. 'We should have put drums on the runway,' said a bitter Clarence Furey, who was at Maleme. 'Hargest should have let us put drums on the airstrip. We told him, but he wouldn't listen.'

§

With his thick slicked-back, wavy hair, thin Clark Gable moustache straight out of *Gone with the Wind* and an iced drink in hand, New Zealand war artist Peter McIntyre cut a handsome, debonair figure poolside in Cairo when W Force retreated to Crete. Bored with painting portraits of brigadiers, he sought permission to join them. Freyberg, who had spotted McIntyre's prodigious talents the previous year and made him an official war artist with the rank of lieutenant, gave his consent. A gifted painter of landscapes in watercolour and portraits in oil was deemed essential to the war effort, whereas stills photographers and movie cameramen were not. As a consequence, there are very few photos of Allied troops on Crete. If you relied on the visual record, you would hardly know they had been there, apart from when Germans took them prisoner. Almost every book published about the Battle for Crete depends on German photographs for its illustrations. Even fiercely patriotic books published in Crete and written in Greek have to suffer the indignity of using images shot through a German lens.

When the New Zealand concept artist Brendan Heffernan prepared a storyboard for a film on Charlie that never went beyond the storyboard stage, all of his reference sources were German and he had to use his imagination to depict Kiwis in action. I saw this imbalance finally being addressed in Crete. A burly young man conducting guided tours of Second World War battlefields showed me his website on his cellphone. In pride of place he had illegally downloaded some of Brendan's stunning images and put them to good use.

With Reich Propaganda Minister Goebbels cracking the whip, German cameramen excelled in documenting their military triumphs. There was an insatiable appetite in Berlin for newsreel footage of lands conquered and enemies vanquished. Propaganda publications included *Signal*, the largest-selling magazine published in Europe during the war; its circulation reached three million in 1943, most of it outside Germany. It was produced by the Wehrmacht in Berlin in twenty languages expressly for people in conquered and occupied territories, and its purpose was to exalt life in the Third Reich, glorify the power and might of German armed forces and reinforce the inevitability of German victory.

The name 'Signal' was chosen because it has the same meaning in virtually every European language so the same masthead could be used everywhere. The editors enjoyed the services of over a thousand cameramen embedded in propaganda units which followed Axis soldiers, sailors and airmen into battle. They were supplied with state-of-the-art Agfa-Gevaert colour cameras fitted with superb precision Leica lenses. As a result, the eight-page photo spreads in *Signal* were filled with some of the most vivid and arresting images taken during the war and went some of the way to satisfying Goebbels' constant craving for heroic images.

The attack on Crete was expected to provide stirring copy. Movie cameramen and stills photographers accompanied German paratroopers in the gliders. Meanwhile the New Zealand Division made do with Peter McIntyre doubled over his pad sketching furiously with charcoal and coloured pastels. Suck on that, Nazi Germany! McIntyre's skills didn't go to waste on Crete. He was commissioned to paint a portrait of the Greek king who had abandoned his palace and fled Athens with the retreating Allied forces, his personal luggage consisting of a good number of very heavy leather suitcases that strong men struggled to lift. This lent weight to the suspicion that he'd fled the palace with more than just a toothbrush, a trusty razor, socks, bespoke shoes and monogrammed shirt — quite possibly he had the Crown Jewels and a hefty quantity of gold bullion as well.

§

For Charlie, 20 May dawned like most of his mornings on Crete. In the grey half-light at the far end of the olive grove, crouching with his pants around his ankles, he had another attack of the squitters. This was possibly made worse by the alcoholic beverages, which came in every colour of the rainbow, that he and Leggy had consumed the previous day in copious quantities in the old Venetian city of Chania, a few miles downhill to the east. The pretty barmaid they were trying to impress hadn't helped. For the first week on the island Charlie had been responsible for a run on the drachma until Leggy realised to his horror that the stolen notes he'd been wasting as toilet paper were valid currency on Crete.

In the lightening skies to the north, German bombers and fighters appeared out of the haze as per usual, but in larger numbers than normal. Charlie nodded. He was expecting this. Bombs and bullets rained down on the dark coast to the east and west of their hideout. The air crumples and thumps, while columns of black smoke billow up from the ship's graveyard of Suda Bay.

Once their ordnance was spent, the planes turned for home and a heavy silence descended again. In the stillness, breakfast is prepared. Leggy makes Charlie rice pudding. 'This'll knock your shits on the head, boss.' Leggy waves some tins proudly. 'Highlander condensed milk. Rare as rocking-horse shit and not cheap. Had to sell your spare boots.' Upham says nothing and accepts the sweet, sticky mess gratefully. The violent stomach cramps don't return, which is a good sign, but the planes do, which is not.

'Holy Jesus! Take a look at this!' someone shouts. Leggy and Charlie take a look. The horizon to the north is filled with dark specks, as dense as swarming bees. The familiar drone is replaced with a low throb that makes the air itself pulse and vibrate like a tuning fork. It grows into a deafening growl that is met with another deafening roar from below as Allied guns open up. Passing over the shoreline, the black specks give birth to hundreds of smaller black specks of their own, which blossom into floating parachutes. The scene has an ethereal beauty. 'They told us at Bullshit Castle the bastards were coming this morning,' Charlie barks. All his men can do is watch paratroopers descend in the distance and listen to all hell breaking loose beyond them. The 20th Battalion are being held in reserve. And if anything is guaranteed to give Charlie the shits, Highlander condensed milk or not, it's being held in reserve.

§

That same dawn a junior British officer is dispatched to Chania with a message for General Freyberg, who at that hour is at his hillside villa with sweeping views to the west and across the bay to the Suda docks. The first wave of German aircraft has been and gone and all is quiet on a lovely late-spring morning, cloudless with no wind. The message delivered, Freyberg kindly invites the runner to stay for breakfast. It's not a sumptuous spread, but it's better than what the junior officer had partaken of for some time so he accepts gratefully. They sit outside on a small verandah, just the two of them. Freyberg hears a growing roar and looking up sees a sky full of dark Ju 52 Junkers transport aircraft towing six gliders each and Ju 52 Junkers disgorging paratroopers ten at a time. Hundreds and hundreds of different-coloured parachutes — psychedelic thistledown — hang in the air.

It's a little after 7.30 a.m. Freyberg continues silently eating his breakfast. The young officer wonders what he should do. It seems impolite to interrupt the general's thoughts. On the other hand, the sight is extraordinary and quite possibly militarily significant. Eventually, he respectfully draws the general's attention to it. Freyberg looks up, glances at his watch, and says evenly, 'They're dead on time,' and returns nonchalantly to eating his breakfast.

Such was the barrage greeting them, the Germans suspected their plans had been intercepted. A captured British colonel was asked by a German officer. 'You knew we were coming today. Who told you?' A Luger was pressed into his stomach. 'You have twenty seconds to tell me.' The question was put to the men captured with him. 'If any of you know, tell me and save this officer's life!' 'Lord Haw-Haw!' shouted one soldier gleefully, and all the prisoners roared with laughter. Lord Haw-Haw was William Joyce, a US-born Briton who broadcast taunting Nazi propaganda to Allied troops from a radio studio in Hamburg. In one broadcast Haw-Haw warned the New Zealanders that the Luftwaffe had a bullet for every leaf and a bomb for every olive tree in Crete. The German officer stormed off in disgust.

The first wave of the German invasion — bound for Maleme airfield, Prison Valley inland from the coast, and the harbour city of Chania — set off at dawn on 20 May 1941 from airfields north of Athens in high spirits, singing rousing battle hymns and convinced of their own rectitude. One German paratrooper wrote in his diary:

Now the shadow of the Junker, for fractions of a second, glides over the huge ruins of the Acropolis, whose pillars

glow in red-golden hues. The sight of this great fortress
and temple has a deep effect on us. We feel or rather are
palpably aware that we too are helping to build great
times and only toughness can look history in the face.

Their appointment with destiny turned into a date from
hell. Nearly half the young men who left Greece that
morning never saw another dawn. The Germans later
admitted they made a number of serious miscalculations.
The New Zealanders were particularly good at melting
into the landscape and German reconnaissance pilots
underestimated the number of Allied troops hidden in olive
groves and orchards in the hills around Maleme and Chania.
They also underestimated the toughness of Commonwealth
soldiers — especially the ferocity of the Maori Battalion.
And they were preposterously deluded when they thought
the famously independent people of Crete, who had
contempt for the Metaxas regime, coupled to a deep loathing
of officials in Athens, plus zero affection for the Greek royal
family, would hail them as liberators.

Dropped from deliberately low heights, paratroopers
descending at the rate of 4 metres a second had very little
time to brace and position their feet correctly to avoid being
killed on impact with the ground. Some landed in irrigation
ponds, rivers and the sea and drowned. Some landed in trees,
leaving them trapped like flies in a web. Punctured by bullets,
many chutes bled air and dropped like stones, white silk
settling softly over mashed bodies like shrouds. Some gliders
set alight by anti-aircraft and tracer fire became flying funeral
pyres, their human cargo writhing balls of flame as they leapt
from aeroplanes, burning to death as they descended.

Other paratroopers twisted and squirmed helplessly in
their harnesses as they floated into merciless, withering
fire. A shot aimed at a paratrooper's boots had a good
chance of hitting him in the chest or abdomen. Aussie and

Kiwi farm boys said it was like shooting ducks. Paratroopers descending within rifle range were as good as dead before they hit the ground. Almost all of them not killed in the air were hit within minutes of landing. Dazed and confused German paratroopers spilling intestines into their jumpsuits lay about shouting plaintively: 'Save me, Anglais, save me! Don't shoot, kamerad, don't shoot! Water, please!'

German paratroopers lucky to be taken alive complained bitterly at the unfairness of being fired upon while still in the air. Some reprimanded the Allies: 'You must wait until we have landed and formed into units before shooting!' The universal response was unprintable. Under Protocol I of the Geneva Conventions attacking parachutists escaping from an aircraft *in distress* is a war crime. Firing on airborne forces who are descending by parachute is not. Nor is firing on someone who asks for time out so he can consult his handy pocketbook copy of the Geneva Conventions.

One unfortunate paratrooper floated down onto parked trucks, toppling a Dixie cooker and sending the contents cascading over pebbles. Enraged drivers devoted more energy and profanity salvaging what they could of their breakfast than dealing to the hapless gatecrasher. The condemned man did not eat a hearty meal. A German sergeant scrambling around on the ground looking for his men made a mental note of the controlled fire and preponderance of single bullet holes in the heads of his dead comrades and concluded that fate had cruelly delivered them into an area stocked with specialist snipers. Not so. Just well-drilled Kiwi farm boys, most of whom were already crack shots with a .303 before entering the war.

It was scarcely any better for Mountain Division troops descending in ungainly gliders that clipped treetops, got tripped by grapevines or cartwheeled across stony riverbeds, sending bruised and confused survivors staggering into a violent world. Word of the carnage got back to

Greece. Aircraft limping back to Athens with their fuselage riddled with bullet holes confirmed the swirling rumour. Some Paratroop Division troops and Mountain Division troops scheduled to take part in the second wave bound for Rethymno later that day refused to board their aircraft and were executed on the spot. Understandably, the insurrection was short-lived and self-corrected in time for the third wave bound for Heraklion.

When Hitler heard the dire news, he ordered Goebbels to conceal the invasion from the German people. Late in the evening at the German headquarters in the Hotel Grand Bretagne in Athens, a shaken, panic-stricken General Student waited with his pistol by his side, ready to use it on himself if the worst came to the worst.

§

I got a better appreciation of the scale and topography of the battlefield from Stelios, my Cretan guide, amateur historian and former paratrooper, when he took me in his disintegrating car to Cemetery Hill, a high point between the coastal plains and distant snows. On top, a large concrete pad with low sides pooled with water from overnight rain. Weeds and shrubs sprouted from cracks. Graffiti covered the walls. A marble plaque that had fallen from its mounting lay face down on wet paving. In the centre a large grey-green plinth splotched with moss was slowly crumbling. Engraved on a stained, dissolving plaque were the words: 'In Memory of the New Zealand servicemen who gave their lives in the struggle for freedom on Crete 1941–1945'.

It's an unlovely, desolate place that Stelios clearly regarded as sacred. He tenderly pressed on me a small limestone rock that I was to take home. In every direction there was countryside big and broad enough for any number of parachutists to fall out of rifle range and out of sight. Gliders had plenty of room to circle like drugged seagulls until they found suitable landing sites. Once safely down, paratroopers and mountain troops scrambled to collect supplies and heavy weapons from the different-coloured canisters that floated down with them. Fully equipped, they organised themselves into units and spread out in attacking formations. Some canisters fell among New Zealanders who helped themselves to German machine guns, chocolate and ammunition, marvelling in disbelief at the Thermos flasks filled with hot coffee. New Zealanders dashed out of hiding and grabbed the swastikas and white sheets acting as drop zone targets and shifted them closer to their positions so they could take better advantage of the bounty raining from the sky. Mostly, though, it just rained dead men and boys.

§

Charlie's frustrated platoon were held in reserve, well back from action, until the Commander of C Company, Denver Fountaine, came running with news that paratroopers had been spotted floating into the gully next to theirs. Taking half a dozen men with him, Charlie raced off through olive trees, up and over the crest of the ridge to where parachutes lay on open ground and dangled from trees. 'Cover me!' hissed Charlie. They went into a drill they had practised repeatedly. Picking their cover, they dropped to the ground and started firing into the area where the chutes lay. As stealthy as a cat after a sparrow, Charlie moved around the flank of the grove and out of sight. Five minutes later they heard a volley of shots. Then an ominous silence, until Charlie emerged out of the olive trees unscathed, dangling a German helmet, and in a voice 'high with excitement' in Sandford's account, told his men that things were jake now.

§

I read this as adrenalin-drenched relief rather than bloodlust. There is no record of Charlie losing sleep over killing Germans, nor is there any record of him exulting in their deaths. Another VC winner, Major Robert Cain, who features in Jeremy Clarkson's documentary on the Victoria Cross, *did* feel exultant after killing his first Germans. He was part of Operation Market Garden, the doomed 1944 airborne assault to take the bridge at Arnhem in the Netherlands. Two of his friends had just been killed. Clarkson quotes from Cain's diary, 'For the first time since childhood my eyes filled with tears. My heart filled with rage.' Rounding a corner, he ran into five Germans and mowed them down with a Bren gun. 'I cannot describe the surge of dreadful and unholy joy I felt.'

Clarence Furey felt differently: 'I'm not proud of taking another man's life. I didn't like it. My immediate thought was what's his mother going to think? She brought him up, suckled him and he gets killed by a bloody New Zealander.'

Norm Jones felt nauseous.

> When I took a snap shot of his head, I did it instinctively, with no more feelings or thoughts than I used to feel shooting a deer or rabbits. Transfixed, I stood staring at his exposed brain bunched out through white splinters of smashed skull. The realisation dawned on me that I had killed a man — a fellow man — a human! I suddenly wanted to be sick and I turned away from the dead German's accusing eyes, retching.

If killing a fellow human being is unnatural to most civilised people, the principal task of all infantry training is to make it second nature. In 1950, the New Zealand Army commissioned *Infantry in Battle: notes on the training and command of New Zealand infantry units,* a top-secret, strictly classified study on how to better achieve this more efficiently in future wars. Some people think about these things so the rest of us don't have to:

The average New Zealander on entering the army has an aversion to killing a fellow man. This aversion will be partially overcome during the training period when he learns to fire automatically at 'enemy figures'. Once he comes under fire, however, especially when he has seen his comrades wounded or killed by enemy fire, it will be submerged by a desire to kill the enemy, if only to save himself. In hot blood the average infantry man will kill without hesitation, and without subsequent misgivings. At ranges over 100 to 200 yards killing becomes much more impersonal and few men will turn away from it. Nevertheless the New Zealander is not unaffected by human feelings, even in the heat of battle. Generally he will prefer to take prisoners rather than to kill.

Charlie:

'There were always three or four men in each section, perhaps twenty in a company, who did the brunt of the actual fighting. I don't think you would ever force or make them actually aim and fire true shots at a human target.'

§

On the first day of the invasion, paratroopers landing in the lightly defended Tavronitis River valley west of Maleme seized the airfield the next day thanks to command failures by New Zealand officers.

Everywhere else the Germans were losing — and they knew it. However, with no wireless sets, few field telephones, most of which were quickly rendered inoperable when cables snapped in the fighting, and with flares, semaphore and runners a poor substitute, the Allied forces exchanged incoherent, incomplete and unduly pessimistic battle assessments. The New Zealanders were winning, but they didn't know it. Not on Point 107 above Maleme airfield where they needed to know it most.

Today Point 107 is the site of the German War Cemetery. In immaculately kept grounds, in neat rows, two men to a plot, simple plaques lie flush with the grass on a gentle rise overlooking the coast where most of them were killed. On a sunny morning, without a breath of wind, much like 20 May 1941, I was the only visitor. It felt lonely and exposed.

Back then, despite its protective screen of olive groves, it felt lonely and exposed to Lieutenant Colonel Les Andrews VC, Commander of the 2nd Battalion holding the Maleme sector. A brave man who had served with distinction in the First World War, Andrews likened the aerial bombardment they endured that day to Passchendaele — a byword for horror. While dreadful enough, it was nothing like the charnel house of the Great War. Nothing ever could be. Andrew's hyperbole suggests that his nerves had shredded. Later that night when he informed the commander of the 5th Brigade further down the coast that he was pulling back, Brigadier James Hargest's limp response, 'If you must, you must', suggests that his nerves were shot as well.

All through the next day a constant stream of clunky black Ju 52 Junkers braving ground fire landed on Maleme airfield at the rate of one every three minutes, making it briefly the busiest airfield in the world. Disregarding wrecked and burnt-out planes lining the small runway, they disgorged more men than a bull can shit, as Charlie could have put it. A good many crashed. Ground crews hauled scores of blazing aircraft off the runway to the airfield perimeter. Nothing was allowed to stem the tide.

Chapter 10

'He'll either get a wooden cross or a Victoria Cross'

When it dawned on Creforce HQ that Crete would be lost unless Maleme was retaken, the 28th Maori Battalion and Charlie's 20th Battalion were tasked with mounting the counter-attack.

With Stukas and Messerschmitts criss-crossing the skies, troop movements during the day would have turned open countryside into a slaughterhouse. Charlie and his men had to contain their impatience while German troops continued arriving and advancing along the coastal plain abandoned by the Allies — taking shelter in farmhouses, occupying the village of Pirgos and setting up machine-gun nests. The Allied counter-attack was planned for later that night.

It was still light when Australian troops assembled at Georgioupolis to be trucked to Chania to take over as reserves for the 28th and 20th Battalions, who would then borrow their vehicles and drive to the attack start line. The New Zealand reserves could have moved forward without the Australians taking their place, but Freyberg was obsessed about a German seaborne invasion. He wanted reserves to fight them on the beaches if the Royal Navy couldn't destroy them at sea.

One of the last Luftwaffe patrols of the day spotted the

Australian trucks lining up and dropped out of the twilight sky to inflict heavy damage. Their scheduled departure of 8 p.m. was delayed until after midnight, with half the trucks originally envisaged. Winding laboriously over the rough road, the Australians then got lost in the maze of narrow Chania streets — as I did myself several times in broad daylight with Google Maps on my phone — eventually reaching the Kiwi reserve forces after 1 a.m. Some historians believe they should have just given the waiting Kiwis a toot and carried on to the start line and mounted the counter-attack themselves. Instead, a swapping of places occurred. Anyone who has participated in collecting children from a school bus will know how messy and time-consuming this can be — let alone in a war zone in the pitch-black. It took ages to get moving.

2nd Lieutenant George Brown of 20th Battalion recalled:

> There was only one road; it was chock-a-block with civilians, miscellaneous people, wounded coming back. We had three officers in our company; Denver Fountaine had a platoon. (He was acting company Commander) I had a platoon (I was acting second-in-command) and Charlie Upham had the third platoon. Denver Fountaine went into Brigadier Hargest of the 5th brigade headquarters, I waited outside, and when he came out I said, 'What's the story?' and he said, 'George, you know as much as I do.' So we took up position on the starting line.

The men taking part were angry and frustrated. Multiple delays not of their making left a diminishing window of darkness in which to cross five miles of enemy-infested territory and retake an airfield now teeming with enemy troops.

Colonel Kippenberger shared their frustration:

> The counterattack to retake Maleme was launched much

too late. It did not get under way until 3.30 a.m. on 22
May. Parts of two battalions — the 20th and 28th (Maori)
Battalion — were used. Charles Upham was leading 15
Platoon of C Company towards the airfield.

At Platanias the troops spread out in a line nearly a mile
wide: B and D Companies on the right hugging the coast, the
Maori Battalion on the left, inland from the road to Maleme,
with C Company and Charlie moving up the middle. Out over
the water they could see flashes and searchlights sweeping
the sky where the Royal Navy were scuttling the German
seaborne invasion — putting paid to Freyberg's worst
fears. Moving west, the New Zealanders strained their eyes
to decipher every shadow and interpret every silhouette.
Complicating matters, they were moving against the grain of
the land. Gullies, streams and culverts ran across their path.
Vines and hedgerows had to be climbed through and several
minefields previously laid by the Maori Battalion had to be
negotiated. A machine gun barked in the distance. A tank
clattered along the road.

§

That rough road is now smooth tarseal, lined on either side
with palms, cafés, villas, backpacker lodges and luxury hotels.
The once scrubby coast is home to playgrounds and the
groomed sand festooned with beach umbrellas. To get a better
sense of what Charlie encountered, I walked over a stretch
of undeveloped coast near Georgioupolis. Marshy creeks
meandered through thick stands of tall bamboo and clumps
of cactus. Thick olive groves hugged hillsides. Cat's cradle
grapevine trellises turned flat ground into obstacle courses.
Loose rock and drains lurked beneath wild herbs and carpets
of buttercup. I wouldn't want to run through it blindfolded.

On my return journey, I discovered that communications

on Crete are still problematic. Approaching a superette, I saw a billboard advertising foreign press. 'You have English newspapers?' I asked a man unloading warm bread from a van.

'But of course, but they are not here yet.'

'What time do they arrive?' I was already planning my afternoon: reading a copy of *The Times* while sipping a frothy cappuccino in the main square.

'Two weeks!'

§

On 22 May 1941 the night was eerie and still. The Kiwis traversed a gully, pushed through a hedge, negotiated a field of grapevines and crossed exposed ground. Tall trees rearing up ominously at the far end provided ideal cover and a clear field of fire down the meadow. They moved forward cautiously, tense and alert, until from deep shadow at the base of the largest tree a machine gun flamed — RATA TAT TAT! Red, illuminated horizontal rain seemed to float past them. Tracer! 'Down! Down!' screamed Charlie. Some of his men toppled with anguished groans. Some dropped without uttering a sound apart from the slap and thud of their bodies.

Colonel Kippenberger:

> About a mile past the start line and while crossing an open field, the men came under fire from a German heavy machine-gun concealed behind a tree about 60 yards to their front. Four members of the platoon were hit. The platoon went into an immediate action drill, diving to the ground and crawling forward under the vocal encouragement of their commander. The sections crawled forward until they were only 25 yards from the machine-gun, from where they kept up a steady fire on the German position. Meanwhile, Upham moved around the open right flank of the machine-gun

position and attacked it with grenades from the rear. He threw three grenades and then ran forward, firing his pistol. Upham stormed the position, killing eight Germans in the process.

Private Melville Hill-Rennie of 20th Battalion also described the scene:

We edged forward on our stomachs until we were within 20 yards of the Nazis, who were tucked away behind a large tree, and then opened fire with our one Tommy gun, one Bren gun and eight rifles. As we kept up the fire the platoon officer cautiously crawled round to the side and slightly to the rear of the tree. Although it was still dark, we could tell by the way the Jerries were shouting to each other that they didn't like the look of the situation. When he got round behind the tree the platoon officer jumped to his feet and hurled three Mills bombs, one right after another, into the nest and then jumped forward with his revolver blazing. Single-handed he wiped out seven Jerries with their Tommy guns and another with a machine-gun. Two machine-gunners managed to hobble away in the darkness, but we got them later.

Charlie had explained his feelings during the incident to Ken Sandford:

It was excitement and a tremendous tension; but above all he was aware of an icy fury possessing him, not a feeling of hot reckless rage but a deliberate deep savagery that began the moment he saw four of his boys roll agonisingly on the ground. The first time they had really seen action and now they were dead or badly wounded. The hatred of it took hold of him, the hatred of war, the hatred of the enemy crouching behind the tree just a few yards away in the semi-darkness.

Charlie called his men forward in a high-pitched yell. When they reached him, his chest was heaving. Breathing heavily, he said they still had a long way to go and should get cracking. He told them to spread out. Re-forming, they moved forward. Up ahead they could make out a house and small shed on the edge of the road. Inside the house, the enemy could see them. A machine gun started barking from a window and another machine gun opened up from the door of the shed. The men dropped to the ground and started firing back — watching for movement.

What they saw in the gloom was Charlie dashing straight past the house to the side of the shed. While his men kept up a covering fire with rifles and a Bren gun, Charlie edged along the wall to the open door where a dead German lay with one arm outstretched. Reaching into the bulging sack slung over his shoulder, Charlie removed a grenade, pulled the pin and leapt forward to place it in the dead man's palm, then leapt back — BOOM! He screamed to his men. 'Come forward! Come on!' That was enough for the enemy. Half a dozen Germans reeled out of the house with their hands in the air. Inside the shed another eight lay badly wounded or dazed by the explosion. Charlie deputised some of his men to take the prisoners and wounded back to the start line. The rest of them had to keep moving towards the village of Pirgos.

Charlie:

We meet resistance in depth — in ditches, behind hedges, in the top and bottom stories of village buildings, fields and gardens on the road beside drome. The wire of 5 Bde hindered our advance. There were also mines and booby traps which got a few of us. We did not know that they were there. There was T.G. [Tommy

gun] and pistol fire and plenty of grenades and a lot of
bayonet work which you don't often get in war.

They were stopped in their tracks by a murderous fusillade
directly across their path, tracer so thick it almost made a
single beam. There was no way through it. Charlie began
shouting. 'It's chest high! That won't hurt anyone! We can
crawl underneath it! Come on!' Like Tom Cruise evading
laser beams in a high-security vault in a *Mission Impossible*
movie, Charlie got down on his hands and knees and crawled
under the red tracer and out the other side. Terrified and
inspired in equal measure, his men took a deep breath
and followed him. They could hear the waspish hiss of the
bullets passing just above their heads. They could feel the
vacuumed suck of something cleaving the air. They could
see the tracer. They kept crawling. An eternity passed. Then
suddenly they were safely on the other side. Relieved and
disbelieving, they got to their feet and raced after the man
they called boss.

Charlie: 'The amount of MG fire was never equalled.
Fortunately, a lot of it was high and the tracers enabled us to
pick our way up and throw in grenades.'

It was getting lighter by the minute. More houses loomed.
Fire rained down from rooftops and lofts. It was particularly
deadly from the window of a corner house. Hit in the
abdomen, one of Charlie's men rolled on the ground in agony.
Charlie screamed, 'Leave him to me! I'll fix the bastard!'

They concentrated their fire on the window where
machine-gun fire came from, while Charlie raced through
the shadows. When he'd run out of cover, he ran straight at
the house with an unpinned grenade in his hand and hurled
it through the open window — BOOM! Pistol drawn, Charlie
ran around the side of the house to the back door, followed
by Leggy, who was armed with a Tommy gun. Alerted by a
cry, Charlie turned to see his diminutive batman struggling

with a towering German. It wasn't safe to fire his pistol. He could have shot the wrong man. Charlie had no choice but to join in the tag-wrestle, beating the German to the ground with his fist. Another German, unarmed and panic-stricken, came running, refusing to stop or surrender when Charlie demanded he put his hands in the air. Charlie had to wrestle him to the ground as well. The German fought back in a frenzy. Charlie subdued him by striking him repeatedly on the side of the head with the butt of his pistol. Another New Zealand officer witnessing this, Peter Maxwell from D Company, was aghast. 'Jesus, Charlie. You could have just shot him. You don't have to be so savage.' There was no time to chat. Charlie urged his men on. The village was swimming into focus like a photograph in a tray of developing fluid. That worked both ways. It meant they were becoming visible as well.

Private Hill-Rennie: 'Jerry had taken up vantage points in the houses. We slowly blasted our way from house to house, wiping out one nest after another, while the snipers kept up a constant, deadly fire.'

Charlie led the door-to-door fighting. They sprayed windows and rooftops with fire, then an NCO kicked in the door and Charlie, or someone else, tossed in a grenade. Before the dust cleared, they dealt to enemy occupants. Charlie snatched a German sub-machine gun off the floor in one cleared house. Company Commander Denver Fountaine, who had caught up with them by then, asked Charlie if he had any ammo. He replied in the negative, but he was confident he would get some soon. Somewhere close a big gun started thumping.

Kippenberger:

At Pyrgos village, near the airfield, the platoon could hear a captured Bofors gun firing. Upham's platoon moved towards the gun until they could fire at the gunner. While his men kept the gunner's head down,

Upham crawled around on his stomach to within 10 yards of the gun, where he lobbed a grenade that killed the gunner and damaged the gun.

Charlie:

We had heavy casualties but the Germans had much heavier. They were unprepared. Some were without trousers, some had no boots on. The Germans were hopeless in the dark. We captured a lot of MGs, 2 Bofors were overrun and the guns destroyed. The POWs went back to 5 Bde.

It was approaching daybreak. They heard mortar and machine-gun fire ahead of them. D Company had made a rapid advance up the coastline and were now meeting stiff resistance. Beyond dense clumps of bamboo, C Company could see the edge of the airfield, and the road to it crossed a culvert. German troops crouching under it sprayed the approach with jittery, indiscriminate fire.

Colonel Jim Burrows arrived from Battalion Headquarters in time to witness Charlie's platoon go about their deadly business. They forced the enemy to keep their heads down with pinpoint aim while Charlie raced in from the side, hurling two grenades and firing his pistol, rendering the culvert mute and still. Everyone in his platoon marvelled at Charlie's seemingly inexhaustible supply of grenades in his haversack. Like circus clowns emerging from a car, they just kept coming and coming. They couldn't marvel for long. Charlie was off again, threading his way between the tall bamboo. On the other side, a German with a machine gun and another German with a rifle were trying to make sense of the unseen, unholy cacophony when Charlie burst through the bamboo curtain.

Again, Fountaine saw it all. Charlie dispatched the startled machine gunner with the last bullet in his pistol, then spun around to deal with the German with a Luger he had picked up earlier. It clicked on an empty chamber. The German had his rifle raised and cocked. Charlie was contemplating his own mortality when a rifle muzzle blasted next to his ear and the German fell to the ground. With his head ringing, dizzy and half deaf, Charlie turned to thank Private 'Puck' Wesley, but Wesley was already rushing forward to relieve the dead Germans of the chocolate they invariably carried in their pockets.

Jim Burrows:

> On the south side of the road the Maoris were carrying out their task in their own inimitable way. It was easy to see how far they had progressed by the flashes and explosions and also by the truly fearsome clamour that went up every time an assault was made on an enemy post. Soon it was daybreak. By 6 a.m. we were encountering aimed fire and movement became more difficult. Planes called up from Athens began to attack us from the air. Dry water courses with their steep banks no longer provided shelter. Planes rocketed overhead firing furiously at everything they could see. By 7.30 we were at a dead halt. I realised that if we went much further over the open ground ahead we would hardly have a man left.

Lieutenant Jack Bain from Headquarters Company had worked his way forward to talk to Charlie. 'What's the guts, Jack?'

'The counter-attack is over, Charlie. We're pulling back!'

Charlie let rip a torrent of invective against the army. The whole show was a stuff-up from start to finish. They could have taken the airfield if they had set off earlier.

Burrows:

> All I could see to do now was get what remained of the

battalion across the road onto high ground. I spoke to the officer in charge of the forward platoon. This was Charles Upham. I told him where I proposed to assemble the battalion. I wanted him to get a message to B and D Companies on the right forward flank and guide them back to our rendezvous.

Knowing it was a hazardous mission, Burrows advised Charlie to send two very good men. Charlie said he would fix it. He crawled across to Sergeant Dave Kirk to discuss who to send. They would be under continuous fire, there and back. The operation looked decidedly dicey. Charlie said he would go. Kirk grabbed a Bren gun and said he was coming with him.

Brigadier Burrows: 'I saw Charles talking to his platoon Sergeant Dave Kirk, then leaving a corporal in charge he and Sergeant Kirk moved away on a mission that gave no promise of survival, much less success.'

In order to reach B and D Companies they had to cross 600 metres of largely open ground to the sea with pockets of Germans everywhere. At a social gathering many years later, laughing and shaking his head in disbelief, Dave Kirk told Charlie's son-in-law, Marty Reynolds, that machine-gun, rifle and tracer fire followed them all the way — shredding vines, exploding cactus, ricocheting off walls and kicking up dirt as they ran, crouched and crawled forward. When a culvert loomed, Kirk was only too happy to dive into it. Charlie dropped down beside him, disgusted and contemptuous: 'I'd sack the bastard who trained them! That was piss-poor shooting!'

Charlie described Kirk as the finest soldier he ever met — he was one of the few men who could fire a Bren gun from the hip like a Tommy gun without losing accuracy. They remained friends for the rest of their days. For his part in this suicidal errand, and for other actions on Crete, Dave Kirk was awarded the Distinguished Conduct Medal.

Charlie shot and killed two more Germans on their journey through no-man's-land. On the eastern tip of the runway, they almost tripped over the bodies of two New Zealand soldiers: bitter proof of what could have been achieved with an earlier start.

Charlie: 'When we reached the 'drome planes were landing, some leaving too, and parachutists were jumping out and getting straight into battle.'

Crete was lost and they knew it. Skirting the runway, they returned along the coast, picking up men who had become isolated from B Company. D Company was nowhere to be seen. Informed by runner of the pull-back, they were on their way to the rendezvous point. Charlie, Kirk and the B Company stragglers needed to head there as well. The only way back was through Pirgos. It meant running the gauntlet again.

Charlie: 'The mortar and machine-gun fire on the open ground was heavy and we were lucky to get back alive.'

There were German dead and Allied dead on the streets of Pirgos. Determined to leave no injured man behind, Charlie ripped a door off its hinges to make a stretcher for Private Bill Fitzgerald, whose terrible wounds left him unable to walk. Charlie, Jack Bain and two others took a corner each and carried Fitzgerald down the street in full view of Germans who had somehow survived the brutal door-to-door battle earlier. Out of decency — and possibly in salute to the insane courage they were witnessing — they held their fire and let the stretcher party pass through to safety. It wasn't his only makeshift stretcher-rescue that morning. Second Lieutenant Brown remembers German bombers and fighters giving his platoon hell. He was hit and lost consciousness:

> I believe we got to the edge of the Aerodrome. I was wounded so I was out of it. There was muck flying everywhere and I lay on the ground. Charlie Upham and Paterson came along and I told them to get the hell out

of it, frightened that they'd get hit, but they went and pulled the door off an old derelict building, placed me on it, and some others came along and helped carry me out of danger.

Another New Zealand soldier who witnessed a solo rescue performed by Charlie that morning recalled the deed later:

Bullets and shrapnel were flying about. A chap walked out of olive trees and across open country. No shirt, shorts blood-smeared. Carrying a badly wounded man. I said to my CSM, 'He'll either get a wooden cross or a Victoria Cross.'

Long after the fact, a British war artist's tribute to Charlie rescuing a wounded comrade on Crete.

By nightfall Charlie's platoon had fallen back to an exposed ridge between Chania and Maleme. In the dark they could hear the Germans moving equipment forward. The 20th Battalion had endured a torrid day. Tomorrow would be even worse.

§

Before dawn the battalion pulled back quietly towards Chania. When the Germans realised what was happening, they gave chase. At Platanias bridge the battalion swung their rifles, machine guns, mortars and artillery around and began hammering their pursuers. Charlie's platoon was rushed to plug the gap between the bridge and the sea, a front 300 yards wide. German attempts to break through along the shore were beaten back. Charlie's thin defensive line came under heavy mortar attack. He heard the whirr of an approaching shell and dived into a ditch as it exploded. Hot metal ripped into the back of his left shoulder. The man standing next to him was blown apart. When the bombardment ended, the pain and bleeding started — or perhaps he just noticed it for the first time. Handing Dave Kirk his pocketknife, Charlie asked him to dig out the metal. When Kirk refused, Charlie pulled rank and made it an order. It was the surgical equivalent of the caning cliché where the headmaster assures the errant schoolboy, 'This is going to hurt me more than it hurts you.' Except in this case it was true.

Kirk gingerly cut into flesh while Charlie hissed at him to get a move on. Kirk prised out one lump of shrapnel. Unable to continue, he lied that the other fragment was too deep. Ordered by a superior officer to report to the regimental aid post, Charlie had the wound dressed there by a medical orderly who informed him that he qualified as walking wounded and was eligible to leave the battle. Charlie snorted at that suggestion and rejoined his depleted platoon with his arm in a sling.

Later that night, exhausted and dispirited, the New Zealanders melted en masse back along the coast to a new defensive line between the village of Galatas and the sea. Charlie's platoon moved into their former lodgings — the olive grove overlooking Chania. Charlie was still suffering from dysentery. Somehow Leggy rustled up a can of condensed milk. Charlie, gaunt and shivering, spooned it straight from the can with his good hand.

Chapter 11

'Perfect pandemonium'

Galatas is nothing like the picture I had of it in my mind's eye. I ignored clues to the contrary in every book I read on Crete and imprinted in my memory it was a cluster of houses on a flat rural road.

I could never figure out why Charlie's platoon participated in a bayonet charge to recapture it. This changed when I saw a road sign for Galatas and swung my rental off the national highway and headed inland to a hilltop village. A one-way road coiled like a snake charmer's python to the summit where a Greek Orthodox church overlooked a small square. To the east farmhouses and hilltop mansions stretched all the way to Chania. To the south lay the White Mountains, Cemetery Hill, Prison Valley and Lake Agia reflecting late-afternoon sunlight like a chrome bumper. To the west, rolling slopes laced with vineyards and dotted with olive trees spread all the way to Maleme airfield, an air force base and the German War Cemetery.

After four days of battle, the Germans owned this coast lock, stock and smoking barrel. To continue their advance into Chania, the Germans had to first get past Galatas. That's why it mattered.

§

On the fifth day Charlie's company were sent forward to protect the northern approaches of the village against repeated enemy assaults that got heavier as the day wore on. Some New Zealand units were forced back. Charlie was determined to hold their ridge. Leaving his men lower down, he crawled to the highest point to study the approaching enemy. Satisfied the terrain worked to their advantage, he signalled his men to join him. The crack 5th German Mountain Division advanced confidently. Too confidently.

Kippenberger:

> At Galatas on May 25 his platoon was heavily engaged when troops in front gave way and came under severe mortar and MG fire. While his platoon stopped under cover of a ridge 2/Lt Upham went forward, observed the enemy and brought the platoon forward when the Germans advanced. They killed over 40 with fire and grenades and forced the remainder to fall back.

Another wave of Germans flowed around their dead, firing in the general direction of Charlie's well-hidden boys. Sandford describes Charlie as being in a state of 'exhilarated defiance' at this point. He paraded up and down just long enough to pinpoint German machine-gun fire, then directed his riflemen to destroy it.

As Private Ken McKegney told it:

> Charlie was telling us to keep down, all the time standing there in the open himself, his arm in a sling. Most of the boys thought it was too hot for us to stay there but they couldn't do much about it with Charlie wandering around as if it didn't matter, lead flying everywhere. Charlie knew that if we didn't stick it out for a few hours the whole division might have gone west.

Sheer weight of numbers prevailed in the end. Germans getting in behind Allied lines wreaked havoc. Under orders to retire with his platoon, Charlie saw a pincer movement unfolding behind him.

Kippenberger: 'He went back to warn other troops that they were being cut off. When he came out himself he was fired on by two Germans.'

Charlie emerged out of an olive grove on the run. Somewhere behind him were two Germans armed with machine guns. Ahead of him was a hundred metres of exposed ground sprinkled with a few trees. He was halfway across when the Germans appeared out of the grove, guns chattering. One of Charlie's men saw him jerk and twist as he fell from view into long grass. He was convinced Charlie had been killed. So were the Germans, but taking no chances, they crept forward cautiously.

Kippenberger: 'He fell and shammed dead, then crawled into a position and having the use of only one arm he rested his rifle in the fork of a tree as the Germans came forward.'

Charlie had just tripped over an exposed root. He squirmed through the grass to a small tree that stood between him and his stalkers. The first branch was low. Charlie used his right hand to lift the heavy rifle into the fork. The Jerries were close, looking for a body. Charlie let them creep closer. He took aim, waited until they were just 2 metres away, then squeezed the trigger — CRACK! The first German toppled to the ground. The second German paused in disbelief over his fallen comrade. It was time enough for Charlie to shift his good hand to the bolt, draw it back and bring another round into the chamber. Pushing it home, he squeezed the trigger again — CRACK! Blood spouting from the middle of his forehead, the second German fell face forward against the muzzle of Charlie's rifle.

Further up the slopes, Colonel Kippenberger was charged with holding Galatas against the German breakthrough with a makeshift force of drivers without trucks, gunners without artillery, the Kiwi Concert Party, plus Cretan irregulars and mainland Greek soldiers armed with ancient rifles. Some of his men broke and ran. Horrified that it might become contagious, the slightly built, undemonstrative small-town lawyer stood in the middle of the maelstrom shouting, 'Stand for New Zealand! Stand, every man who is a soldier!' He sheepishly admitted later that he couldn't think of anything else to say. It was hardly 'We few, we happy few, we band of brothers!' like Henry V before the battle of Agincourt, but it was enough. It stopped a trickling retreat from becoming a complete gushing rout and made him a legend in the New Zealand Division.

Kippenberger waited until dusk before launching a counter-attack. With reinforcements from the 28th Battalion, Charlie's platoon, and two British tanks, they charged back into the village with all guns blazing and Maori war chants electrifying the air. Unbidden, locals, including mothers and grandmothers, armed with knives, reap hooks, pitchforks, hoes and axes joined in, screaming like banshees.

Kippenberger:

There was a tremendous amount of bayonet work in Galatas. For 15 minutes there was perfect pandemonium in the village, an indescribable uproar, screams, grenade bursts and the deafening rattle of rifles, Brens and Tommy guns. The narrow cobbled street was carpeted with the dead, nearly all Germans. Every door and window had been smashed in, and dead Germans sprawled in every room by the street, with wounded on both sides walking, crawling or propped against the walls everywhere.

Chased down streets, over walls and across backyards, Germans fled in terror. But everyone knew that once they had gotten over their shock and called for reinforcements they would be back.

§

A large painting depicting a scene of the fighting hangs on the wall of the antechamber attached to the church at Galatas. Holding a rock aloft, a bearded Cretan wearing a beret, sleeveless jerkin, breeches and knee-high leather boots stands over a cowering German. Trapped in his harness, as helpless as a bug on its back, the paratrooper is about to get his head stoved in.

Beneath this violent image, sweet old ladies in black shawls eyed me suspiciously when I entered asking for directions to Stelios Tripalitakis's war museum. Recognising my accent, an old man beamed and ushered me back into the square where I rang Stelios again. 'Stay put!' he yelled. 'STAY PUT!' 'Sniper!' yelled the old man when I got off the phone, pointing with boyish glee to the church tower above us. For just a moment I caught glimpses of the gleeful boy who witnessed the battle. He told me how his mother baked bread for Kiwi soldiers and he delivered it to their barricades.

A belching car lurched up and Stelios leapt out. He had his book with him that featured a large collection of black-and-white photographs taken during the invasion. Included were shots of charred, rubble-strewn Galatas streets alongside shots of the same streets today, leafy and quiet. Stelios walked me to the spot where a dead Maori soldier lay in one of the photos. Despite the captions being in Greek, I purchased two copies. It was the least I could do.

Stelios spends every spare moment scouring lofts, combing old battlefields with metal detectors and diving coastal waters searching for military relics and, with a bit of luck, the Crown Jewels of Greece. His bigger relics, rusting engine cowlings, chassis, motorbikes and the like, have taken over his lawn, garage and basement. Upstairs the living room is filled floor to ceiling with badges, buckles, helmets, guns and dressmakers' dummies clothed in German and British uniforms. He knows his swelling collection tests his family's patience, but with a passion bordering on fever he wants young Cretans and young New Zealanders to never forget what happened here. You get the impression that if his wife were ever to say, 'Stelios, either this shit goes, or I do!' he would call her a cab.

I had occasion to use the bathroom and was unnerved to discover that all the porcelain fittings — hand-basin, bath and toilet bowl — were a ripe faecal brown. This is taking camouflage to new and unnecessary heights. From my brief exposure I am not in the least surprised that this look has not taken the world by storm.

§

The retaking of Galatas was short-lived. With German victory on Crete assured, the only course left to the Allies was to withdraw to evacuation ports and await rescue by the Royal Navy, so Kippenberger's forces slipped away in the dead of night. Troops in the eastern sector retreated to Heraklion. Troops in the western sector trekked in a wretched column over the White Mountains to the tiny fishing port of Sphakia on the south coast, a 60-kilometre journey through twisting gorges, across exposed plateaus, and up barren slopes through snow in some places to a vertiginous drop at the far end where far below white cubes, a lone monastery and a stone breakwater hugged a wild shore.

It was nerve-wracking enough in my rental, descending endless hairpin bends with goats appearing out of the mist without warning. And I wasn't being chased by crack alpine troops or Messerschmitts. Charlie's men made good time to Sphakia, their skeletal leader urging them on with promises of a slap-up meal at Shepheard's when they got back to Cairo.

In a cosy taverna on the wharf, I sipped a beer and nibbled delicious freshly baked baklava, looking out at massive misty cliff faces vanishing into low cloud. Clearly visible, massive caverns were eaten into the base. Whipped by salt spray, thousands of Allied soldiers huddled here for days hoping and praying to get off the island. A cordon of armed guards forced them back from the wharf, telling them to wait their turn, everyone aware that not everyone would get a turn. Belligerence became blind panic when rifle fire reverberated around the hills and bullets ricocheted off the stone jetty. Had the Germans broken through? Puffs of smoke were spotted in the gully running down from the crest of the encircling hills. Fifty heavily armed Germans had managed to outflank the New Zealand rearguard and sneak down the steep ravine. Men from the 18th Battalion were sent to block escape across the eastern shoulder. Men from the 20th Battalion guarded the mouth of the ravine.

In a move anticipating the movie *Ghostbusters* ('Who you gonna call?'), Charlie and a small firing party were summoned by Freyberg and dispatched to the western shoulder to deal to the enemy — meaning a steep 600-foot ascent over jagged rock and a journey inland of two miles. It took two hours to get into position. Charlie wouldn't stop until they were behind and above the infiltrating party, who were exchanging fire with the New Zealanders below. Charlie picked a ledge so steep he had to hold the Bren gunner by his legs as he leant over the lip to fire. Halfway through, stopping to swap magazines, they swapped places. Taken completely by surprise, the Germans broke from rhododendron bushes in search of better cover from the plunging fire. There wasn't any.

Kippenberger:

On the 30th of May at SPHAKIA his platoon was ordered to deal with a party of the enemy which had advanced down a ravine to near force headquarters. Though in

an exhausted condition he climbed the steep hill to
the west of the ravine, placed men in position on the
slope overlooking the ravine and himself went to the
top with a Bren gun and two Riflemen. By clever tactics
he induced the enemy party to expose itself then at a
range of 500 yards shot 22 and caused the remainder to
disperse in panic.

That dusk Kippenberger instructed Charlie's men to not let
him out of their sight. Sick and delirious, Charlie was babbling
about staying behind to continue fighting. There was a scare
when he went missing. He was found in a cluster of houses
abandoned by the locals when the Germans had started dive-
bombing their village. Starving mules, crazy with terror, were
tethered in a yard. Charlie set them free, saving them from
being killed, cooked and eaten by men crowding the port in
increasing numbers. When it was dark, semaphore blinked
from a frigate out at sea.

Fountaine: 'I had to hold Charles and literally drag him
through a cordon of marines.'

Half an hour later Charlie was on board a crowded boat
heading for a destroyer anchored in deeper water, a shrunken,
diminished, tearful figure — heartbroken that good men
were being left behind and bitter that he wasn't allowed to
stay with them. His men were grateful for the black night and
crashing waves. No one wanted to see him like that. Charlie
was beyond caring if anyone saw him and wept freely.

On my last day on Crete, I paid my respects to the men who
never made it as far as Sphakia, visiting the Commonwealth War
Cemetery on the shores of Suda Bay where achingly sad rows
of white headstones stand at attention facing out to sea. Boys
whose remains couldn't be identified are remembered simply
as A SOLDIER OF THE 1939–1945 WAR. The ones that could be
identified were younger than my own sons. And always will be.

§

For years a silver Cretan dagger occupied pride of place in Charlie and Molly's lounge. He said it reminded him of their sacrifice and courage. He admired the bravery of the Greeks, particularly the Cretan women:

'The way those women dealt to German paratroopers with stones, pitchforks and daggers in the fields after they landed is something I'll never forget. The Cretan people were the heroes of the German occupation, not us. We had it easy. Many of us were gone eleven days after Student's paratroopers landed. The Cretan people had nowhere to go. Many of them were executed at the hands of the Germans during the occupation for harbouring New Zealanders.'

Chapter 12

'It's meant for the men'

The apportioning of blame for the loss of Crete began before the returning, defeated troops had even set foot on gangways in Port Alexandria.

Bitter debate rang out in barracks, bars and briefing rooms in Cairo, Whitehall and Wellington. One British officer described it as everyone pouring shit on everyone else. Freyberg copped most of it. The tragedy weighed heavily on him for the rest of his days. Close to death, he made a plea in mitigation to his son, Paul, who became his authorised biographer — he wanted it understood that he was forbidden from making full use of Ultra intelligence.

The apportioning of acclaim was more dignified and discreet. Kippenberger and Burrows agreed that Charlie's deeds merited the highest possible award. Oral testimony and sworn statements were obtained from a number of eyewitnesses, including Denver Fountaine and Dave Kirk. Alone in the battalion orderly room, Kippenberger prepared a twelve-page citation for Charlie in longhand:

> During the operations in Crete this officer performed
> a series of remarkable exploits, showing outstanding
> leadership, tactical skill and utter indifference to
> danger. He showed superb coolness, great skill

and dash and complete disregard of danger. His
conduct and leadership inspired his platoon to fight
magnificently throughout and in fact was an inspiration
to the Battalion . . .

Second Lieutenant Bert Steele, who had been on the same OCTU
course in Cairo with Charlie, was called into Kippenberger's
tent and asked to read an early draft of the citation:

'Well, Bert, what do you think that is worth? I am
recommending him for the Victoria Cross.' I was a
comparatively inexperienced soldier and a VC was
beyond my comprehension. In retrospect I now consider
no VC was more justly deserved.

Further south in dusty Helwan Camp, Charlie finally admitted
himself to hospital, where he was treated for dysentery and
chronic sinus problems and had his wounds attended to. A
bullet lodged in flesh above his ankle popped out of its own
accord like a burst pimple. In the bed next to him, recovering
from sinus surgery, was another junior officer, Noel Gardiner
from the 27th Machine Gun Battalion. A Taranaki boy from
the back of beyond, and a farm valuer like Charlie, they got
on well. Gardiner's descriptions of his fellow patient in his
war memoir *Freyberg's Circus* are touching and insightful:

Much of what Upham told us in that hospital is now in the
history books. As we first heard it, it sounded incredible.
We didn't know that a VC was coming through for him,
but we could judge from his bearing and demeanour
that he was a born soldier and leader. Like the Ancient
Mariner of our schoolboy reading, he had story 'that in
him burned'. It simply had to come out. Day after day,
in the colourful idiom of the high-country shepherd,
Upham blasted off, never boastfully but always with a

deep hatred for the Germans. As he saw it, they had
ridden roughshod over all the recognised conventions
of war. Although he spoke always in a quiet, modest
way, he told enthralling stories of lone forays into and
behind the German lines. He held our minds as he crept
through a cornfield on Crete making a stealthy approach
to an enemy machine-gun nest in a small blockhouse.
He went as cautiously as though he was stalking a deer
in the South Island foothills. As he told it, the Huns were
unaware they were being stalked. Having crawled to
within throwing distance he half-rose from cover to let fly
with two hand-grenades. Annihilation of this machine-
gun nest was instant.

The survivors of his platoon kept coming in, in threes
and fours, to sit on his bed and swap yarns. And they
had so much to talk about. These visits gave Upham so
much pleasure. The way Upham's men respected him
had a profound influence on my mind, for I realised that
unconcealed admiration of this sort could only be earned
by an exceptional man. I knew that men would follow a
leader whom they have learned to trust.

Looking back, I realise I was fortunate to have
encountered Upham when I did. Although he would
never have suspected it at the time, he helped me to be
a better soldier. Immediately it was announced that he
won the VC Upham closed up and you could hardly get a
word out of him . . .

Back on his feet, true to his word, Charlie treated his men
to a feast at Shepheard's, earning disapproving frowns from
braided high brass taken aback at having to share the opulent
dining hall with a junior officer and a scruffy band of 'other
ranks'. If military tradition was strictly observed, a long
table would have been set for every member of his platoon,
including the men still hospitalised or left above and below

ground in Crete. Their empty chairs would have been tilted forward against a white tablecloth as if kneeling in prayer. When absent friends were toasted, only six men stood and raised their glasses in tribute.

Around this time Charlie sent an undated postcard home to unnamed people, most probably his parents. In a photograph taken in a busy street he is wearing a hat, smoking a pipe, and dressed in a pressed and spotless army uniform, no small achievement in Egypt. No rank or insignia were attached, which suggests it had just been issued. His face is gaunt and his frame fuse-wire thin. My guess is he is not long out of hospital. On the back Charlie writes: 'This postcard was taken by a street photographer in Cairo. I do hope you are both very well.' Clearly, Charlie isn't. His mother and father would have been shocked at his drastic weight loss.

Meanwhile his VC recommendation progressed quietly up the chain of command, eventually landing on a desk at Buckingham Palace, where it was signed off by King George VI and made public in the *London Gazette* on 10 October 1941. From Charlie's perspective, a bad day was about to get worse. He'd lost his service revolver while on training manoeuvres in the Baggush desert, a cardinal sin. Destroying, abandoning or losing military hardware is the sole prerogative of generals. Charlie's boys had been scouring the sands for their worried boss, contemplating nicking someone else's gun — they had blown the doors off a Greek bank after all — when the news came through at 9 p.m. on the BBC: 'The Victoria Cross has been awarded to an officer of the New Zealand Military Forces, Second Lieutenant Charles Hazlitt Upham, for gallantry in Crete...'

Denial and isolation, anger, bargaining, depression and acceptance are the five universally accepted stages of grief. In Kippenberger's and Sandford's accounts of Charlie's response to the news, they could be describing a man struggling with bereavement. Sandford:

He seemed neither excited nor overcome. Just slightly puzzled, almost defensive. 'It's meant for the men,' he said harshly. 'My men — by God they could fight!' He began talking rapidly, almost wildly, about the merits of his platoon, as if trying to postpone the fact that he himself had been singled out.

Out in the desert that night Charlie withdrew into himself, making one excuse after another for not going to the officers' mess to join in the noisy celebrations. Sandford: 'It is doubtful if Upham was ever less happy.'

Back in New Zealand, Charlie's former adjutant from Burnham Camp, Captain Frank Davis, broke the news to his parents in their Christchurch home ahead of official publication:

Both Mr and Mrs Upham were a little incredulous.
Mr Upham had been deeply disappointed that his son, Charles, had not followed him into law. He reckoned on him being a farmer and a soldier of average ability, but not a VC winner.

His letters home make no mention of his VC. The only time he does bring it up is in a letter to Molly — begging her not to include the letters VC after his name when she addressed envelopes.

When the New Zealand Mobile Broadcasting Unit trundled into the Baggush camp with the express purpose of interviewing him, Charlie posted Leggy Le Gros at the entrance of his dugout to explain he was indisposed. Kippenberger had to intervene. Charlie's stubborn insistence that any broadcast would be self-aggrandising was worn down by his commander's argument that this might be his only chance to pay tribute to his men. Charlie consented, but only if he could write down precisely what he wanted to say. Nothing less. Nothing more. Retiring to his dugout, he emerged hours later with a wad of sweat-soaked notes held in shaking hands.

The original broadcast tape is held in national archives. It took three attempts to record it. The first two were ruined when Charlie made mistakes and let forth a stream of expletives. Reading at a fast clip, his voice thin and nervous, he sounds like the father of the bride at a wedding who just wants to get this nightmarish ordeal over and done with:

'I wish to thank all those who have sent me cables from New Zealand and England and I have been very fortunate indeed, having the very best of commanders above me and the very best of NCOs and men in my own platoon, as well as right throughout the New Zealand Division. It was very easy to do any job under those circumstances. It was the men in my own battalion, not myself, who earned the distinction. Their morale was the highest in the whole army. Nothing could stop them, especially my battalion, and company commanders. We left many friends killed over there. Men who we will never forget. I will mention the names of some of our own Company — Major Wilson; Sgt. Wallace; Sgt. Mussen; Cpl. Herbert; Cpl. Malloch; L/Cpl. Skilton; Privates Allen; Atkins; Boyd; Burns; Brown-Pride; Gilligan; Hislop; Watson; and Woods; not to mention Sgt. John Hinton and hundreds of others left wounded in Greece and Crete. I hope the people in New Zealand remember them, lying in hospitals and prisons all over Europe. Do all you can to send them food and clothing. These men were not captured whole and unharmed like the Italians we ourselves took, but were wounded and sick men who struggled and fought right on to the last. After the war we must do all in our power to help the Greeks with food and clothing and stud stock to help build up her country

again. The Greeks were very staunch friends of the New
Zealand soldiers and hundreds of us owe our lives to
the big-heartedness of these people. The Division over
here is growing from strength to strength and the morale
of our own troops is unsurpassed. You will hear more
from us again. We have a great little army up here in
the sandhills. I would like the New Zealand Government
to know that it is impossible to send over too much
New Zealand tobacco to the troops. It is very much
appreciated here.

Kia ora.'

There are few better examples of Greek big-heartedness than
the story told by a driver in the New Zealand Army Services
Corps taken prisoner at Sphakia in May 1941, Rex Thompson:

A Hitler Youth Brigade arrived for overseas experience
and they put them more or less in charge of the camp.
They were real little horrors and threw their weight
about. An elderly Cretan lady walked past. She had a bag
and bread in it so she threw some over the fence. There
was a general scuffle for it. One of these Hitler Youths
told her to get off, but she just looked at him and threw
another loaf. He clubbed her down with the butt of his
rifle. She was out for quite a while. It just about caused
a riot. They had to fire machine guns over our heads.
The boy disappeared. She eventually got up. She put her
hand into her bag and threw another loaf.

Yarns like this would have suited the broadcaster more.
The interviewer turned to Kippenberger to provide an
impassioned postscript:

'I am speaking as Upham's Commanding Officer. Upham
is the first New Zealand officer to get the award of

the Victoria Cross probably since the Maori Wars. He
is very distressed, genuinely distressed that he has
been singled out for this award, as he has the idea
that a great many men who served well and gallantly
deserved to get it instead of himself. Nevertheless every
man in the company and every man in the battalion is
satisfied that the award was made to the right man.
He was unquestionably the paladin of the battalion,
unquestionably the finest fighting soldier that it had
throughout the operations. The exploits for which he
has been awarded the Cross, a whole series of dazzling
exploits, any one of which deserve an award. One thing
has been missed out from the citation. No reference has
been made to the fact that during the whole affair he
was suffering from dysentery very badly indeed. He had
contracted it some five weeks before in Greece. He was
unable to eat bully beef and biscuits; which were the
only ration in Crete. He lived simply on milk which the
men of his platoon found for him, tinned milk, and kept
him going on that and nibbling biscuits. He was a walking
skeleton when the affair ended.'

On 4 November 1941, on a sandy plateau overlooking the
glittering Mediterranean, Commander in Chief Middle East
General Sir Claude Auchinleck presented Charlie with his
VC ribbon at a ceremonial parade. The hefty Auchinleck
leaned over him. Charlie, who had been sick with nerves
for hours beforehand, stood grim-faced and ramrod erect.
People about to be shot by firing squad have looked happier.
As the ribbon was pinned to his shirt, the two men had the
following exchange:

'Congratulations, Upham. New Zealand will be very proud
that you have won this decoration.'

'I didn't win it, sir.'

'Then if you didn't, Upham, I don't know who did.'

Kippenberger and several other senior officers blinked rapidly and swallowed hard when they noticed that Charlie was wearing bright yellow socks. Their alarm increased when Charlie forgot to salute. He marched several paces back across the parade ground before remembering and hastily correcting this oversight. If legend is to be believed, Auchinleck may well have been used to this by then. Driving through the camp earlier in the day in an open-topped staff car with Freyberg, he allegedly remarked, 'Your chaps don't seem to salute, General.' To which Freyberg purportedly replied, 'Not a lot, sir. I'll grant you that, but they're very friendly. If you give them a wave, I think you'll find they wave back.' In other versions the bigwig is General Wavell, Montgomery or Winston Churchill.

Charlie was too self-conscious to wear his VC ribbon. Both Kippenberger and Freyberg ordered him several times to sew it onto his battle tunic. Freyberg upbraided him sharply that not to do so was an insult to the king. Freyberg may well have been stark naked at the time. Peter McIntyre records that, fond of a morning dip, the former swimming champion would often emerge from his dugout wearing nothing but a pith helmet, his massive body a riotous welter of angry battle scars — Freyberg himself explained matter-of-factly to shocked onlookers that bullets passing through your body left exit wounds as well as entry wounds. Striding purposefully towards the Mediterranean, he would cheerfully engage startled men in casual conversation. His opening gambit was to ask their name and where they came from. When they stammered out a reply, even if it was Ulan Bator or the Outer Hebrides, he would invariably claim, 'I knew your father. Good man. Give him my regards.'

Peter McIntyre says that Freyberg was deeply superstitious. He once saw him bow three times to the moon on leaving a club in Cairo, shocking passing British Tommies who thought the towering, highly decorated general was bowing to them.

Charlie with his sisters Esther (left) and Agatha at No. 2 Gloucester Street, Christchurch, circa 1913. Charlie would never look this tidy again. The seeds of his 'approach with caution' look were already forming.

Charlie loved animals. It was mutual. In the Egyptian Western Desert on the night he heard he'd won his first VC, Charlie returned to his tent to find that the regimental cat, 'Mrs Rommel', had given birth to a litter of kittens on his cot. Rather than disturb them, Charlie folded his battle tunic into a pillow, grabbed a spare blanket and went outside and slept on the sands under the stars.

Charlie in a team picture of Lincoln College First XV. What he lacked in size, strength and speed, Charlie made up for in wiry, raw-boned enthusiasm and steely determination. He had no equal as a sideline barracker when it came to decibel level and colourful exhortation.

CHARLES UPHAM COLLECTION

Charlie in Colombo en route to Egypt. He made sure he got on the very first boat to war so as not to miss any of the action. He loved calling into exotic places. No matter how far from home, his pipe was seldom far from his mouth.

CHARLES UPHAM COLLECTION

Charlie was so quick off the mark he went to war before Second World War uniforms were ready and arrived in Cairo dressed as an infantry sergeant from the First World War.

CHARLES UPHAM COLLECTION

The Free French Forces soldiers are every bit as scruffy as Charlie and his driver. Their lack of spit and polish would have endeared them to him enormously.

Charlie was so weakened and debilitated by chronic dysentery during the Greek campaign his men got him a donkey to move around on and scavenged for tins of condensed milk to bind his intestines.

The Nazi propaganda magazine *Signal* embedded photographers with frontline Wehrmacht and Luftwaffe forces to capture images of the all-conquering Nazi war machine, like this shot of Dornier bombers flying over the Acropolis after the downfall of Greece just prior to the invasion of Crete.

Evacuation from Greece. Enjoying total air superiority, with more men, munitions and weapons at their disposal, the Germans forced Allied troops into a mad and desperate scramble to southern ports and beaches, where they abandoned and destroyed all manner of machines and munitions before boarding crowded rescue vessels.

Arrival in Crete. Rather than heading back to Egypt, evacuated troops were deposited on the island of Crete. Their rest and recreation were short-lived. They were ordered to hold it against a likely German invasion — no easy task given all the gear they had left behind in Greece and with only a handful of fighter aircraft to pit against the might of the Luftwaffe.

Charlie photographed in a Cairo street, post Crete, shortly after discharge from Helwan Camp hospital, where he was treated for dysentery, sinus problems and battle wounds. He's whippet-thin in a uniform so new no insignia have yet been attached. The photo was sent with a postcard to his parents hoping they were well.

Charlie captioned this photograph, 'fat tailed sheep crossing irrigation canal near Cairo'. He makes no mention of the pyramids in the background.

Charlie with Lieutenant Colonel Howard Kippenberger and Major Ray Lynch about to receive their medals at Baggush Camp in northern Egypt, 1941. Charlie's socks are paler than the other recipients' because they are canary-yellow instead of regulation, standard-issue olive-green.

Charlie congratulated by his platoon sergeant after the ceremony.

Charlie receives his VC from British General Sir Claude Auchinleck, November 1941.
He forgot to salute afterwards until he had retreated several paces.

Charlie days after winning his VC. Already heartily sick of all the fuss and attention, he told Army photographer Harold Paton that he could take one shot and one shot only — and be quick about it. This is it. The eye blazing under the helmet says everything.

Charlie with Lieutenant Colonel Howard Kippenberger, October or November 1941. Kip is immaculate, Charlie is an unmade bed.

Charlie with 'Leggy' Le Gros and wild dog 'Star' that befriended them, as wild animals seemed to with Charlie.

Briefing in the Western Desert, late 1941. Charlie with Major Ralph Peterson, Kip, and Brigadier Lindsay Inglis who agreed that a second citation needed to be drawn up advocating that Charlie be awarded a Bar to his first VC.

Iconic image of Charlie in helmet and battledress famously used to great effect on the cover of *Mark of the Lion*.

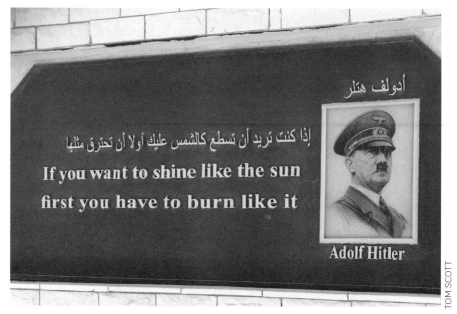

Hitler quote on bas-relief sculpture on the inner courtyard wall of the El Alamein Second World War Military Museum, in Egypt.

Field Marshal Erwin Rommel, the Desert Fox. Much admired by New Zealand soldiers, who he complimented fulsomely in return. He sometimes drank Chablis with captured POWs. Here he is drinking coffee, which the Wehrmacht kept piping hot in sturdy metal Thermos flasks.

Aerial view of the sprawling Weinsberg POW camp in south-west Germany.

Weinsberg's double-skinned perimeter fence that Charlie attempted to scale in broad daylight.

Charlie tangled in coiled barbed wire between the inner and outer fences when his escape bid failed. The photo was taken by Camp Commandant Hauptmann Knapp, who shortly afterwards sent Charlie to Colditz prison.

Colditz Castle, Oflag IV-C, a POW camp for Allied officers who were repeat escapees and/or persistent troublemakers, sitting on the bluff high above the Mulde River in the Leipzig district of Saxony.

Above: Charlie standing rigidly to attention in front of King George VI as his lengthy second VC citation is read out at his royal investiture at Buckingham Palace, 1945. At left, waiting his turn, is fellow New Zealand VC winner Sergeant Jack Hinton.
Below: Charlie and Jack Hinton outside Buckingham Palace after the ceremony.

King George VI chats to Charlie at inspection during the ceremony celebrating victory in London, June 1946.

GETTY IMAGES

When the news of Charlie's VC came through, McIntyre was sent across to the 20th Battalion to sketch him. Men who had been on Crete with him gathered round, keeping up a ribald commentary. Charlie didn't mind that, but he was acutely embarrassed at having his portrait done.

Charlie's aversion to publicity and dismay at being singled out for any form of attention escalated as his fame spread beyond North Africa. Fleet Street newspapers went into raptures. Visiting New Zealand dignitaries made trips into the desert to be photographed with the VC hero only to find Charlie had gone bush, prompting Kippenberger, tongue in cheek, to send him a warning: 'Next time I'll charge you with cowardice.'

Charlie was not in a receptive mood when official 2NZEF photographer Harold Paton arrived to take his picture. Charlie barked that he could take one shot then fuck off. He is sitting on the ground eating something out of a can with a spoon. Only one eye is visible. It burns like a laser. It's a perfect shot. Paton knew it, quickly pressed the button and fucked off.

After the presentation, Kippenberger wrote to Christ's College praising their former pupil:

> Upham is an outstanding officer of whom you may be justly proud. His head is not in any way turned nor likely to be. It really has been rather pathetic watching him meet the attacks of photographers and reporters, he did it very well, though with desperate reluctance. I am sure you will not think it a presumption on my part to congratulate the College on this decoration, which General Freyberg told me was about the best earned he had ever known.

When he got wind of moves to send him back to New Zealand to inspire the home front, to be fêted and paraded, Charlie was devastated. He made a special trip to Cairo to talk to the Acting Military Secretary, Captain Guy Rhodes, an old friend from Crete and Greece campaigns, and tearfully pleaded to be allowed to stay in Egypt with his men. He lobbied others as well and in due course he was advised he could remain. His joy was short-lived when a few weeks later his men went into battle without him.

On 18 November 1941, a pitch-black night pouring with rain, and with lightning flashes illuminating the desert in a ghostly blue glow, the New Zealand Division departed Baggush to participate in the huge Allied assault to relieve the siege of Tobruk — Operation Crusader. With no headlights and no one smoking, following a route marked at intervals with dim green lights facing back, and with red lights on the rear of some vehicles to keep the trucks in line, a massive convoy of men, munitions and machines headed up the coast to the Libyan border. Charlie watched in a state of molten rage as the never-ending stream of red lights vanished into the distance until the desert was dark and silent again. He had been designated 'LOB': left out of battle.

Kippenberger:

> From his experiences in Crete he had developed a hatred for the enemy. He was bitter about Army shortcomings and about the two miserable withdrawals. Yet he believed his men were superior to the Germans in fighting ability. He was fretting for more action. He really was too anxious to get at the enemy again. I thought his mood was too dangerous. I left him out because I thought he would get himself killed too quickly.

All battles are good to be left out of and this one especially so. Not that Charlie saw it that way. In one exchange the 20th Battalion was overrun by Axis forces and Charlie could well have been among the many men captured or killed. In brutal, see-saw engagements, both sides inflicted terrible carnage on each other. In multiple tank clashes, the Wehrmacht suffered their first terrestrial defeats of the war. Outnumbered and over-extended, Rommel's forces abandoned the Cyrenaican coast in north-eastern Libya and limped back to defensive positions in the west of the country. The New Zealand Division led the eventual breakthrough to Tobruk. When a land transport corridor had been secured to the port, the Allies returned to Egypt, claiming the narrowest of victories on points.

Kippenberger: 'I don't think the New Zealand troops ever fought so well. Auchinleck came to see me in hospital and said we'd done the finest fighting he'd ever known, and he meant it.'

For all its ferocity, both sides were surprisingly chivalrous, Rommel insisting that Allied wounded be treated the same as German casualties, and they buried each other's dead. Swarming blowflies made this a necessity as well as a courtesy. In *Gunner Inglorious*, Jim Henderson graphically describes doing the honours for two Germans:

> The caps of the Afrika Korps are still on their heads. One mouth is open in a humourless grin, with teeth dead-white against a purple-black sponge of tongue. Their arms are still around each other, so we leave them that way. Ralph and I can't find any identity discs. Their jackets and trousers pockets contain only cigarettes, a jack-knife, some twine, two handkerchiefs and a photograph. This might help identify one of the poor cows, so we put it aside and start shovelling sand and rocks upon them. Heck, they stink! The sand mounts up, their boots and ankles and knees and thighs are covered and we're starting to chuck earth on to their torsos. 'Hang on, Ralph,' I say suddenly and get the two handkerchiefs and place them over the faces the colour

of varnished skirting board. I didn't like to think of dirt crashing down rudely on to those faces and going all roughly into eyes and nostrils and throat and ears.

If you were lucky, you died instantly. A friend of Norm Jones wasn't so fortunate:

Explosions began to rock the burning carrier. The outline of Scotty's head and shoulders could still be seen inside the inferno. Hobson and the others had tried to get him out but the flames were too hot and sitting right on top of the ruptured petrol tanks he'd be a goner anyway. Following the explosion Scotty's 'body' had stood up and fallen over the side of the carrier, and was now wriggling and writhing like a sidewinder snake through the burning sand, screaming like a burning rabbit coming out of a gorse fire. He was burnt black from his head to his boots; every stitch of clothing burnt off, his hair the same. His eyes were burnt blind, his knees and elbows were shattered, his buttocks, crutch and thighs ripped and gaping with open wounds. He'd have bled to death from his atrocious wounds but they'd been seared black and cauterized by the flames, and only frothy bubbles of red blood were suppurating through his charred flesh. His elbows and knees were laid open, his crutch and testicles gone! I began to cry. I couldn't help myself. Hobson and Hamish, Corporal Wood and his driver bent over Scotty, took hold of a blanket corner each and like pallbearers carried him slowly to Wood's carrier and laid him gently on top. Scotty never moved nor uttered a sound. For God's sake, what had I to blubber about? Body juices previously cauterised had begun to seep and stink from his charred wounds. I was looking at his face, which wasn't any longer a face, when he spoke quite clearly and lucidly.

'Is that you, Jonesy?'

I bent over his sightless eyes, closer to the lips that weren't lips.

'Yes, it's me, Scotty. It's Jonesy.'

'I can't see, Jonesy!'

'You're asleep, Scotty. Go back to sleep, Scotty.'

'We're moving. Where am I going, Jonesy?'

'You're going home, Scotty. You'll be there when you wake up.'

'Home, Jonesy?'

'Yeah, home, Scotty. Go back to sleep, Scotty!'

Scotty never made another sound. He was dead when they lifted him from the carrier. He'd gone home.

When he calmed down, Charlie busied himself at Baggush getting the camp ready for his returning men. The badly knocked-about New Zealand Division were restocked with reinforcements from New Zealand. Charlie was promoted to captain and put in charge of C Company. He managed to get some leave in Alexandria, but was otherwise getting bored and restless.

In February 1942, the New Zealand Division was trucked and railed across the Sinai Desert, up through the Holy Lands to Aleppo in Northern Syria, the oldest continuously inhabited city on earth — a city so fabled Shakespeare was able to refer to it in *Macbeth* and *Othello* and punters standing in the straw and sawdust pit of the Globe theatre in Elizabethan London knew its significance. The New Zealanders' prime task was to make lots of noise on training exercises, to be a highly visible presence and dispel any notion the Turks might have of joining the war on Germany's side and pouring over the border. The interlude gave the New Zealand Division a chance to absorb the lessons of Operation Crusader, to rethink their fighting doctrine and better coordinate their infantry and artillery tactics.

On leave they swam in the Med, floated in the Dead Sea, skied snowfields in Lebanon, flirted with lovely girls in Tel Aviv, bartered in Beirut bazaars and marvelled at ancient monuments. Charlie took lots of snaps. Photographs taken of him show weight slowly returning to his frame. If not a lotus-eating sojourn, it was close. The aroma of sweet oranges, cedar and thyme hung in the balmy air. Returning to his dugout one night, Charlie found a cat nursing a litter of newborn kittens on his camp stretcher. Rather than disturb them, he happily slept outside under the stars. He befriended a puppy and sent a postcard home of him cuddling it.

It was too good to last, and it didn't. In late May 1942 Rommel launched another offensive. The Allies had more tanks and more artillery, but by shrewdly concentrating his forces against isolated and separated Allied formations, Rommel sent the British Eighth Army packing and captured Tobruk. The New Zealanders were on night manoeuvres in Syria when they got the call.

The previous defenders of the garrison port of Tobruk, gutsy Aussies and tough Poles, who'd held out for a year, had been replaced by South African troops under the command of General Klopper, who gave the order to surrender despite outnumbering the encircling Germans. Years later at a Christ's College Board of Governors meeting, the appointment of a new staff member with the surname 'Klopper' came up. Charlie, who had hitherto given the appearance of being dormant, erupted like a volcano, with eyes blazing, 'No relation to the bastard who threw in the towel at Tobruk, is he?' Assured that he wasn't, Charlie subsided and went back into hibernation.

Bundled out of Libya, the British retreated along the Egyptian coast and the New Zealand Division raced helter-skelter west around the rim of the Mediterranean, where they met the bedraggled, disorganised Eighth Army streaming east. Lieutenant General Sir Leonard Thornton would later write:

It took us only about five or six days I suppose to move all those hundreds and thousands of kilometres back into the Western Desert. And as we went up into the desert from Alexandria up that narrow and well-known Desert Road towards the East, the 8th Army and the Air Force were coming pell-mell back down the road and it was, shall we say, not exactly riotous but it was certainly a very disorganised retreat. And morale had fallen to pieces so it was quite a challenge. The Kiwis rather liked the idea that they were going to save the situation, so we went in the most orderly way we could up alongside the road mostly against the stream of traffic coming back from the disordered battles that had occurred further to the east.

On a road between Maadi and Suez, a petrol tanker and a giant Italian truck loaded with flour smashed head on. According to one eyewitness, flour showered skyward and petrol poured across the ground — petrol fumes joining flour granules in the air — a volatile mix, effectively poor man's gunpowder. The eyewitness and another New Zealander, a recently arrived medical orderly who had never dealt with anything like this before, were struggling to free one of the drivers from a fume-filled mangled cab when Charlie materialised to lend a hand:

'Is he dead?' demanded the new captain.

'I don't I think so, sir,' came the medical orderly's hesitant reply.

'Is he dead or alive?' snapped Charlie, who wanted a definitive answer.

'He's dead, sir.'

'Then there's nothing we can do for him. Let's fuck off!'

Chapter 13

'This show tonight will make bloody history!'

There was scant chance of me having a fateful head-on collision. I headed for the Alamein coast in a chauffeured Peugeot down the silky-smooth Cairo–Alexandria freeway, four lanes wide in either direction, eight lanes in all — stretching as far as the eye could see in a straight line.

It could double as the world's biggest runway, which is doubtless the intention. The freeway is flanked on either side with dual-carriage roads for heavy vehicles and exclusive military use during an emergency.

'The army own Egypt. This is *their* country,' said my driver Amir with a sly grin. 'Until we are attacked or in trouble, then suddenly it is *our* country again.' We passed whole new cities under construction, orange groves, olive orchards, fields of flowers and banana crops, grazing goats and cattle. Then the landscape changed from green to amber as abruptly as a traffic light and suddenly we were in open desert. Walled estates with gatehouses the size of palaces had long driveways running to palaces the size of small cities.

I asked Amir to take me to his favourite roadside café for lunch. We pulled into a McDonald's car park. Shaking his head, Amir led me up the road to an enclosed pedestrian bridge straddling the freeway. The spiral staircases at either end were open. On every landing cigarette butts, old shoes, cans, cardboard cartons and sand eddied out of the wind. Toothless old women and mothers cradling infants squatted in the rubbish with outstretched blackened hands begging for money. Amir had a fit when I reached for my wallet. 'NEVER SHOW YOUR MONEY!' Lunch was delicious charcoal chicken, pita bread, fresh cucumber, sweet tomatoes and rich black coffee. I dreaded the return journey. I gave Amir money for the meal and told him to give the change to the women. It can't have been enough. One of them broke into English and began wailing like a police siren, 'I beg you! I beg you! I beg you! I beg you! I beg you!', and the harrowing cries followed us all the way to the car.

Heading north again, the magnificent country estates thinned out and another wall loomed up. It ran unbroken for many miles, punctuated every so often by high gates and watchtowers where women with baskets formed long queues. 'Military prison,' explained Amir with a broad grin, barely able to contain his delight, adding, '[President Mohamed] Morsi was locked up here.' The wall kept going for another 10 kilometres. It must be one of the few prisons anywhere where inmates can suffer from claustrophobia and agoraphobia at the same time. Then it ended and we were cruising through empty desert again.

I jotted down 'P.J. O'Rourke' in my notebook. Covering the first Gulf War for *Rolling Stone*, the American satirist hitched a ride out of Iraq on board an RNZAF C-130 Hercules, delighting in the Kiwi pilot's droll description of the endless, flat, featureless landscape as 'Wall to wall, fuck all!' It fitted the Egyptian desert as well — save for the occasional concrete bus shelter popping up in the middle of nowhere. 'For the Bedouin when they take public transport,' explained Amir. Black bags placed back from the verge at regular intervals intrigued me. 'Petrol for people who run out of gas,' said

Amir. Rommel would have loved this arrangement.

I asked Amir to play me his favourite road-trip music. Something that sounded like Sting's 'Desert Rose', minus Sting, blasted at deafening, filling-rattling volume. 'What do you like most about the desert?' I shouted. 'The peace and quiet!' he shouted back. As we approached the sea, scores of mysterious grey cones marched across the olive-green and brown rocky, scrubby plains. We passed one close up — a quarry with mounds of gravel and aggregate waiting to be trucked to a building site 8 kilometres wide and 50 kilometres long. All along the Alamein shore new cities in various stages of construction and completion are springing up. Inner harbours and marinas are being gouged into the bedrock of the coast. It's gobsmacking in scale and ambition. Dusty, bustling and confusing.

Amir couldn't find my hotel and started screaming at Google Maps on his cellphone. 'YOU LIE! YOU LIE! WHY ARE YOU LYING TO ME? I AM AN EGYPTIAN, NOT AN INDIAN!' He eventually located it in a gated beach resort just as a sandstorm arrived. Within minutes the plush homes, lush lawns, tall palms and inland waterways had vanished completely. Being the off-season, the elegant hotel was all but empty. A team of lovely people at reception set about organising cars and drivers to take me on tours of the war graves and the Alamein War Museum. The battlefields of Ruweisat Ridge and Minqar Qaim were out of bounds due to unexploded ordnance. Some 23 million mines were laid in Egypt during the Second World War, and most of them remain hidden in the ground, decaying slowly. Camels and Bedouin putting a foot wrong are still being blown to shreds. I told them I had no problem with not going there.

What I couldn't understand was their reluctance to take me to the Italian hospital and bunker complex inland from the El Alamein–Bahariya Desert road. The excuses kept changing — an oil company was drilling there, the road was closed for repairs, the military was conducting live ammunition exercises. Whatever, it wasn't safe. Nor could I get a driver to take me to Rommel's cave at Mersa Matruh, where he directed operations from caverns once used to store grain in Roman times. Converted into a museum dedicated to Rommel, the cave houses personal effects, including his leather coat, compass, field telephone and maps donated by his son, Manfred.

Mersa Matruh was where a copy of Peter McIntyre's charcoal sketch of Winston Churchill was pinned to the wall in a bar. It became the custom of those passing through to sign it. When the Allies retreated and the Germans overran and occupied the ancient harbour town, they never took it down or defaced it. Instead they added their own signatures. When the Allies retook Mersa Matruh, it was still there. A retreating German had paused long enough to write across it: '*Auf Wiedersehen*'. Nightclubs in Alexandria and Cairo were less sentimental and more pragmatic. As the fortunes of the desert war ebbed and flowed, bars named Spitfires in Alexandria and Cairo changed their name to Messerschmitt bars then back again.

§

Ten days after upping sticks in Aleppo, the New Zealand Division reached Mersa Matruh Bay — famous for its white sands, clear blue water, sponge diving and beautiful rock pool where Cleopatra skinny-dipped with Mark Antony. Not swayed by its charms, Freyberg refused to stay there. He feared that, ringed as it is by low hills, it could easily become another Tobruk. After the shambles of Operation Crusader, where more New Zealanders were captured or taken prisoner than in any other campaign fought by the New Zealand Division in the war, he didn't want to be shackled to the Eighth Army. Preferring autonomy and operational flexibility, he sought and was given permission to move his men 20 miles inland to a sloping escarpment at Minqar Qaim to head off any German advance taking a southern route to the Nile Delta.

Ground as hard as concrete made digging slit trenches all but impossible. Weapon pits had to be blasted or jack-hammered out of solid rock. Stones and sand had to be scraped together to form low-walled structures called sangars — which afforded only meagre protection. Heavy artillery was set up on slopes facing west. On the scrubby, undulating, rubble-strewn plains below, sappers assisted by Indian troops laid mines. It was slow, dangerous work. New mines were being laid beside an old unmarked minefield. Several men were blown to pieces. Flares lit up the twilight sky in the west. The Germans were coming. It would be a close-run thing to get the mines laid in time. The 20th Battalion assisted and stood guard, with Charlie pacing back and forth like a caged big cat.

They were climbing onto trucks to drive back to the escarpment when Charlie recognised a familiar whine and yelled at his men to head for a wadi (a dry channel) some yards away. Twenty Stukas came screaming out of the sinking sun to pound their column. Charlie leapt back to his feet, urging his men to engage them with small arms, but the Luftwaffe wheeled away. Overnight, radio reports painted a confused picture. Rommel's Afrika Korps were advancing on multiple fronts. Middle East High Command were issuing orders to make a stand at Mersa Matruh *and* to retreat to Alamein. The New Zealand Division stayed put.

At 7.30 the next morning the 21st Panzer Division and the German 90th Light Infantry Division began advancing from their overnight positions, halting when they reached the newly laid minefield. German sappers were called forward to clear a pathway. Alighting under fire, they scrambled back into rock and scrub, where they were hard to spot. When the

Germans came within range, Kiwi 25-pounders opened up and a thumping exchange of high-explosive shells began and continued all morning. Three miles to the north, shimmering in the heat haze, a breakaway enemy column was spotted moving east. Led by tanks, several hundred trucks laden with infantry passed by — then swung south, cutting off escape to the east. The New Zealand Division was being encircled.

All afternoon the noose tightened. They would have to break out that night — if they survived that long. During a lull in the firing, Charlie drove a 3-ton truck down the escarpment and parked it behind his company, facing the enemy on the plains. Sitting on the bonnet surveying the strangely quiet battlefield, he turned to his Company Sergeant Major Bob May with a request: 'Bob, there's a Primus in the back. What about boiling up? I reckon we won't have time later.'

No sooner had May climbed into the back than there was a loud splintering crash and the truck rocked sideways. Deep in the interior, a startled May wanted to know what was happening. Charlie explained that a shell had gone through the windscreen and asked how far away the cup of tea was. The next shot smashed the tailboard. When May suggested it might be time to leave, Charlie told him to get a wriggle on, as near misses didn't count. But German tanks did, appearing out of the haze and swirling in large numbers, accompanied by crack Panzer Grenadiers on foot — a nightmarish apparition charging straight at them.

'HOLD IT! HOLD IT!' Charlie screamed to his men. New Zealand infantry and anti-tank gunners waited until the range was down to 400 yards before opening up a thunderous fusillade. Tanks veered away and grenadiers dived into hollows and behind boulders and returned fire, forcing the New Zealanders to keep their heads down. Not Charlie. He began racing from slit trench to sangar, from section to section, with German mortar and small-arms' fire kicking up plumes of sand and stone in his wake. Dashing through smoke and dust on crouching runs, he was very fortunate not to be struck by friendly fire as he repeatedly crossed in front of New Zealand guns shooting almost parallel to the ground. The commander of an anti-tank platoon captured the scene poetically to Sandford: 'Charlie came across the desert leaning over holding his soft hat against the bullets as if against the wind . . .'

His actions are recorded in the official 20th Battalion history:

> Upham with characteristic coolness moved around his company on foot, crossing open ground swept by small arms and mortar fire steadying one platoon which was under shellfire and encouraging his men; he set an example appreciated by all who saw it, except perhaps the field gunners whose 25-pounders were firing over C Company's positions over open sights.

In his terrific, authoritative *Breakout: Minqar Qaim, North Africa, 1942*, Colin Cameron repeats a Minqar Qaim reunion yarn told by Charlie about being asked by 5 Field Regiment where to place their anti-tank guns:

> 'Dig one behind us,' he told the officer.
> 'We can't put it in there. It would deafen you all.'
> 'We're not bloody reinforcements,' Upham replied. 'We know what noise is.'
> The gun was duly sited.
> The first round went off. A sheet of flame shot out the end. A cloud of dust came up around us and no one could see a thing. We had a hell of a time. I wish to God I hadn't told the bloke to put it there!

A platoon on the exposed front line rose out of their trench and began falling back in dribs and dabs. The retreat was stopped by Charlie: 'What the hell are you doing? How many casualties have you had?' When told none, he said, 'Go back. Let me know when you have had thirty per cent casualties and we'll think about it!' When a runner was needed to take a message out to a platoon on a distant flank, Charlie took it. His advice to anyone else exposing themselves unnecessarily was a harsh bark: 'Keep your rump down, you fool! Or you'll spend the rest of your life sleeping on your stomach!'

Charlie told Sandford that he took risks on Minqar Qaim because German fire was inaccurate and too low. When his company mortars ran out of ammunition, he had no qualms about running back and forth through shellfire with fresh supplies. Wireless sets on Minqar Qaim had limited range and had to be cleared of dust and sand before every transmission. If the person you wanted to speak to was Charlie, there was a good chance he wasn't at home. Colonel 'Gentleman Jim' Burrows noted:

> He was always a hard man to get on the phone. He never seemed to be at Company HQ. Someone would have to go for him, or he would come on the line breathless, as if he had been running hard . . .

When a heavy German machine gun somewhere beyond the minefields pinned down one of his platoons, Charlie called for another 3-ton truck and had it driven through the firestorm and parked forward of the forward positions to draw fire. Sheltering in slit trenches and sangars, his men looked on in awe, disbelief and dismay as Charlie, binoculars in hand, clambered up onto the roof of the cab where he stood legs akimbo, calculating range and directing 20th Battalion machine-gun and anti-tank-gun fire at enemy positions.

Peter Llewellyn was one witness: 'A hidden Spandau was giving trouble so he drew its fire. The range was too great for Brens but a three-inch mortar finally did the trick.'

Some of his men speculated that the Germans may have thought he was an artillery operations commander and they withheld fire in case Charlie directed artillery fire onto them. The danger Charlie was deliberately courting angered others. Terry Madsen screamed at him: 'GET DOWN, YOU IDIOT! THEY'LL HIT YOU!' Eyes glued to his binoculars, Charlie shouted back: 'They've been trying all day. Haven't hit me yet.'

Charlie rationalised his behaviour later: 'An officer needed height to determine the course of the battle in the flat desert. It also made one vulnerable to sniper fire. I don't think anyone was hit, but you could hear the bloody bullets pinging around you.'

In a letter to Sandford, Madsen described the scene vividly:

> The ground to our front was very flat and as the enemy was advancing out of the sun — hot as hell, everything shimmering and mirage like. It was difficult to judge if what we could see were trucks, tanks or even just patches of scrub. Charlie wanted to know, so with no heroics he simply stood up on the cab of the truck observing, his binoculars winking in the sun. It was the most cold-bloodedly brave, matter of fact display of guts I can imagine. There was no hurried peep and a quick dive for cover — he stood fully erect for what seemed like hours — but of course wasn't — until he had thoroughly satisfied himself that he knew all that was necessary then got down.

Freyberg was not so lucky. Later that afternoon while checking on the aftermath of a German infantry attack repelled by 28th Battalion, the general was struck in the neck by a flying shell splinter. Given morphine and heavily bandaged, he lay semi-conscious in a shallow trench ringed with sandbags under a canvas awning.

Brigadier Lindsay Inglis took charge of the New Zealand Division with Colonel Jim Burrows as his second in command. They set the breakout for half an hour after midnight. It needed to be a surprise. There would be no warning and no artillery. It would be led by infantry with bayonets fixed. Sappers would follow close behind in case the enemy had laid mines. Casualties would be collected by stretcher-bearers moving behind their own units. Red and green Very lights would signal that an escape route wide and deep enough for the whole division to drive through had been cut through the enemy lines a mile to their east.

The midsummer nights were short so they had to be swift and decisive to get well clear of the enemy before daylight. Officers were briefed at an 8 p.m. meeting and left to instruct their men, which didn't take long as the plan was simple. No provision was made for an alternative plan in case of failure. Only personal items, paybooks, guns and spare ammunition were to be taken. Everything else was to be left behind. Soldiers who had been hoarding bottles of grog weren't about to let it fall into enemy hands. Warm beer was polished off and men quietly wished each other luck and shook hands in the dark. Everyone knew the operation was a huge gamble that had to be taken. They didn't have enough ammunition to repel panzer attacks on three sides the following day and surrender was not an option. Some men managed to lie down on the hard ground and get some sleep. Some Maori soldiers gathered around a radio heard a taunting propaganda broadcast from Lord Haw-Haw: 'What are the Kiwis going to do now, because kiwis can't fly? Try flying out of this lot!'

Haw-Haw was far away in Hamburg. Germans closer to the action did not share his confidence and were markedly less cocksure. An officer in 21 Panzer Division noted glumly in their daily battle report that very night: 'Units of the enemy resist most stubbornly; our tank attack gains ground slowly.'

Any hopes he had that the next twenty-four hours would see a huge improvement were about to be cruelly dashed.

At the appointed hour, troop transports, canteen trucks, artillery, petrol tankers, water tankers, ambulances, staff cars and other vehicles lined up in columns on the start line. The 20th Battalion were fifteen minutes late getting there. Charlie had an explanation for the delay: 'C company had patrols out looking for enemy creeping up for a night attack as well as probing for mines. It took time to get them all back in.'

The 28th Battalion were later still. A bright moon was rising when they finally got under way an hour and a quarter late.

Stepping like lace, making a soft rhythmic crunch, the infantry advanced a thousand yards before enemy sentries spotted something and raised the alarm. A couple of shots were fired, people shouted anxiously then the whole front erupted in flame. Rifles, machine guns, mortars and anti-tank guns started chattering and thumping. Red tracer criss-crossed their path. A seemingly impenetrable curtain of hot metal greeted them. Decimation if not complete annihilation seemed inevitable. Colonel Burrows:

> An amazing and thrilling thing happened. To a man the whole brigade charged forward. No orders were given; no urging forward by officers and NCOs. With shouting, cheering and war cries every man broke into a run as if he knew exactly what was expected of him.

Clarence Furey was injured in the charge:

> What I can see to this day is a wall of fire. I thought how are we going to get through this? It's chaos. What a bloody slaughter. We went through a field hospital. It shouldn't have been that far forward. Behind me a brand new soldier with a Tommy gun was a bit jittery. I think he shot me.

With men dropping to the ground on either side of him, Charlie led the 20th from the front. Leaving the shooting and bayoneting to his men, he snatched grenades from the small arsenal in his stuffed haversack and hurled them on the run at trucks and tanks parked in their path. In preparation, Charlie had changed from grenades with seven-second fuses to grenades with four-second fuses, making them a close-quarters weapon. Somehow, above the detonations, erupting munitions, exploding petrol tanks, gunfire, roaring flame, cursing and screaming, his men could hear him urging them on.

In slit trenches most of the Germans still had their boots off. Some were undressed. Some Germans who attempted to surrender were disregarded. A sobbing German teenager was spared. Some Germans sprinted into the dark. Others ran to revving trucks, which was their undoing. Others fought back, fiercely pouring petrol onto the sand and lighting it to make barriers of flame and driving wheeled and half-tracked vehicles at their attackers, only to be met with bullets and grenades. The strongest resistance was met among the tightly parked German transport.

No one knows how many trucks Charlie destroyed that night. Asked after the war, he was not much help: 'Perhaps six or seven . . .' Others say more. He fired into cabs and lobbed grenades onto trays packed with troops. He was seen running so hard after one departing truck that German soldiers on board thought he was one of them and one of their number reached out to hoist him on board. Charlie responded to this act of compassion by throwing two grenades onto the packed tray, killing all those on board and receiving cuts on his face and hands from blast fragments. He said:

'Fleeing vehicles were stuck in soft sand with men
hanging onto the sides while their drivers revved to try
to get out. Very few did. One good soldier was firing his

machine gun from beneath a truck. It drove away leaving him in the open and I dispatched him with a grenade.'

The 20th Battalion gatecrashed an officers' enclave and mobile headquarters. Charlie fired into fleeing staff cars. Opening the rear of one, he tossed in a grenade and slammed it shut, blowing the door off. Using bayonets, rifles, Tommy guns, grenades and Brens fired from the hip, the New Zealanders created a corridor through the inferno to open ground on the other side. Flares signalling success went up and the rest of the New Zealand Division came hurtling through.

Major General Inglis:

> For a mile and a half we ran through and past and over Germans who were so shaken by the massive trucks and guns drawing down on them out of the dark that not one of them fired a shot at us. Some of them were dashing about in their shirt tails. One could see the dim shapes of many parked vehicles, but there was none directly in front of us. After three miles we halted to let the columns close up; but we could hear the enemy still shooting himself up away behind us.

They paused to pick up infantry and gather their wounded before turning southwards to elude any German pursuit and dispersing into the squid-ink vastness. Charlie was too pumped with adrenalin to notice that he was soaked in blood and peppered with grenade fragments, exclaiming excitedly to all and sundry: 'This show tonight will make bloody history! We rocked the bastards that time!'

Charlie and Leggy Le Gros were picked up by a staff car: 'Follow that convoy!' shouted Charlie, pointing to vanishing lights. Everyone was exhausted. Charlie and Leggy were soon fast asleep. The driver nodded off at the wheel and they drove on aimlessly for quite some time, which you can do on a vast trackless plain. When the driver woke up, there was no sign of the convoy. He sheepishly informed his passengers. 'I don't give a bugger,' replied Charlie and went back to sleep.

§

There were many fearless deeds performed during the breakout, Charlie's actions supreme among them. Colonel Burrows wrote later:

> Officers, NCOs and men were talking freely about his actions during a night assault. From several I heard how Charles had led a rush to a truckload of Germans who were trying to get up speed through soft sand. With one hand on the tail board he tossed in a grenade getting slightly wounded from the explosion.

Burrows waited until the exhilaration and raw emotion of Minqar Qaim had subsided before speaking to men who had witnessed Charlie in action. After solemn deliberation, he sought out Kippenberger and Inglis at the 5th Brigade HQ. There was something he needed to say to both of them. Only Kippenberger was there, but Burrows had to get it off his chest and blurted it out: 'Kip, you heard about Charlie, I suppose?'

'Yes,' said Kippenberger, 'who hasn't?'

Burrows hesitated. What he was about to suggest had never happened to any combat soldier before.

'Kip, Charlie's got to have another VC for Minqar Qaim.'

Kippenberger agreed and passed the suggestion on to Inglis. A tough, hard-drinking man, as red-faced and as bulbous-nosed as W.C. Fields, Inglis' nickname was 'Whisky Bill'. Famous for his heated disagreements with Freyberg, he agreed with Kippenberger and Burrows and requested that a formal recommendation for a Bar to Charlie's VC be drawn up.

In the immediate aftermath of the breakout, the diary of the Afrika Korps noted curtly: '1 Battalion Panzer Grenadiers has suffered very heavy casualties as the enemy succeeded in surprising the battalion and cutting it to pieces in hand-to-hand fighting.' Rommel was initially sanguine, paying the Kiwis a compliment of sorts, writing: 'The British units already badly mauled again suffered heavy losses. Even the New Zealand Division newly moved up from Syria could not stave off a fresh defeat.'

When the gruesome details of the breakout at Minqar Qaim emerged, Rommel's tone changed. In a letter of 2 July 1942 to Field Marshal Kesselring, he wrote: 'The intention is first of all to hold the front and regroup in such a manner that the New Zealand Division can be encircled and destroyed.'

When Brigadier George Clifton was captured, he was brought before an angry Rommel who accused the New Zealand Division of gangster methods — eighty injured men, medical orderlies and doctors in tented hospitals and ambulances had been bayoneted to death. Some multiple times. Overkill, literally. His generals said the New Zealand Division behaved like Bolsheviks drunk on vodka. Rommel thundered that any further acts of this kind would be answered with immediate reprisals — shorthand for execution of captured Allied soldiers. Clifton swiftly explained that many Germans played dead and rose to shoot the first wave of attackers in the back after they had passed. As a consequence, succeeding waves of New Zealanders gave no quarter and stuck every man who failed to stand and surrender.

As for the stabbing of German wounded and medics, their regimental aid post and ambulances were set right behind the first line of German vehicles among slit trenches. In the dark, in the blinding flashes, strobing fire, choking smoke, swirling dust, noise, chaos and confusion, it was difficult in a split second to differentiate one German from another. Rommel conceded this could be the case and calmed down sufficiently to be amused by Clifton's admission of shame and horror at the prospect of being captured by Italians, and his relief when a German officer showed up to accept his surrender.

Some in the 28th Battalion were not amused by reports that Clifton had suggested that Maori soldiers were responsible for the worst of the bayoneting. Sergeant Bill Rickard from 28th Battalion insisted later that Maori *and* Pakeha soldiers participated equally:

> 'That was the worst blooming slaughter I've ever seen in my life. Fullas were coming out of the back of those trucks on the ends of bayonets. Man, I saw some Pakeha there, Jeez, they were worse than the Maoris, they were getting stuck into those fullas . . .'

Years later, Burrows told a group of North Canterbury soldiers that the essence of those hot vital minutes was self-preservation: 'Our blokes didn't swing away from the fighting.' Also present, Charlie agreed: 'It was a soldiers' battle. Officers had no say. Morale was high and the objective was to get through.'

Ken Longmore took part in the breakout at Minqar Qaim and remembered Charlie's actions:

> 'Charlie was in his element that night, chasing German trucks, hurling grenades. We were lucky we got out. Some of their blokes had thirty bayonet wounds. In the morning the Germans would have shot us just like in the movies.'

I interviewed Ken in his retirement home on my return from Europe and North Africa. Traffic was light and I got to the rest home in suburban Lower Hutt fifteen minutes early. I had plenty to read. I could have waited in the car, but I thought this guy is a centurion — why take the risk? Ken Longmore was waiting for me in the foyer — clearly, he didn't want to take the risk either. His massive hands rested on the handle of his walking stick. His strong handshake was the last echo of the keen tennis player he'd been all his life (the racquets would have looked like ping-pong bats in his big hands). He was dressed in an ironed check shirt, pressed trousers, comfortable shoes, and with his trimmed moustache, shards of white hair falling over his temple and clear eyes, he looked much younger than his 100 years. Only his laboured shuffle gave him away.

Ken had been a prisoner of war at Campo PG 47 at Modena in Italy and Oflag VA at Weinsberg in Germany with Charlie, Major Bob Wood who became a lifelong friend of Charlie and Lieutenant Bruce Robertson, who didn't. Robertson kept thoughtful, descriptive, detailed diaries in which he describes Charlie as a brooding, unapproachable, unnerving presence. Lightly edited by his daughter Rosanne Robertson, they were published in 2010 in an insight-rich and touching book, *For the Duration*. It was Rosanne who put me onto Ken.

Ken was a warm man but there was no hiding or disguising his coolness when I brought up the subject of Charlie. 'You didn't like him?' I asked tentatively. 'Who could?' he replied emphatically. Although he was unstinting in his admiration for Charlie's fearlessness at Minqar Qaim, he had mixed feelings about Charlie's ceaseless, borderline reckless behaviour as a POW which could have gotten other POWs injured or killed. 'We were scared of him at times, but mind you, so were the Germans!'

§

After the breakout from Minqar Qaim, the New Zealanders were left defending a narrow strip of land running between an impassable sandy basin in the Sahara Desert and the Mediterranean Sea. This vast basin — the Qattara

Depression, the largest in the Sahara — has sheer sides in places that drop 200 metres to the sandy floor. It lies below sea level in the Western Desert of Egypt. Ancient Egyptians regarded it as the land of the hereafter. It was once filled with water. Latter-day Egyptians want to fill it with water again as part of a hydro-electric project gargantuan in scale and ambition. The basin floor is covered with salt pans, salt marshes and soft, talcum-powder dunes. Peter McIntyre, an eloquent painter with words as well as oils, was briefly attached to the Long Range Desert Group, one of the few units able to traverse and survive the Qattara Depression. He described it memorably: 'The desert lay in quivering heat, like a dead planet. Hills of black and red rock broke in scab-like blotches through the sand.'

Freezing at night, scorching by day, it is impassable except for modified vehicles. Denying direct access to Cairo, it obliges all would-be conquerors from the west to negotiate a narrow strip of land less than 40 miles wide and 60 miles long — pretty much the bulk of the building site that consumes much of the Alamein coast today.

It was here that the New Zealand Division fled after Minqar Qaim. It was here that General Bernard Montgomery made a stand, waiting patiently behind massive minefields while the Afrika Korps, their supply lines sorely stretched, wilted. Monty insisted on building a three-to-one superiority in men and armaments before attacking in what purists call the Third Battle of Alamein. Thanks to Ultra, Monty knew that Rommel was sick and convalescing in Italy — a good omen and the perfect time to strike. The Afrika Korps were routed. Chased west without respite, six months later the Germans surrendered in North Africa.

Churchill marked this turning point in the war with a famous speech in London's Mansion House. In the BBC tape recording you can hear him savouring the words in his mouth like boiled lollies: 'Ah, this is not the end. It is not even the beginning of the end. But it is perhaps the end of the beginning.'

§

From my personal observation, it is the beginning of the end for the roadside memorials marking the Axis and Allied front lines at Alamein as of 23 October 1942. In a state of disrepair, a concrete slab with the Afrika Korps logo — a palm with a swastika on its trunk — bears the warning: 'FORWARD GERMAN MINEFIELD'. This is the closest Rommel got to Cairo. About 200 yards east another memorial barely 100 kilometres from Alexandria marks the line where the Allies stopped his onslaught. It is about to be smothered completely in rubble from new motorway construction. You can just make out half a lion and read the words: 'FORWARD BRITISH MINEFIELD'. I don't imagine either memorial will survive much longer. *C'est la vie.* This is the land of the Ozymandias, King of Kings, after all. In a sonnet by Shelley the once mighty Pharaoh is reduced to two trunkless legs of stone standing in a sandy plain.

So far at least the German dead have been spared that ignominy. German sacrifices are commemorated inside a grim octagonal fortress of rough-hewn blocks with bulging buttresses, set back from the motorway on a low rise overlooking the sea. A towering, windowless chamber houses two massive medieval sarcophagi carved from stone the colour of pewter: the final resting place of the remains of 4280 men slain during the battle of El Alamein.

Five kilometres along the coast, the Italian memorial is a tower of smooth stone situated on another lonely dune overlooking a soothing shore. Inside, bathed in soft light, a hall of remembrance has inscriptions to the 4800 soldiers who were able to be identified. There is a separate dedication to 38,000 men whose bodies were never found or which remain unknown.

Further inland, the Commonwealth War Cemetery is open to the sky — an English county churchyard on steroids with sand instead of lawn. Row upon row of engraved headstones separated at regular intervals by ornamental trees, flowering shrubs and banks of red roses cover a wide, serene slope facing south towards a desert as vast as the sea filling the horizon to the north. All told, some 7367 men are buried here and another 11,945 whose bodies are still missing are commemorated. The day I paid my respects someone had written in a spidery hand in the visitors' book: 'Thanks, Dad.'

The cemetery is next door to the Alamein War Museum. A Spitfire on a plinth, tanks, half-tracks and artillery portees of the Allied and Axis forces, all painted the same unifying khaki, surround a rectangular courtyard, the inner wall of which is lined with bas-relief sculptures of battle scenes and portraits of Rommel and Churchill, *plus* a large plaque featuring a coloured image of Hitler, the rough slouching beast himself — Charlie's mad dog, alongside one of his quotes that was paradoxically blood-chilling despite the subject matter and noon-day sun showering photons and infrared rays from above: 'If you want to shine like the sun first you have to burn like it.' Criminal, lunatic, ferocious single-mindedness has seldom been better expressed.

Inside the courtyard, four separate halls are devoted to Commonwealth, Italian, German and Egyptian soldiers. Alongside the photographs, flags, maps, weapons, uniforms, motorbikes and side-cars, a framed information panel on one wall grabbed my attention:

> As far as is possible in war, the desert campaign was fought in an atmosphere of chivalry without hate, soldier to soldier. The common struggle against the desert created a bond of camaraderie between enemies and there was a concern on the battlefield to see that opposing troops didn't suffer through lack of water or through the absence of medical aid.

This struck me as fanciful until I remembered Charlie's actions on Ruweisat Ridge. After his shattered left arm had been bandaged, after refusing morphine because he wanted to keep his wits about him, Charlie began disabling the breech mechanism of a captured German 88-mm field gun. His Company Sergeant Major Bob May joined him and together they rendered it inoperable. The injured and shaken German gun crew were lying nearby, their wounds neatly dressed by their captors. 'Those Nazi bastards don't look so clever now!' remarked Charlie, before shuffling over to them. May feared the worst and was astonished when Charlie offered each of them a long draught from his own water bottle.

A second quote made my mouth dry, throat tickle and eyes glisten. The Egyptian curators have singled out one country for special mention: 'The New Zealanders were first class Infantry who gained an enviable reputation for their fighting qualities.' Afrika Korps papers captured after their final defeat included a document Rommel issued to his senior officers on the relative merits of Allied troops in North Africa — he placed the New Zealanders at the top of his list. Rommel's description of them could have been written with Charlie in mind:

> They were quiet men, not given to boasting and possessing a firmness of spirit that came from thoroughly digested experience. Perhaps, some day, someone will write this division's history. It ought to be the best reading of the war.

Unwittingly, Montgomery agreed with his old foe. In his foreword to Freyberg's reports on the Battle of El Alamein, known as the *Blue Books* because of the colour of their covers, Monty wrote in December 1942:

> The battle of Egypt was won by the good fighting

qualities of the soldiers of the Empire. Of all the soldiers none were finer than the fighting men from New Zealand. The Division was splendidly led and fought magnificently; the full story of its achievements will make men and women in the home country thrill with pride.

The legendary Australian war correspondent Alan Moorehead was equally generous when writing about the New Zealand Division in *African Trilogy*: 'By common consent they were regarded as the finest infantry formation in the Middle East', and in *The End in Africa* he waxed lyrical about an encounter on a desert road:

> We hit the New Zealand Division coming head on towards us in the way the enemy would see it coming. They rolled by with their tanks and their guns and armoured cars, the finest troops of their kind in the world, the outflanking experts, the men who had fought the Germans in the desert for two years, the victors of half a dozen pitched battles. They were too gaunt and lean to be handsome, too hard and sinewy to be graceful, too youthful and physical to be complete. But if you ever wish to see the most resilient and practised fighter of the Anglo-Saxon armies this was he.

The most purple prose was penned by a New Zealander, Lieutenant Colonel John Mulgan MC, who served with the British forces as second in command of an English infantry regiment. In his book *Report on Experience*, he describes coming across his fellow countrymen in the Western Desert in 1942:

> They were mature men these New Zealanders of the desert, quiet and shrewd and sceptical. They had confidence in themselves such as New Zealanders rarely

have. It seemed to me, meeting them again, friends grown a little older, more self-assured, hearing again those soft, inflected voices, the repetitions of slow, drawling slang, that perhaps to have produced these men for this one time would be New Zealand's destiny. Everything that was good from that small remote country had gone into them — sunshine and strength, good sense, patience, the versatility of practical men. And they marched into history.

These eulogies and accolades came at a huge cost. At the close of hostilities in North Africa, the total casualties (killed and wounded) suffered by the Second New Zealand Division amounted to 19,000 men out of the 43,500 dispatched to the Middle East. That is almost one in two. One of them was Charlie, barely a month after the bloody breakout at Minqar Qaim.

Chapter 14

'Go on, give them hell!'

On 14 July 1942, the New Zealand 4th and 5th Divisions, assisted by 18th Indian Infantry Brigade, led the night-time attack to capture enemy-held Ruweisat Ridge, a poor man's Uluru barely rising 40 feet above the surrounding Alamein desert.

Ten miles in length, running east to west, sitting halfway between the coast and the impassable talcum-powder sands of the Qattara Depression, the long, low, wide ridge was deemed strategically essential. The order from British High Command to take it came at the end of a tough few weeks for the New Zealand Division.

According to the official history, *20 Battalion and Armoured Regiment*:

> All were showing the strain of the campaign. Boots and
> web gear were streaked with white salt from many days
> of sweating toil. Shirts and shorts in which men had
> worked and slept for several weeks without being able
> to change were hard and wrinkled with perspiration.
> Everyone looked much thinner, some near the point of
> exhaustion, others drawn but tough looking with that
> sun-browned hardness that comes with life in the desert.
> Quite a number with bandages over desert sores, some

were limping, but all had a sort of Agincourt grimness that boded ill for somebody out in front.

The New Zealanders crossed the start line at 11 p.m., heading six miles north-west across undulating land guided by the clear North Star. The leading battalions went two and a half miles before striking the first enemy posts, encountering far stiffer resistance than expected from an enemy who hated night fighting. With bullets, grenades and bayonets, the New Zealanders forced their way ahead, not entirely sure how the battle was unfolding. When they heard tanks start up, they hoped they were theirs, but they weren't.

Adding to the confusion were the sheer number of Italians surrendering. In the dark an infantry lieutenant called out to a provost sergeant to take fifty prisoners off his hands. 'I've already got a thousand here, sir, and I'm the only one in charge.' Then he thought about it, 'Tack 'em on, sir. Another fifty won't matter.' Radios weren't working and telephone lines had failed. Back at the start line with nothing to go on apart from distant flashes, rifle fire and revving tanks, Burrows asked the Commander of 20th Battalion, Ian Manson, to send a couple of reliable men forward to find out what was happening. Charlie's 20th was one of the battalions held in reserve.

Burrows:

Ian told Charles Upham what I wanted, and Charles of course went himself, taking a gunner officer, Doug Green. They set off on the wildest jeep ride that I imagine the desert had ever seen. Doug's account of this escapade is a story in itself and I seem to remember him saying we would have to lasso him before he would go anywhere with Charles again.

Charlie summarised this trip for the Battalion history:

I could not find 19 Battalion when going forward and
18 and 21 Battalions were in confusion. So were the
Germans. They were getting trucks out and pulling
guns back by hand and ropes. All this went on under
cover of fire from tanks, which in groups of three were
covering the withdrawal. It was a very colourful show
with flares going up, tanks firing, and red tracer bullets
from machine guns. There was some barbed wire that
gave trouble, and some trenches, too. We had to stop
and lift the Jeep out of shallow trenches and often had
to disentangle poor efforts at wiring. The enemy helped,
thinking we were some of them.

There was much more to it than this masterpiece of com-
pression and understatement. After handing his company
over to his Company Sergeant Major Bob May, Charlie headed
off into the dark battlefield with Green at the wheel and
another soldier, Colin McLerlan, in tow. They immediately
came under fire from enemy dugouts and weapons pockets
somehow missed earlier by the New Zealand advance.
Charlie decided two could play that game and ordered Green
to cruise around until he could see a machine-gun nest
whose crew had been killed. He did as instructed and pulled
alongside an abandoned nest. Leaping out, Charlie grabbed
a heavy machine gun complete with tripod and ammunition.
Mounting it on the bonnet of their jeep, Charlie urged Green
forward, firing at everything that threatened them while his
hapless driver weaved away from shots that seemed to come
at them from all directions.

Up ahead they could just make out the dark smudge of
Ruweisat Ridge. Searching for 18th and 19th Battalions, they
skirted and startled Germans and Italians in various states of
alarm and confusion. Half-tracks, trucks and tanks coughed
into life, orders were shouted, flares sent up and red tracer
was fired randomly and blindly into the black night. Several

times they sank in soft sand up to their axles and had to put their shoulders to the tailboard and push themselves free. The second time they came to a complete stop next to a pocket of Axis infantry. As both sides used vehicles they had captured from each other, Charlie hated tin helmets and never wore them, and with the Spandau resting on the bonnet, in the dark their identity was ambiguous. When Green cocked his Tommy gun, Charlie restrained him: 'They're only bloody Wops. Let's get the jeep out.' Green and McLerlan lent their weight, all the time expecting a bullet in the back. On the third occasion when more weight was needed, Charlie pulled out his pistol and indicated forcefully to watching Italians that they should lend a hand as well, which they did.

On a fourth occasion they toppled sideways into an Italian dugout that Green hadn't seen in time. Charlie climbed out, gesturing angrily. Interpreting this as culpability, the Italians hastily righted their jeep and pushed them clear. Charlie knew they had been pushing their luck as well and called it a day while it was still night. With their jeep trailing a long afterbirth of tangled barbed wire, Charlie reported to Burrows.

The good news was the New Zealanders had taken the sparsely held ridge. The bad news was they had unwittingly punched their way through the Axis defence line to get there. In essence, they had done the enemy's job for them — getting themselves surrounded. Reaching the undulating ridge at different points along its length, they found themselves scattered and isolated from each other. The low rise was more trap than redoubt — more leg-iron than foothold.

Charlie headed home through a cluttered battlefield as the sky was getting lighter by the minute. Hearing the news, Burrows and his supporting units rushed forward. A wide, shallow basin filled with enemy troops lay between them and their countrymen isolated on the ridge. German small-arms' fire opened up on their left. Burrows ordered the 20th Battalion to go in with bayonets. Charlie's C Company just happened to be closest. It was a straight sprint down a long slope into the teeth of enemy fire — crimson red and gold surf breaking on a black shore. Charlie led the charge, shouting to his men at the top of his voice: 'Come on, C Company! Come on!'

Sandford: 'As Upham ran he saw them all running with him, unhesitating and unflinching, "What men they were! What bloody heroes," he thought, a savage pride possessing and coursing through him.'

Burrows:

> I recognised the voices of many men, among them Charles Upham's, and there was a surge of soldiers towards the enemy posts. Soon A and D Companies were equally briskly employed and I knew that these last enemy posts were being properly cared for.

Above the din and clamour, Beau Cottrell also heard Charlie: 'When Italians were surrendering the Germans fired on them. I can remember Charlie's voice. "Go on, give them hell!" I can remember him roaring his head off as he went straight at them.'

Two of Charlie's platoon commanders were killed immediately. Men on either side of him toppled sideways, lifeless. Then it was his turn to smack into the hard ground — knocked off his feet by the thump of machine-gun bullets ripping through his upper left bicep and smashing his left elbow. Getting to his feet, he carried on dropping grenades into foxholes until he reached parked German vehicles. He climbed on top of tanks or armoured cars — recollections differ — and dropped grenades through their hatches; 'Charlie being mad,' noted one of his men at the time, as if this was all the explanation needed for such daring. When they reached slit trenches it was merciless fighting, no quarter given, no quarter received.

Charlie ran on and destroyed a machine-gun post with

grenades. Another machine-gun nest further out continued firing. Charlie led the rush to silence it. Then like a switch being thrown the battlefield fell silent.

A full-page obituary, published on 23 November 1994 in *The Times* of London, described Charlie's actions that night:

> Although shot through the elbow he personally destroyed a tank, four machine guns and a number of trucks, capturing the German positions and some valuable tactical maps. Observers of his performance have since described him as being possessed of an almost divinely inspired rage as he strode forward destroying everything in his path.

Burrows:

> With daylight there were the most astonishing scenes of enemy panic and confusion. There was transport dispersed over miles of desert, troops, most of them Italian, were wandering aimlessly about completely disorganised. Except for the late arrival of our tanks I felt quite satisfied with the situation as it was at this stage.

German tanks that could, backed away from engagement. Over a hundred Italians and forty Germans were taken prisoner and they captured a German intelligence truck full of battle maps. Even with his smashed arm, Charlie felt elated, exclaiming: 'This is the greatest victory yet!'

Charlie accepted a truck ride to a regimental aid post tent higher up the broad ridge where he got his mangled arm bandaged. Then a sobering sight on the plain below reminded everyone of their perilous situation — a long column of dejected men, the bulk of 22nd Battalion, who had successfully taken ground on Ruweisat Ridge two miles to their east, were being marched in a long column west, flanked by German tanks, acting like sheepdogs, herding them across the plain.

Ken Longmore was taken prisoner that same morning. His truck was blown up by a shell, killing his driver instantly. Ken crawled out of the wreck onto the sand without a scratch on him. He knew the game was up and hastily buried his revolver and a Mills bomb. He had a marked map that he didn't want to fall into enemy hands. A fully laden Bren-gun carrier beating a retreat rushed past, refusing to stop. Ken threw the map after it. It wafted and floated like a dart before dropping into the open top. Ken beamed at the memory, 'Just like in the movies!' — Ken's go-to analogy when telling a story about the war. Ken was cradling a dying soldier in his arms when Italian and German troops picked him up. Again — just like in the movies.

§

I switched on National Radio one Saturday morning and caught Kim Hill talking to a gruff and lively old geezer, who said that Charlie Upham had been a good friend of his. They served alongside each other in North Africa and were in POW camps together in Italy, and after the war became closer friends still. His family enjoyed lovely picnics on the Upham farm and when Charlie came to Christchurch on business, he used Bob's office as a base. The voice was that of Major Bob Wood. He told Kim he was the last of his generation. 'Absolutely none are still alive. I'm pretty fit. I'm pretty lucky.' Kim ended by saying, 'And that was Bob Wood, ninety-seven.' Bob chipped in quickly. 'And still dangerous!' That did it. I had to talk to him.

From Kim's producer I got his contact details. He lived on the northern New South Wales coast of Australia. I rang to see if I could fly across and talk to him. He agreed without hesitation and in the next breath insisted that I stay with him. I didn't let on, but I wasn't keen. The prospect of being trapped for three days with a near centurion didn't appeal. The chances of his plumbing being in full working order had to be low. I had visions of a cluttered, stuffy bungalow with a bar heater on full blast, a La-Z-Boy rocker positioned inches from a booming television and a fridge full of food growing fur, but Bob wouldn't take no for an answer. I was staying with him and that was that. No further correspondence would be entered into.

Night was falling when I pulled up full of trepidation in my rental outside his home in the coastal village of Sawtell, and I was pleasantly surprised to find neat flower beds and trim lawns fronting a modern apartment block built on a rise. When I rang the bell there were no protracted, shuffling footsteps and no waiting for multiple deadlocks to be released. The door flew open instantly and a short, slightly built man with a merry smile and twinkling eyes shook my hand warmly. Bob was wearing an ironed shirt and tie, a buttoned-up cardigan, pressed slacks, polished shoes, and his luxuriant snow-white locks were combed and brilliantined into submission. He ushered me into an elegant open-plan kitchen and living room with sweeping views of the darkening coastline, joking that on a good day he could see New Zealand. We would talk later; first dinner was ready.

Bob had been cooking for me. He removed crumbed lamb cutlets from the oven and served them with boiled spuds, carrots and peas. Pudding followed. Bob apologised for no longer cooking desserts — the cheesecake had been purchased at a local supermarket. My contribution was a Central Otago pinot noir and a bottle of duty-free Jameson's. We talked well into the night, laughing like drains at times. He was an utter delight.

Bob told me how his company had been surrounded by Germans on Ruweisat Ridge. In the ensuing fire-fight, his voluminous 'Bombay Bloomers' shorts were shredded with bullets that somehow missed his crutch, pelvis and legs completely. 'I was pretty skinny back then,' Bob laughed. His spare shirts, which I'd put money on were perfectly folded in the kit bag on his back, were blown to pieces by a mortar and he copped a piece of hot metal in his arm. It could have been much, much worse and Bob couldn't believe his good fortune. The snappy dresser felt the loss of his fresh laundry almost as keenly as the searing flesh wound. Battlegrounds are not marked out like sports fields with touchlines and in-goal areas, so New Zealanders not captured immediately were able to melt away into folds in the ridge and slip down to the plain.

Nursing his wounded arm, Bob and three Kiwi companions, one of them a tall, fit former All Black, Ron Bush, laid low all the next day until they saw a column of Bedford lorries churning up dust on a desert trail. They stood up and ran towards them, sliding down a sand dune and waving joyously to their saviours. The trucks came to a complete halt, canvas covers were pulled aside and well-armed German troops poured out of the captured British vehicles.

They were taken to an Axis staging post also serving as Rommel's forward HQ. Dusk was falling when an open-topped staff car with an escort of half-tracks arrived and the Desert Fox himself alighted. Informed that the prisoners were New Zealanders, Rommel requested they join him for a glass of chilled Chablis. In perfect English, he commended the fighting quality of New Zealand troops and said he couldn't understand why they had travelled so far from home to fight in a war. Bob told him that he was a long way from Germany. Despite being almost completely devoid of a sense of humour according to his generals, Rommel took it well and told them to enjoy the wine. It would be the last they would be tasting for quite some time.

Charlie's capture was not so courtly. All day long, scorching sun blazed down on the exposed ridge and German gunners pounded away relentlessly, picking off parked trucks, armoured cars and artillery pieces. When tanks finally started clanking up the long slope, they were German. Of the British armour promised for first light, there was no sign. Earlier in the day, barely able to contain his frustration, in a car running on three cylinders and only capable of ten miles an hour, Kippenberger went in search of the British tank regiment:

> After ages we reached a mass of tanks. In every turret someone was standing gazing through glasses at the smoke rising from Ruweisat Ridge four miles away. I spoke to a regimental commander who referred me to his Brigadier. The Brigadier received me coolly. I did my best not to appear agitated, said I was a commander of the 5th New Zealand Infantry Brigade, that we were on Ruweisat Ridge and we were being attacked in the rear by tanks when I left an hour before. Would he move up and help? He said he would send a reconnaissance tank. I said there was no time, would he send his whole brigade? General Lumsden drove up. I gave him exactly the same information. Without answering he walked around to the back of his car, unfastened a shovel and with it killed a scorpion with several blows.

It doesn't take much reading between the lines of Kippenberger's tart, acerbic account to gather the impression that he wasn't impressed with Lumsden's attitude and, had circumstances permitted, given half a chance, he would have taken to the English general with a shovel himself — like the housewives, mothers and grandmothers he had witnessed in Galatas dealing to German paratroopers with garden hoes, hammers and axes.

British tanks were eventually sent in at 4 p.m. It was too little too late. The Germans were ready for them and they were easily repelled. With his throbbing arm in a sling, his pipe clamped between his teeth, Charlie left the comparative safety of the aid post tent to totter across the fire-torn ridge to be with his men. En route, a mortar exploded close to him. Shrapnel buckled his legs and he toppled to the ground. All around him New Zealanders were rising out of sangars with their hands in the air as German tanks and infantry bore down on them. Charlie urged his men still standing to take the trucks and make a dash for it. Some did. Others stayed and shared a last smoke with him. Charlie offered his pips to a private to make himself an officer and thus avoid becoming a POW in a work camp and having to assist the Nazi war effort on a farm or factory. The private had to decline. He had already promoted himself in his paybook and didn't want to risk another forgery.

Charlie took the opposite tack with himself. Knowing that the Germans had a fetish about decorations and medals, and preferring non-preferential treatment, Charlie ripped the VC ribbon off his tunic and let it flit away across the sands. A German tank neared, its barrel swivelling in their direction. The commander in the turret waved them to their feet with their hands up. Charlie could only raise one arm. It was 5 p.m., 15 July 1942. His companions helped him to his feet and raised his arms.

§

Molly was nursing in Wellington when she got a telegram from Mrs Upham that said starkly: 'CHARLES MISSING'.

Dismay, concern and utter disbelief swept through the New Zealand Division when word of Charlie's death or capture spread like wildfire through the ranks. It was a huge relief on 16 October 1942 to receive official word that he had been captured and was still alive — *The Times* of London published a short article saying he was a prisoner of war in Italy.

After surrendering, Charlie and other wounded who couldn't walk spent an agonising day in the open while the battle for Ruweisat Ridge raged violently around them. When victory was complete, Axis soldiers ordered them into the back of covered trucks. They formed a column and, bumping and lurching, followed the setting sun west. Flies tagging along for the ride laid eggs in open wounds and already putrefying flesh.

Lieutenant Kuru Waaka of 28th Battalion:

> You'd kill a fly, you'd smell like a corpse. That's why you never killed flies. You'd only kill one fly and that'd be the last because the smell was terrible. They'd eat anything, and there were plenty of corpses around.

After drinks with Rommel, Bob Wood and his companions were trucked in the same direction as Charlie. Demoralised, hungry and thirsty but otherwise healthy prisoners were packed fifty to a truck and fifty to a trailer. Italian troops drove the trucks and were the guards. They overnighted in foul dungeons in Benghazi where there was not enough water, barely any food and no toilet facilities.

Two days later Bob's convoy pulled up alongside a convoy of flag-flying Italian vehicles, Lancia cars and Fiat trucks parked in the middle of nowhere. Their Italian drivers and guards began excitedly shouting, 'Il Duce! Il Duce!' A short, bull-necked, ball-bearing-shaped man who looked like he had been pumped under pressure into an olive-green tunic, jodhpurs and gleaming jackboots, with a machine pistol strapped to his waist, strutted about in front of an open-topped staff car. Il Duce, 'The Leader' — Benito Mussolini himself. At Bob's command, New Zealand soldiers, many of them suffering from dysentery, others just desperate to empty their bowels, lined up, did an about turn, lowered their shorts, crouched and crapped in unison. Ron Bush added a rousing haka for good measure.

§

Bob left reading material for me on a small writing desk in the guest wing of his house. On top was a stapled-together photocopy of Bob's escape diary. Beneath it, beautifully bound in embossed leather, was *The War Diaries of Count Galeazzo Ciano* — Mussolini's son-in-law and foreign minister. The Count is just a footnote in history now, a handsome, preening background presence in photographs of Mussolini with Hitler and Mussolini with Neville Chamberlain, but he had an acute eye and wrote with a slippery skill. One of his quotes speaks to sports coaches the world over and always will: 'Victory has a thousand fathers, but defeat is an orphan.' A repentant, chastened President Kennedy famously borrowed it during a White House press conference in the wake of the humiliating failure of the CIA-planned, funded and mounted ill-fated invasion of Cuba in 1961 that did not trigger a popular uprising and overthrow of the Castro regime as they had fatuously and over-optimistically expected.

Bob had marked diary pages for me with pink Post-it slips. The excerpts made entertaining reading, helped hugely by the fact that Mussolini was only too willing to share every malicious thought, every vain ambition, every petty grievance and every bruised feeling with Ciano, who relished being entrusted with the bats from his father-in-law's belfry and judiciously and meticulously jotted them all down. On nearly every page you sense Ciano bracing himself for and savouring in advance the rapturous applause and thunderous ovation due to him in due course:

JULY 21, 1942. The Duce is in good humour, especially as he is satisfied that in the space of two or three weeks we can resume our forward march in Egypt and reach the great goals of the Delta and the Canal. He is so certain of it that he has left his personal baggage in Libya as guarantee of a quick return . . .

That of course did not happen. I like to think that to this day somewhere in Libya a trunk of Mussolini's underpants are crumbling to dust in the dry heat — possibly alongside an abandoned Louis Vuitton toiletry bag belonging to the late Colonel Gaddafi containing tubes of black hair dye. Mussolini's wounded indignation over German driving habits in a following paragraph had me laughing out loud. I could visualise the scene like an out-take from an *Indiana Jones* movie:

> Naturally, Mussolini has been absorbing the anti-Rommel talk of the Italian commander in Libya, and he takes it out on the German Marshal who, by the way, did not pay him a visit during the three weeks and more Mussolini spent there. The attitude of the soldiers is also insolent. German motor vehicles do not yield the right of way to anyone, even to our generals, and at the slightest opportunity of acquiring a little booty they take everything . . .

Further down was the paragraph that Bob wanted me to read: 'He told me that he had found groups of fierce-looking New Zealand prisoners "who were so far from reassuring that he always kept his gun close at hand".'

I told Bob in the morning that I loved the reference to fierce-looking New Zealand prisoners. 'That was us!' he chortled gleefully. 'That was the mass crap!'

Their Italian guards quickly herded them back onto the lorries and trailers after this gross insolence and they accelerated away while the Duce was still gasping for breath. From Tripoli, Bob was transported by air to Bari on the heel of Italy's boot and later held in a transit camp at Sulmona further north. He was then railed to Campo PG 47 on the outskirts of Modena on the southern lip of the broad Po Valley of northern Italy, where he got to know Charlie well.

§

Charlie's path to Modena was more circuitous and eventful than Bob's. Two days after capture, he fetched up in a tent hospital at El Daba. In the cot beside him was an old Christ's College schoolmate, Beau Cottrell, whose Achilles tendon had been blown away. It was here that Charlie threw his watch at Beau when Beau's was stolen from his wrist. It was here that Charlie kicked up a huge fuss until wounded non-commissioned soldiers got the same water rations and same treatment as officers. Next stop was Mersa Matruh and the crude concrete underground Italian hospital operating theatre, an updated Dante's Inferno — dank, dark, sweltering, crowded and suffocating. Screams bounced off the walls. The floor was awash with blood, urine and body waste. Corpses and drums overflowing with severed limbs awaited removal. In the gloom the suffering, the dying, and the decomposing were hard to tell apart.

Charlie, who had spent days slipping in and out of delirium — being woken by searing pain one minute then blacking out from even worse pain seconds later — is suddenly fully and permanently alert, taking in his nightmare surroundings. He looks at his broken limb. The bone protruding from bloody bandages crawling with maggots is a worry. The man on the stretcher beside him has both legs shattered, and good flesh above the ground mince has been marked with chalk for amputation. Orderlies lift his stretcher and tip him onto a blood-smeared operating table. A hinged blade contraption resembling a large paper guillotine that bookbinders use is positioned directly above one of the chalk marks.

Charlie is suddenly conscious of a similar line drawn on his own arm just above the foul bandages. 'Jesus Christ!' he mutters, rubbing at it furiously with his good hand. The pain is excruciating. The chalk smears but remains visible. Up on the operating table, the man's eyes bulge in terror when the blood-splattered surgeon positions a blade black with blood directly over a chalk line. His loud protests are reduced to a pitiful muffle when orderlies clamp their hands tightly over his mouth. The surgeon takes a deep breath then thrusts the blade down with all his strength. Blood sprays everywhere. The man jerks upright, gurgling and choking. A grimacing orderly advances on the spurting stump with a red-hot iron. Flesh sizzles and smokes. The man convulses, dies of shock, and slaps back on the table.

The exhausted surgeon wipes his temple, smearing yet more blood across his face. '*Il prossimo!*' he says, pointing to Charlie. Orderlies reach for him. Charlie shakes his head, kicking them away, screaming, 'No thanks! Fuck off! Fuck off the lot of you!' The surgeon, irritated with the orderlies, barks '*Rapidamente! Rapidamente!*' The orderlies reach for Charlie again. Half-sitting, he pushes himself back with his legs. Despite his boots slipping in the gore, he manages to wriggle clear, screaming, 'Don't touch me! DON'T FUCKING TOUCH ME!' The surgeon shakes his head in resignation. 'You kaput! You finito! *Comprendere?*' Charlie nods. He is taken away and sometime later a British doctor, a POW, gently cleans his wounds, sets his splintered humerus as best he can, dresses the arm in clean bandages and wraps it in a plaster cast, probably saving him from toxic shock and death.

Charlie:

'They were set on doing me and thought they were doing me a service. I never could stand pain and although I thought the arm should come off — it was very painful and maggoty, I knew I couldn't stand up to that and that's why I didn't let them. I was too damn scared . . .'

Charlie sailed to Italy from Mersa Matruh, too weak and frail to fully appreciate Rommel's cave on the inner harbour or Cleopatra's pool on the outer coast. Walking up the gangway, he was stark, bollocky naked, as Mark Antony had been on this shore, but unlike the lusting Roman general it wasn't of his own volition. Not wanting prisoners with lice in their hair or filth on their clothes, Charlie's head was shaved and he had to limp up the gangway wearing only his identity discs and a plaster cast in a sling, his anger and humiliation burning more than his wounds.

Jim Henderson had taken a similar hospital ship cruise to southern Italy some months earlier and found the sea air more bracing than anticipated:

> Suddenly I am aware of an overpowering stench. It is disgusting and utterly nauseating, and in vain I turn my head from left to right in an attempt to escape it. What thing on earth could smell in such a fashion, I wonder; there must be some filthy refuse unaccountably left in this ward. But the ship seems so clean and neat, that is impossible. Suddenly the realization strikes that it is I, my body, my own flesh become putrid. I shudder in ashamed anger . . .

If Charlie's faith in humanity was shaken walking up the gangplank in Mersa Matruh, it was restored a little in the port of Reggio in the toe of Italy's boot. Italian soldiers disembarked first to loud cheers from crowds lining the streets. Italian wounded that followed were greeted with wailing and sobbing. There was more applause for German troops. At the tail end of the parade, shoeless in shirt and shorts, wearing handcuffs, came Charlie. The entire population of the city seemed to press close, booing, hissing and shouting abuse at him.

Sandford:

> All except one. For as the procession neared its
> destination Upham saw a little Italian girl run out

from the crowd, a child of six or seven perhaps quite
uncomprehending the reason for this demonstration.
All she saw was a ragged-looking man stumbling along
ill, barefooted, one wrist fastened to the other and with
one arm in plaster. She ran towards him. In the cradle
made by his two arms the little girl gently laid a bag of
fresh sweet pears. Then shyly she turned and ran back
into the crowd.

I cried quietly in my bed when I read that passage in *Mark
of the Lion* at about three in the morning when I was
sixteen. I needed my faith in human nature restored at that
point also. Charlie told Sandford that all he remembers
of the interminable, uncomfortable, jolting train journey
up the Tyrrhenian Sea coast north to Naples was sharing a
compartment with German officers who offered him their
food but not their wine. When the time was right, Charlie
contrived to accidentally bump the table, spilling wine into
several laps. It dampened the mood in the carriage, but
Charlie felt better. From Naples it was a short road trip inland
to a hospital at Caserta.

In 1942 all the POW hospitals in southern Italy were
overcrowded and under-resourced. Doctors did their best
and nursing sisters came in two brands, saints and monsters,
mostly the former. When Red Cross parcels began arriving
with goodies that could be bartered illegally, conditions
improved slightly.

Henderson:

For six months no vegetables or fruit had been given the
patients. Edible greenery was said to be unprocurable
in the locality, yet black marketeers could and did bring
onions, shallots, lettuce and also eggs in exchange for
English tea, cigarettes or underwear. A priest had illicit
trading down to a fine art. Inside his voluminous gown

he had sewn a series of pockets from which he would produce vegetables, cigarettes and varieties of wines. These would be rapidly bartered for English articles, which disappeared hastily into the gown, and the priest, bestowing a benediction, would depart in peace. 'The Holy Bludger,' we called him. So it came to pass sundry woollen garments would fly in triumph from the favoured clothes lines of the village. The good citizens of Altamura who had received no British clothing murmured amongst themselves and complained to Rome. Whereupon, an English-speaking detective came down to investigate the forbidden trading. He set himself up in a little office, and sent for a prisoner.

'I believe a certain amount of trading is going on in this hospital between prisoners and Italians,' began the detective.

'Certainly,' replied the prisoner, himself a keen trader, mistaking this approach for preliminary black-market negotiations. 'What do you want — coffee or underpants?'

Charlie's condition did not improve, stricken first by jaundice then debilitating, chronic toothache. The VC hero was fearful of dentists and he was buggered if he was going to let an Italian poke around in his mouth. Everyone's morale and physical well-being suffered as food rations and medical attention shrank. Keeping his mates alive kept Charlie alive. Along with Beau Cottrell, he shared a room with five grievously wounded men whose health deteriorated as the dreary months dragged by. Charlie did his best to cheer them up, spinning long yarns to fill the endless nights.

§

Snow flurries past the window, blanketing terracotta roof

tops and cobbled streets. Lighting his pipe, Charlie sits between the beds of Cottrell and the fast-fading Major Lynch.

'Did I ever tell you about the time I worked as a shepherd for Black Jack Burns in the back of beyond? Jesus, he was a hard bastard was Jack. Muscles in his shit they reckon.'

'I don't think so, Charlie. Tell us again.'

'We were dagging some stringy ewes one day when one of the old girls kicked my hand and I cut myself pretty badly with the clippers. Getting sheep shit in the wound, as you can imagine. If we'd been closer to town I might have buggered off to a quack, got a tetanus jab and had it stitched. Instead I went up to Jack, spraying blood everywhere, fully expecting him to tell me to run it under a cold tap, but Jack was all care and compassion. Took me by surprise, to tell the truth, you don't associate care and compassion with Black Jack Burns. Clearly I had misjudged the bastard.'

The men are all ears.

Charlie takes a puff on his pipe before continuing.

'Black Jack took one look and whistled. "Jesus, Charlie! You'd better get yourself down to the first-aid kit, pronto." And he pointed to the far end of the woolshed where a white cabinet with a red cross painted on it sort of glowed like a beacon in the gloom.'

The major's sunken eyes are filled with delight — Charlie takes another contented puff on his pipe.

Cottrell can't wait.

'And?'

'And what?' Charlie feigns incomprehension.

'What happened next?'

'Oh yeah, right. So I hot-foot it down there, open it up, and the bloody thing is empty. Well, almost empty. Apart from a card with writing on it. That's all. Just a card with a couple of words scribbled on it in pencil. Fat fucking use.'

Charlie shrugs, appearing to have finished the story.

Cottrell takes the bait — 'What did it say?'

'What did what say?'

'What did it say on the card?

Charlie smiles.

'"Harden up!" It said, "Harden up".'

'Get outta here!' laughs Cottrell.

'Don't worry, I intend to . . . When I feel better. You won't see me for dust.'

Major Lynch smiles happily.

'Thanks, Charlie. Goodnight, gentlemen.'

§

Before submitting *Mark of the Lion* for publication, Sandford sent the manuscript to a number of Charlie's mates to check accuracy and tone. Several asked him to remove the blood-donation story from Castel San Pietro hospital as they felt it didn't put Charlie in a good light. An English boy called Jimmy, who didn't seem to have anything wrong with him apart from a large, unpleasant-looking stye in his eye, was getting on everyone's nerves with his constant bragging about sexual conquests. When blood donors were called for, Jimmy asked innocently what it felt like to give blood. Charlie told him it was exactly the same sensation as ejaculation. Jimmy raced off, keen to contribute. Everyone roared with laughter when Jimmy shuffled back in sheepishly and called Charlie a bloody lying bugger.

§

The major was the first to go. Of the six patients in that Caserta hospital room, only Charlie and Beau Cottrell came out alive. After the war, Beau became Charlie's personal lawyer. The Upham and Cottrell families holidayed at the same North Canterbury beach. The Upham tent was only big enough for Molly and the girls so Charlie cheerfully slept outside. Beau's daughter Anna remembers Charlie being gruff and funny and riding bucking broncos at the Cheviot gymkhana, holding on with his one good arm. Looking on, her father would grin and shake his head in disbelief. 'He's mad! He's a bloody mad bugger!'

Judging from the entries in Beau's war diaries, Charlie was a mad bugger — in terms of his wild audacity and rebelliousness — back then as well. This touching excerpt is from Caserta when Beau learnt that Charlie was about to be transferred:

> **16th September 1942:** Dear old Charlie Upham is going. He has been my constant companion ever since Mersa Matruh & our friendship has become very close & real & we shall both miss each other equally. Somehow we're so different that in diverse ways we've both leaned a good deal on each other & for me I know there will be an unbridgeable gap once he has gone.

Charlie was transferred by rail across the Apennines to another POW hospital in the small town of Castel San Pietro in northern Italy. Sometime before Christmas, Beau was transferred there as well. The food was good, the medical attention adequate and the nursing nuns could not have been kinder. Slowly Charlie's strength and rebellious spirit began to return.

> **23rd December 1942:** Had a party tonight. Charlie got drunk & stripped off and did a Maori haka much to everyone's amusement.

> **3rd January 1943:** It's Sunday afternoon and Laurie and I have just been for a walk outside in the snow. It was very cold but still it's always good to get some fresh air. Charlie Upham and Humphrey are playing 'Knock' and Jack Carlton writing a letter beside them. Jack & Charlie

are as usual squabbling like a couple of barmaids. How bored we all are with life but everyone is making a definite effort to be cheerful and bright.

7th January 1943: Quite unexpectedly yesterday old Charlie and Ernie Shaw left. This is the second time I have said cheerio to Charlie since I've been in hospital and for the second time I've wept under the bedclothes after he's gone. It's weak and childish I know — but then that is just our state of mind in this dreary unreal existence.

Chapter 15

'I refuse to be shot by a corporal!'

Old Charlie didn't go far. Just up the line, via Bologna, famous for its sausage, to Modena, a boutique, medieval town famous for its balsamic vinegar.

The Ducal Palace bell-towers and cathedral spires were visible from Campo PG 47 located on the outskirts in picturesque vineyard country. Purpose-built as army barracks, it was ringed with walls and watchtowers and became an Allied officers' POW camp during the war. It was well-appointed with marble ablution blocks, a small infirmary, a concert hall and asphalt parade grounds where the Modena Turf Club held race meetings.

In *For the Duration*, fellow prisoner Bruce Robertson writes there was no turf and no horses. Just toy mounts ridden by colourfully dressed jockeys. The track was 60 metres long and divided into squares. Progress square to square was determined by drawing cards. There was a tote on average turning over 700 lira a race meeting and the betting was frenzied. A makeshift jazz band was usually tootling joyfully. The cheering got louder as the finishing post approached, horses and riders bunching as the exact card was required to get over the line. Lining the perimeter fence and leaning out the watchtowers, Italian guards got as swept up in the excitement as their crazy prisoners.

Variations on the Modena Turf Club were played out in POW camps across Italy and Germany. In Campo 57, for example, Ken Brown from Palmerston North could do a pitch-perfect, cadence-correct imitation of a race caller's commentary. Horses' names were manufactured, bloodlines set, form noted, conditions underfoot established, odds calculated and bets laid. Men would lie on their bunks in great excitement while Ken went out into the corridor and through a homemade loud-hailer delivered a commentary. Clutching their betting slips, cheering their picks on, men swore you couldn't tell it from the real thing back home. For a few joyous minutes, they *were* back home.

Charlie arrived in Modena to a warm welcome from fellow New Zealanders. Bob got to know the man who had previously been only a distant, almost mythical figure. He was still terribly weak and emaciated and bore little resemblance to the whirling dervish of VC legend. He participated half-heartedly in sports only because he needed to get stronger physically. He refused to do anything that suggested he had accepted his fate and that his shooting war was over. Others could attend lectures, play contract bridge, study archaeology and mount musicals if they so wanted, but he preferred to plot escapes, patrol the perimeter and goad the guards.

After a late-night drinking session Charlie and some mates became loud and abusive — louder and more abusive still when an Italian officer came to see what the commotion was about. When Charlie grabbed the Italian by the throat, only the swift intervention of his mates, who pulled him away apologising that Captain Upham was drunk and had mistaken him for someone else, saved his bacon. Cooling off in the punishment block, which was outside the wire, Charlie noted that the ceiling was plasterboard. On a subsequent visit to solitary confinement Charlie upended a steel bed frame and used it as a battering ram to punch a hole in the ceiling. With one arm virtually useless, it took huge, excruciating effort and several failed attempts. He was in the attic crawl space desperately trying to loosen roofing tiles from the inside when guards burst into his cell.

The sinus problems which plagued him in North Africa came back and, with them, blinding headaches. Twice he blacked out from the pain and was sent to the camp hospital for treatment. He was unwell and in and out of the camp hospital during the American landings in Sicily, Mussolini's fall, and the turbulent events leading up to the signing of the armistice between Italy and the Allies.

When the war in North Africa ended and the Allies were poised to invade Sicily, the War Office in London began considering how best to deal with thousands of captured British and Commonwealth troops languishing in POW camps the length and breadth of Italy. Senior British Officers (SBOs) contacted through clandestine channels were advised to keep their men in the camps until collected by Allied forces. Italy would be a place of dangerous turmoil, chaos and confusion when the Allies came ashore all guns blazing, and all things considered it would be tidier if POWs on the run didn't clutter the battlefields. Allied troops landed at Calabria in south-west Italy on 3 September, the day on which the armistice with Italy was secretly signed. It took another five days for news of the armistice to reach most camps. Some Italian commandants deliberately withheld the news for fear it would encourage rebellions or mass escapes. In the event, it was received phlegmatically, almost with disbelief, though there were scenes of wild rejoicing in some camps.

Bruce Robertson wrote:

8 September: The camp is in an uproar. Armistice has been declared and Italy has capitulated as from 4 p.m. today. We knew nothing of it as we stood and watched the usual soccer game after dinner. Suddenly however there was a disturbance down by the wire. I thought it was a brawl or an altercation between two sentries. Cheering broke out and the crowd rushed the wire as the news was passed through. Then our commandant was called out to the Italian commandant and when he returned he laconically announced the bare facts. Nothing is known as to what the Germans will do. A fine issue of wine at this moment is being handed out and there promises to be some parties judging by the noise which is swelling.

Some men seized the opportunity to escape, others went out-side the wire briefly to pick grapes in nearby fields or to sample the local wine, but most went back to their games of bridge or reading. Many lay wide awake that night, excited and unable to sleep. The deadening routine of camp life had sapped many of them of their initiative and they were caught in two minds. So were SBOs, toying with disobeying War Office orders, which were explicit — all personnel were to stay put. They were to organise themselves into military units and await orders; arms and assistance would be flown in. Officers at officers' camps were to be prepared to take command of nearby other ranks' camps.

This, however, was a dangerous fantasy with tragic conse-quences. The orders had been formulated several months earlier and bore no relation to the situation on the ground, where the Allied advance was stemmed by natural barriers and frenzied, fanatical German rearguard action. There was deluded talk that POWs and Italian guards might team up and defend camps against the Germans.

Bruce Robertson:

9 September: It has been an interesting day. Last night was very hilarious and we sat up till midnight discussing

the situation. During the morning the Italians have been
gradually deserting by climbing over the fences and
disappearing. A few were shot at by the remaining guards
but gradually they left the sentry boxes also as the news
came through the Jerrys were going to take over the
camp. Meanwhile we had talk by the SBO who advised
those to go over the wall who wished, but he suggested
we would probably be better off inside.

Some POWS started chancing their arm. An Italian father
and son, and the boy's uncle, were tending vines just outside
fences when the boy found a live grenade and innocently
pulled the pin. The explosion unnerved the camp. Were
the Germans there already? Hushed guards and prisoners
crowded the wire when the brothers, yelling and screaming,
rushed the gates carrying the boy, who had flesh hanging off
him like bark on a gum tree. In the small hospital, Kiwi and
South African doctors who had dealt with worse in North
Africa worked frantically to save the boy's life, but his injuries
and blood loss were too severe. The wailing father carried
his dead son out the camp gate accompanied by *two* sobbing
uncles, one more than before.

Halfway down the short road into Modena, the additional
uncle took a sudden left turn and disappeared into the vineyard in a crouching run. It was the right move.

Bruce Robertson:

11 **September:** This morning the worst has happened.
It has been announced that we are to move to Germany
immediately. We have backed the wrong horse and
should have gone over the wall when the opportunity
presented itself. Many have gone however and good luck
to them. We shall see what the future holds for us.

Passivity, naivety and blind obedience to authority resulted in thousands of able-bodied Allied soldiers being transported to camps inside territory controlled by the Third Reich. After twenty days on the move under German armed guard, Bruce Robertson was considerably less philosophical, writing on 29 September: 'Churchill had ordered in the armistice terms that no prisoners were to be removed from Italy, but the greasy yellow livered wops sold us out. Their name will stink for all time.'

The Germans emptied Modena Camp in batches, marching 800 POWS to the railway station to be trained north, leaving the remainder, some skeleton staff and the seriously ill to be trucked north later. Charlie walked from the hospital into the main compound in his pyjamas. The hospital would have been easy for him to slip away from, but it was run by the Red Cross and Charlie didn't want them punished for his escape, or to jeopardise privileges for other prisoners.

Five days later, a convoy of twenty open-topped, high-sided army trucks pulled into the camp. There was an SS man driving and an SS guard in every truck. Every second truck was mounted with a heavy machine gun and stocked with SS guards. They headed 60 miles north to the Mantua railhead along unsealed back roads and soon everyone was covered in white dust. Ghosts on the move. It was dusk when they reached the Po River. Bruce Robertson noted: 'As we crossed the Po River one of our members jumped over the side of his vehicle. He was unlucky and was caught again after some uproarious shouting. He was unharmed.'

There are no prizes for guessing the escapee was Charlie, and it was a miracle he was unharmed.

§

As luck would have it, dusk was falling when I reached the Po River, heading south from Germany. Earlier that day, I had departed Leipzig Hauptbahnhof railway station with no discernible jerk of the carriage and in complete silence. Buildings flashing past were the only proof we were moving and soon we were flying along at 230 kilometres per hour. Coal-fired power stations and wind farms marched across manicured and nearly treeless countryside. I read, wrote, snoozed, sipped wine, entered and exited three countries before crossing the glorious Brenner Pass into Italy. Though I can't be absolutely sure about this. There were no border posts and no one asked to see my travel documents the entire journey. This is the miracle and wonder of modern Europe.

Another miracle was reaching the Po River at the same time of day as Charlie's truck convoy did, albeit from the opposite direction. I don't know why, but I had always imagined Charlie leaping off a truck at the crest of a leafy rise and dashing down a *Sound of Music* glade to dense forest before a lucky shot clipped his heel and sent him tumbling. It was shocking to see how low the Po River stopbanks were and how exposed the floodplain was that he ran across. Scattered gnarly olive groves, skinny Lombardy poplars and threadbare willows 100 yards away would have afforded him next to no cover, not that this put him off.

Pushing through other prisoners to get to the rear of the tray, he gripped the tailboard when they reached the top of the low embankment — momentarily putting their vehicle out of sight of the forward guard truck and the one labouring up the gradient behind them. As Charlie's truck gathered speed down the other side, opening up a gap on the guard truck still grinding up the incline behind them, Charlie took a deep breath and leapt over the side.

It was insane. Only fading light and poor shooting saved him. Bullets hummed past his ears. One struck his boot heel, sending him crashing face forward, and he crawled into a tangle of vegetation and vines hoping the approaching night would swallow him. Nine SS guards fanning out across the field missed him. A tenth, lagging behind, spotted him rising to his hands and knees and with a triumphant whoop booted him in the backside. Charlie was frog-marched back to the trucks where the soldier who captured him was screamed at by the SS platoon leader in charge for not shooting him on sight. Years later, Bob Wood loved repeating Charlie's curt response to being told he was bloody lucky: 'Fuck off! That bullet completely rooted my best boots!'

Bob and a mate, Hugh Flower, avoided being taken to Germany by shimmying up a drainpipe to the roof, removing tiles and hiding in the cramped, baking ceiling space for three days until the final batch of POWs departed on 13 September and Campo PG 47 fell silent. Bob and Hugh descended after dark, crossed the empty compound and began scaling the 10-foot perimeter wall. A burst of automatic arms elsewhere in the camp was unnerving. Dropping like cats to the ground, they sprinted into the night.

The plan was to rejoin the New Zealand Division on the opposite coast, which meant avoiding German troops, the Carabinieri military police, Fascist bands, Communist partisans and freelance brigands and crossing the rugged, icy Apennines in winter. Switzerland was closest, but Bob liked to joke that he gave it a swerve because his sister lived there. While holidaying in Europe before the war, she became trapped in Geneva by the sudden collapse of France and ended up working for the Red Cross, supplying POW camps with all manner of requests. She told Bob that it was almost impossible to meet the demand for piano accordions, the one instrument I would have thought breached the Geneva Convention on torture.

As it happens, Campo PG 47 was easier to escape from than find. I arrived at Modena Station at 10 p.m. and caught a cab to Canalgrande Hotel. The driver was from North Africa, but I gave it a go and asked him about Modena POW camp anyway, to get a head start for the next day. He had never heard of it. Nor had the hotel receptionist, nor had the sweet staff at the Mexican restaurant — the only place I could find open at that end of town at that time of night.

Next morning, I tried the information centre in the exquisite Piazza Grande in the centre of town. The raven-haired, bespectacled beauty behind the counter with the kind of glacially perfect face you only see in optometrists' ads informed me crisply that there had never been a POW camp in Modena. I pointed to photographs on a website on my phone, but she wasn't having it. 'How can I put this?' she said coolly. 'You are thinking of Campo di Fossoli, the transit camps for Jews.' I wasn't and persisted. 'How can I put this?' she persisted irritably. 'You are mistaken.'

Back on the pavement, I accosted strangers at random and even asked at the front desk of the local military academy with no luck. Finally, I met a lovely local who confirmed that there had indeed been a Modena POW camp, but it had long gone, leaving no trace. He was sure the information centre could point me to a plaque. They weren't overly pleased to see me again. 'We have other attractions in Modena like the Balsamic Vinegar Museum, the Museum of Balances and Scales, and Pavarotti's birthplace,' glared the optician model through her stylish glasses, while waving a brochure. 'How can I put this?' I replied under my breath.

I had a train to catch to Bologna and then a high-speed train to take to Florence. It took me under and through Italy's main divide in less than forty minutes. A more circuitous journey over the mountains would take Bob and Hugh Flowers three months after their escape from Campo PG 47 in Modena.

Bob told me he was so excited to be free he didn't sleep a wink for the first three nights of their freedom. As soon as they could, they traded their distinctive army uniforms for rough peasant clobber. Hugging the central massif, skirting villages, sticking to charcoal burners' paths and alpine trails, they wended their way south, living off the land where they could and descending on isolated farmhouses when they couldn't. Almost invariably they were given food and shelter for the night. Bunking in barns with cattle was cosy and comfortable enough provided both parties refrained from topping and tailing in their sleep. They never stayed more than one night in one place in case someone was tempted to dob them in for the reward.

One morning they were resting in a sun-dappled glade when a gleaming pony trap driven by a stylish gentleman dressed top to bottom in Harris tweed clip-clopped towards them. They hailed him in bad Italian and he replied in perfect Etonian English. The Marquis of Gundi. His Lordship invited them to his isolated, elegantly decaying and fraying mansion in the forest. All the servants seemed to have left and dust-sheets covered much of the furniture. Their tattered and torn clothing so pained the Marquis he ushered them into his walk-in dressing room and invited them to help themselves from his massive collection of bespoke suits, cautioning that wearing civilian clothes could result in them being shot as spies if they were captured.

Always a sharp dresser, Bob was sorely tempted. They could have continued on their way looking like minor royalty on a grouse shoot but, showing admirable restraint, they limited themselves to new boots, clean underwear and warm socks. They were grateful for toothbrushes as their teeth were getting rather furry. The marquis also gave them soap, razor blades, cigarettes and toothpaste, asking solicitously if they were sure they didn't want a little toilet paper. Bob declined, only to regret it later. It would have made rolling their own cigarettes that much easier. After bathing, shaving, wining and dining handsomely, they were on their way.

The contrast with another meal two months later could not have been starker. On a bleak plateau under leaden skies, they came across a peasant digging potatoes in a snow-covered field. They asked for shelter and he escorted them mutely to his dirt-poor house where his thin, tubercular son was hunched over the fire in a kitchen filled with oak branches. Bob and Hugh helped the farmer and his family strip the leaves off for cattle fodder. When the potatoes had boiled long enough, the steaming pot was lifted off the grate and slapped onto the table and the family ate straight from it — inviting Bob and Hugh to join them. Bob and Hugh exchanged looks then insisted on paying for the meal. The farmer and his wife sobbed when they handed them some of their precious lira.

With winter closing, the brutal, hulking Maiella massif in the central Apennines stood between them and the advancing Allies. On 11 December 1943, they began climbing in moonlight towards the snowline. To use Bob's vernacular, they spotted a 'Hun' phone line running up the gorge and proceeded cautiously around the next ridge. Hearing a noise, they stopped in the nick of time as German alpine troops emerged from well-camouflaged tents in the deep snow just yards ahead of them. Slipping into beech trees, they made their way around the Germans and clambered off-trail towards a rocky saddle where they began a tricky, nerve-wracking, exhausting descent and ran into British airborne troops who were scouting ahead of the advance.

They cadged a ride to the New Zealand Division, where they were dispatched on the double to the 4th Field Ambulance Shower Unit and instructed to remove their filthy rags. Standing naked in pouring rain, they were daubed with carbolic-soaked cloth attached to the end of long sticks. The rain diluted the carbolic. The hardy, defiant lice, which oxen never seemed to mind, survived, requiring the procedure to be repeated several times. General Freyberg made a point of meeting every returning POW. Clean-shaven, hair gleaming with Brylcreem and kitted out in a new uniform, Bob was ushered into Tiny's caravan and handed 100 cigarettes. 'Wood, you say? From Wellington. I knew your father. Give him my regards . . .'

Meanwhile, the New Zealand Division continued their

bruising, brutal advance up Italy, taking what was left of Florence after the retreating German Army had blown up all but one of the beautiful medieval bridges over the Arno River and partially destroyed many buildings in the glorious city centre. When it had been safely secured, the Americans decided a victory parade headed by the elite US Marines was in order. The Americans had arrived after most of the brutal, infantry-soldier, door-to-door cleaning out had been completed by New Zealanders. Nevertheless, the Italian campaign was being run by US Army Command. Legend has it that at the front of the Florence parade came the US Marines with a large banner bearing their emblem and the words 'US Marines. Second-to-None'. Behind them marched New Zealanders hoisting a large sheet on which was written the word 'None'.

§

After the Gestapo prison, the Jewish museum and mass graves of Vilnius, I needed to recalibrate my moral compass and see the best of what human beings are capable of. Michelangelo's statue of *David* in the Accademia Gallery in Florence fits that description. The English biographer, critic, leading Bloomsbury wit and author of *Eminent Victorians* Lytton Strachey once wrote of the towering 5.16-metre-tall statue: 'No other artwork, ancient or modern, Greek or Latin, is equal to it in any respect — with such proportion, beauty and excellence did Michelangelo finish it.'

Flamboyant and openly gay at a time when homosexuality was a crime in Britain, Strachey was brought before a tribunal considering his exemption from military service in the Great War on conscientious grounds. 'Tell me, Mr Strachey,' asked the chairman triumphantly, 'what would you do if you saw a German soldier trying to violate your sister?' Strachey was too nimble for him: 'I would interpose my body between them.' Having learnt nothing from this exchange, a woman on the panel leapt in. 'Civilisation, Mr Strachey, isn't that worth fighting for?' 'Madame, I am the civilisation they are fighting for!'

When Michelangelo and Leonardo da Vinci worked, lived and loved here, Florence was civilisation's epicentre and the Accademia Gallery ground zero. I stood stock-still and marvelled at *David* for the longest time. When I circled it, Italian women seated together on the far side, looking up, made me smile. A gorgeous teenager, her beautiful mother and her wizened gran were savouring David's gluteals with something approaching lust. In pale stone made flesh the statue confirmed what I thought I had seen in photographs — Charlie did have the same wide, generous curl to his top lip. If David had been holding a grenade instead of a slingshot and wearing a tin helmet draped in camouflage netting, the similarity would have been uncanny.

While Bob and Hugh were ambling through alpine meadows heady with the scent of wild flowers, thyme and fennel, Charlie, Bruce Robertson and other POWs, forty at a time, were jammed into squalid, pitch-black, poorly ventilated cattle-cars with no latrine facilities. Charlie said later it was enough to send a man dotty. Staring through the narrow slats in the cattle-car walls at the most beautiful countryside he had ever seen threw him a lifeline. A grim five-day train journey delivered them to Stalag VIII-B at Lamsdorf in Silesia. It was a sprawling, unruly holding pen filled with 30,000 POWs, near the Polish border, where Charlie got issued with the German identity tag that he wore until the end of the war. The stamped inscription reads:

STALAG VIII B
Nr 28487

Tag Nr 28487 is part of a private collection in South

Canterbury alongside other precious Upham memorabilia. Knowing Charlie wore the rectangular slice of metal near his heart lent it a curious power somehow, and I found it more moving than any other item on display, including his VCs. I had taken to wearing my body tags stamped with my SCOTT T number K 392 and blood group A NEG that the American Coastguard insisted I wear on a beaded chain, like rosary beads, around my neck, on a C-130 Hercules flight from McMurdo Station on Ross Island to the Amundsen-Scott Station at the South Pole, when I was filming a documentary in Antarctica. In the event of things going pear-shaped on the Polar Plateau, rescue crews finding me still breathing in the wreckage and in need of a transfusion would know instantly what blood type I required. If it was too late for that, they could separate the dog tags, place the longer chain around my neck and hang the small one from my big toe, making identification that much easier later for mortuary staff pulling open refrigerated drawers.

§

From Stalag VIII-B at Lamsdorf, prisoner Nr 28487 was put on a train to Stalag VC at Offenberg for a short stay before finally fetching up in Oflag VA, a prison camp for French and Commonwealth officers at Weinsberg in the German state of Baden-Württemberg in lush south-central Germany.

I knew precisely where the town of Weinsberg was located well before I saw it. I was being driven from the neighbouring city of Heilbronn in a bright yellow taxi when, through a gap in the undulating countryside, I recognised the hill behind the town from a sketch drawn by an Allied POW. A perfectly symmetrical cone had horizontal grapevines near the top that resembled a striped blouse and long vertical grapevines that made the pleats of a skirt. Sure enough, circling the base of the fairy-tale cone, we came across a genteel, well-heeled

A prisoner's woodcut sketch of the distinctive cone, covered in vineyards and topped with a fort, rising up above Weinsberg town.

hamlet full of spreading trees, handsome homes and neatly parked Audis.

Weinsberg, flattened during the war and rebuilt, is different from in Charlie's day, though I doubt that my hotel has changed much. Every surface not a muddy apricot was a dull clotted cream, and vice versa. It had never seen better days. It was this ugly the day it opened. It was a relief to drop my bags and go in search of Oflag VA. It wasn't marked on any of my maps, so I would have to ask the locals.

In a licensed premises called Choppo's Pub For Friends, I asked Florian, a cheroot-smoking, cheerful-looking young man with a wispy *Laughing Cavalier* moustache and beard if he spoke English. 'But of course,' he replied in the bemused manner people adopt when speaking to people for whom English is their only language and their third or fourth. He had lived in Weinsberg all his life and had never heard of a POW camp. He canvassed the bar for me. Heads shook. The resident intellectual, an intense bespectacled man, googled a German website which confirmed that Oflag VA had been located here during the war. It gave no address. They were all surprised. Florian wanted to know why I was asking so I told him about Charlie's last escape attempt in broad daylight.

A haversack over his shoulder, Charlie walked straight towards the fence and the tripwire delineating a strip of ground inside the perimeter that was strictly out of bounds. Once during a game of soccer, a ball had bounced into this narrow no-man's-land and an excited player bounding over the wire to retrieve it died in a hail of bullets. A few weeks later a prisoner got up in the morning, shaved carefully, combed his hair neatly, straightened his jacket, calmly told his friends that he was leaving and walked up to the tripwire and stepped over deliberately to his death. What Charlie was planning was crazy, but he had done his homework. There was one less guard on duty on *this* day on *this* particular boundary. As a consequence, perimeter sentries walking past each other in opposite directions created a blind spot. As prearranged, Charlie's mates staged a realistic brawl beneath the nearest watchtower when Charlie reached the tripwire.

Florian translated for the bar. They leant forward keenly and I continued. With the guards' attention trained else-where, Charlie stepped into forbidden territory and nimbly mounted the 10-foot fence. Watching POWS braced themselves for a volley of shots, but the diversion worked. Charlie reached the top wire of the inner fence and was readying himself for the leap across the divide, when — PING! A staple flew out of a post and the wire beneath his boots sagged. Charlie hurled himself forward, flailing desperately at the second fence, but he couldn't get a decent grip and the wire slipped through his fingers — CRASH/SPRONG! He dropped into concertina coils of barbed wire that ran between the two fences. Guards shouted, whistles blew. A young sentry with a rifle came running. As did the brawlers keeping pace with them on the other side of the wire, screaming and shouting, 'DON'T SHOOT! DON'T SHOOT!' POWS came running from every direction, ignoring the tripwire rule and crowding the fence next to Charlie, imploring, 'YOU'VE GOT HIM! HE CAN'T ESCAPE NOW! HE'S TRAPPED! DON'T SHOOT! DON'T SHOOT!'

The young sentry had his rifle cocked and barrel raised. His orders were clear. He was to shoot any prisoner caught in the act of escape. An older POW barked at him in fluent German, 'Don't even think about it, boy! Don't you dare shoot him! You hear me!' The young sentry heard him and lowered his rifle.

Florian did the honours and the bar was hugely relieved and desperate to know what happened next, so I continued:

Brandishing a Luger, an older corporal came running, shouting, 'I WILL FINISH HIM! I WILL FINISH HIM!' Charlie casually slipped a cigarette between his lips and, lighting it, growled, 'I refuse to be shot by a corporal! Bring back an officer. Fuck off!' Florian stopped me in mid-flight to translate. The bar looked sick. 'What did the corporal do?' asked Florian anxiously. I told him and Florian translated with a grin: 'He fucked off!' The bar clapped.

Ken Longmore saw it all. He was sitting on a chair in the sun when he noticed someone with a haversack over his shoulders walk purposefully towards the wire. He couldn't see his face, but he knew immediately that it was Charlie. He could hardly believe it when Charlie stepped over the tripwire and started climbing the inner fence. I asked Ken if he heard the commotion other prisoners were creating around the corner to distract the guards. Ken didn't hear a thing. He was too transfixed watching Charlie getting ready to jump, then falling into the barbed wire. That's when he noticed the shouting. People came running from every direction, crowding the fence, begging the bewildered sixteen-year-old guard with a rifle not to shoot. The boy hesitated and the moment was lost. An angry older corporal arrived, with pistol drawn to do the deed. Ken joined in the pleading. Charlie casually pulled a cigarette from his pocket and lit it. Again, the moment was lost. Ken remembers the Commandant, Hauptmann Knapp, arriving, getting terribly excited that it was Upham, and dashing back to his office to fetch his camera.

When Florian told the bar the commandant took a photo, they cheered and lined up shots of schnapps for me. I left considerably worse for wear in search of the elusive camp, weaving through lengthening shadows up peaceful streets using the conical hill behind the town as my lodestar. Overhead in a clear twilight sky, jet-engine contrails traced white paths towards Frankfurt. On a clear day like this, prisoners heard a drone on the horizon that grew louder and louder. It was joined by wailing air-raid sirens in Weinsberg and ack-ack battery fire in Heilbronn. The air began to vibrate and the sky darkened with swarms of Allied bombers on a daytime raid. The German people had thought that no enemy aircraft would ever cross the Rhine in daylight. Cheering prisoners were quickly herded back into their huts by shaken guards. Like a stubborn ram, Charlie remained out in the open sucking on his pipe until forced indoors at bayonet point, where he taunted the guards from the doorway. 'No planes across the Rhine, eh? What are they then? Fucking ducks?'

When I eventually saw the street sign, I couldn't help but wonder what sort of genius you have to be to even attempt a German crossword puzzle. It read in bold capitals, DOKUMENTATIONSSTÄTTE LAGER WEINSBERG and pointed down a sloping, dead-end street to a large children's playground and a kindergarten. What I didn't know, until I checked aerial photos later, was that the luxurious townhouses I walked past stand on ground once filled with wooden barracks.

All that is left of the sprawling Weinsberg camp is a

modest, nondescript wooden shed with barred windows that once stood outside the original perimeter fence. It could be a Scout hut in any small town in New Zealand. Inside there is a small museum of sorts with photographs around the wall and some exhibits. A Charlie Upham commemorative postage stamp has been blown up to the size of an LP cover. You'd need an envelope the size of a sleeping bag for it to be of any use. There is nothing outside to indicate opening times and no after-hours number. It's doing its best to be forgotten, and it seems to be working if the clientele in Choppo's are anything to go by.

Before I left Florian, he shook my hand and declared with feeling that he was born in Weinsberg and that he wanted to die in Weinsberg. Standing beside the little building in the peaceful, shady cul-de-sac, it occurred to me that Florian's most fervent wish nearly came true for Charlie on at least four occasions: once after spitting in Hauptmann Knapp's face when the commandant attempted to pin a substitute VC ribbon on the breast of his tunic. A second time when a guard in the exercise yard of the punishment block outside the fence was momentarily distracted and he manged to get a hundred yards in noisy clogs down the road away from the camp before running into guards coming in the opposite direction. Three if you count the guard in a watchtower having his sights trained on Charlie the whole time but didn't pull the trigger because he recognised him and couldn't help but admire the hopeless boldness of the act, plus he could see he was about to be captured. And a fourth time following the failed leap when both the young sentry and the corporal declined to shoot him as he was tangled up in barbed wire. At a push you could make it five if you include Hauptman Knapp screaming and shouting at the young sentry and the corporal for not shooting Charlie when they had the chance and it was legally permissible to do so and the corporal eventually snapped, hissing back: 'Sir, the prisoner is in his cell, and you have your pistol!'

A tarseal footpath winds between willows into the town centre. The tree-lined creek that broadens into a duck pond backs onto encroaching vineyards. It's beautiful and serenely calm this evening. Muslim mums in head scarves pushing prams ambled through the park. I retraced Charlie's steps taken under armed escort to the handsome railway station.

The swollen nose of the elderly sergeant in charge was so cobwebbed with broken capillaries, Charlie dubbed him Blue Nose. The official history of Oflag VA records: 'Very few new prisoners joined us, but there was one who deserves mention. He was Capt Charles Upham, VC, a New Zealander, greatly admired by his comrades-in-arms.' The morning Charlie was moved to another camp one of his closest comrades in arms, 'Judge' Holmes, who later became a High Court judge in South Africa, cooked him a breakfast of hot porridge. Holmes wrote later to Sandford: 'Captain Upham had many friends amongst the South Africans. It was a privilege to enjoy his friendship. I think the whole camp was sorry to see him leave.'

Not the whole camp. Not by a long shot. Charlie was greatly admired by his comrades in arms — and by the Germans — but he was by no means universally adored. Many of his fellow POWs didn't warm to him and were frightened of him — again a feeling shared by many of the Germans. In *For the Duration*, Bruce Robertson describes a man of such smouldering intensity it rendered him unapproachable. Early on when his sense of humour was still intact, he was capable of practical jokes, like the desert island map he drew to provoke the guards, and the fake letter he wrote to John Riddiford who ran Romneys on his North Island farm in preference to Charlie's favoured Corriedale breed. Ostensibly from his farm manager, Riddiford got a letter that read:

Dear Mr Riddiford, I decided to sell all your romneys. I only got 15 bob a head for them I have replaced them with corriedales at 35s each and I'm afraid we had to shoot all the old dogs including your favourite Spot.

Riddiford recoiled in horror until he caught sight of the beaming perpetrator. 'Charlie, you utter fucking bastard!' Feigning terror, Charlie fled from the room. He pulled a similar stunt on the Germans, writing a letter to his parents that he knew full well would be intercepted by Hauptmann Knapp:

> Dear Mother,
> Don't expect me home for a week or two, I have a few accounts to settle around here.
> Chas

This mischievous, playful Charlie Upham sank slowly from view like a boulder in a vat of treacle as his incarceration dragged on and was replaced with despondency, bitterness and despair. The old Charlie resurfaced back in New Zealand, but less frequently — it took some coaxing and then only in private among trusted friends, in woolshed smoko rooms, on fishing trips or after a few beers at a reunion.

§

For many years a familiar figure wearing a beanie jammed on his head loped up and down the touchlines at All Blacks test matches, feet splayed like Charlie Chaplin, large hands pressing a telephoto lens the size of a bazooka to Humphrey Bogart basset-hound eyes. Additional cameras, tripods, light meters and bags flapped from impossibly broad shoulders — a legendary sports photographer and Olympic gold medal-level raconteur, Peter Bush was the nephew of former All Black Ron Bush, who had been captured at Ruweisat Ridge with Bob Wood and was in Weinsberg with Charlie.

In 1996 I interviewed Bushy in his cosy Island Bay crow's nest overlooking Cook Strait for a television documentary

I was making on Sir Edmund Hillary. Bushy told me about the time he was in the sanctum of sanctums, the All Blacks' dressing room after a tough test against the French. Back in the days before television replays, French rugby props were well versed in the dark art of gender realignment by boot sprig. After a brutal game, too battered and bruised to shower or talk, the All Blacks slumped on benches. With his gimlet eye for detail, Bushy recalled Sir Ed striding in wearing a *stained* gabardine raincoat and the spent All Blacks immediately hauling themselves to their feet to applaud.

When our interview was over, Bushy and I crossed to the picture windows to take in the glorious views of the South Island, the Seaward Kaikouras and, blanketed in snow, Mt Tapuae-o-Uenuku which Ed climbed on his own when he was in aircrew basic training at Delta Camp in Marlborough in 1944. From the top of Tappy, you look down on the high, wild back country that Charlie used to work on as a shepherd before the war and catch glimpses of the North Canterbury coast where he farmed afterwards. For some reason I mentioned this to Bushy, and he glowered and barked, 'My uncle was in the boob with Upham and couldn't stand the man.' Bushy wanted to leave it at that. Of course, I wanted to know more. Bushy said there were a number of things, but one incident in particular angered his uncle — the VC ribbon spitting incident.

Roll call had sounded one morning for an extraordinary assembly. Prisoners congregating in the compound were suspicious about this break in routine. Someone in the know whispered something to the man next to them, who passed it on, and soon a bow wave of alarm rippled through the ranks — apparently the Germans were replacing the VC ribbon that Charlie had thrown away at Ruweisat Ridge. There was muttered agreement that this was not a good idea. Charlie didn't like receiving his VC in the first place and he sure as shit wouldn't want to receive a replacement ribbon from the Krauts. Brave men swallowed — hoping and praying that Charlie wouldn't do anything rash or silly. He'd done enough mad shit already — needlessly challenging and provoking guards to the point where only swift intervention and profuse apologies from other prisoners prevented him from being shot.

Standing out in front on his own, Charlie was close to the main gate through which the spruced-up Hauptmann Knapp and a spick-and-span armed escort marched, coming to a precision halt in front of Charlie. The commandant gave a Nazi salute then stepped forward with a deep crimson ribbon in his gloved hands. Before he could pin it onto Charlie's tunic, Charlie spat a ball of phlegm in his face. POWs gasped and shrank back, fearing the worst. The escort worked the bolts of their rifles. The commandant reached down to where the holster of his Luger was attached to a belt around the waist of his greatcoat. POWs braced themselves. The gloved hand had another destination. Reaching into a pocket, he removed a white handkerchief, wiped the mucus off his face, clicked his heels and walked away. The guards followed, dragging Charlie with them for yet another thirty days in solitary. POWs slunk away shaking their heads — Upham was a crazy bastard who was going to get himself shot one day and others killed in the process when the Germans opened fire.

Not that you would have known any of this from his bland postcards home. There was no reading in between the lines. Running them through Ultra would have left you none the wiser as to what was happening.

Kriegsgefangenenlager
Write very clearly, short and legibly to avoid delay in censorship

Postmarked Oflag VA, Weinsberg
24 Aug 44

Dear Pum,

A letter from Hon dated the 23rd today. I hope you and little Robert & Brian are both well. By the time you get this you will be out of the hospital. I hope Brian is well & likes the army. How are young Llewellyn & little Mary? I hope they are all well also all at Gloucester street & Paul & her family. I hope to be home very soon.

Love C.

I went back to Bushy to interview him for this book. Terribly unwell and terribly thin, he moved slowly with the aid of two walking sticks, his clothes flapping like washing on a line from his still impossibly broad shoulders. No longer trusting his oral recall, he had painstakingly typed out his Uncle Ron's story for me. It was all there, including drinking white wine in North Africa with Rommel. I could have hugged him, except I was afraid he might snap in my arms.

Not in Bushy's class as a photographer, obviously, but after taking the famous photo of Charlie in the coiled wire and telling him that he was a brave man, Knapp retreated to his office and had the young sentry and old corporal brought before him, whereupon he proceeded to scream and shout — berating them for not shooting Charlie when they had the chance. The Senior British Officer, Colonel De Beer, arrived to see him shortly after this and came straight to the point: 'All I want to say is this. This man Upham is the ace soldier of the British Empire. If anything happens to him, I will see that you are held personally responsible after the war.'

Knapp decided it was time to make Charlie someone else's problem. German High Command had a special place for persistent troublemakers and repeat escapees. Being 'the ace soldier of the British Empire' was a plus. It made Charlie's transfer so much easier.

Ken Longmore remembered Charlie's departure. He didn't really want to say it — he didn't want to speak ill of a war hero, but he felt he had to tell me — the Germans were glad to see the back of Charlie *and so were a lot of POWs.* Ken's energy and sunny disposition flagged after this admission. His clear eyes moistened and reddened. I promptly poured him a hefty glass of Jameson's and proposed a toast to his old comrades in the Second Echelon. We clinked glasses. He perked up and told me how much he enjoyed a television sitcom that was set during the war. He couldn't remember the name.

I ran through the list:

'*Dad's Army*?'

'No, that wasn't it.'

' *'Allo 'Allo!*?'

'No! The one set in a prisoner of war camp.'

'*The Two Ronnies* — *Colditz*?'

'Not that one.'

Ken was getting frustrated.

'You know! You know! The one with the vain commandant and the fat, bumbling guard in the helmet!'

I couldn't believe it.

'You don't mean *Hogan's Heroes*?'

Ken beamed happily.

'Yes. Yes. That one! I loved it!'

Chapter 16

'Please don't cause any trouble, Charlie'

'I was in Colditz with Charles Upham but I did not know him intimately. I can only say that he appeared to be the sort of person who would relish tearing up Germans with his bare hands.'
— **MIKE MORRISON, COLDITZ POW**

I don't make a song and dance about it. That's not my style, but for a time I was held captive under lock and key in the most infamous German POW camp of them all, Colditz Castle. Schloss Colditz, Oflag IV-C, or, to give it its full title, Kriegsgefangenenlager offizer Sonderlager 4C, a name which unaccountably has fallen out of common usage.

The castle is a bulky edifice dominating the small, drowsy town of the same name that straddles the Mulde River as it ambles through Upper Saxony. Sitting on a cliff-top 30 metres above a bend in the river, the castle itself climbs another 20 metres. The walls at the base are 2 metres thick. Building works first began in 1158, and the completed structure was destroyed by fire several times. It was rebuilt in 1504 in Renaissance style with the addition of ornate towers in a valiant but futile attempt to approximate the charm of a French château. Surrounded by ancient forest, it became a grand hunting lodge for various nobles. Even today on the winding roads in and around Colditz village there are signs cautioning motorists to watch out for deer. I spent several hours gazing out the window of an electric bus and never saw a ruminant of any description, domestic or feral. There were no farmers or hikers either. Just hamlets with churches with witch's-hat steeples. The fenceless countryside and cobbled streets were curiously empty — as if the police had issued a warning urging people to stay indoors. A coronavirus lockdown or just another Sunday in former East Germany — take your pick.

When hunting gave way to farming, Schloss Colditz fell into disrepair. For a time, it became a poorhouse until it was requisitioned by the state for use as a lunatic asylum, only shutting its doors at the end of the First World War. When Hitler came to power, the doors opened again and slammed shut again on opponents of the Nazi regime. Conditions were so brutal, locals who had happily tolerated a lunatic asylum in their midst for the best part of a century complained to Berlin and it was closed. A year later it was back in business as a hostel for the *Arbeitsdienst* — the compulsory labour force for teenage boys who did unpaid menial jobs for the greater glory of the Reich. Every morning, picks and spades on their shoulders, they marched off to clear more ditches and shovel more shit in perfect formation and full throat, the eaves and cobbles of Colditz reverberating to the honking strains of the 'Horst-Wessel-Lied' song whose lyrics roughly translate to: 'All we are saying . . . is give war a chance.'

They marched off for good in 1939 when Germany attacked Poland and very quickly ran out of suitable accommodation for Polish prisoners of war. A medieval castle with multiple stone skins much like a Russian doll wasn't ideal. The German High Command were not thrilled, but so urgent was the need they had little choice. Later it became a *Sonderlager* or 'special camp' for Allied POWS — men from the United Kingdom and the Commonwealth dominions as well as Americans, French,

Polish, Czechs, Dutch and Serbians. In the main these were recidivist lags with form, men with a history of escape attempts. The Germans hoped that their forbidding fortress would prove escape proof. It didn't.

My journey to Colditz and subsequent incarceration began, like Charlie's, in Weinsberg. He travelled east and north, across a rail network badly buckled and broken by relentless Allied bombing. Delayed by diversions and halted by repair work, it took over three days. My journey by rail, bus, plane and rental car took less than twenty-four hours. It began when I came downstairs to the combined front desk, lounge and dining room of the Hotel Weibertreu. The lemon-lipped owner silently poured me filtered coffee. Telecommunication workers in identical orange overalls sat incommunicado in opposite corners of the room as if they'd just had a blazing row. I have paid respects to the dead in funeral parlours more festive than this, a thought which put me off the assortment of sliced cold meats, sausage and cheese and I settled for tinned peaches and rice bubbles.

My master plan was to catch a taxi back to Heilbronn and take the bus to Stuttgart Airport, but when I asked lemon-lips if she could call me a cab or point me to a cab rank, she broke into a smile for the very first time and announced triumphantly with the fluency of a BBC newsreader or Oxford don, 'I can't help you. I have no English.' Demoralised, I paid the bill and turned towards the door, at which point she thrust out a hand palm uppermost and shouted 'SCHLÜSSEL!' It took a moment, but I twigged she meant the room key attached to a brass plate the size and weight of a skillet in my pocket. I was sorely tempted to say, 'Sorry, I don't speak German,' and keep walking, except the Schlüssel was so heavy I risked dislocating my hip crossing uneven ground so I meekly handed it back.

Outside, I headed for the railway station, hoping there might be a taxi rank there. Two studious, bearded young men of Middle Eastern extraction, sensing my anxiety, asked if they could help. I explained about needing a taxi to Heilbronn to catch a bus. They said they were catching a train there in a few minutes and it was a fraction of the price. They helped me purchase a ticket from a vending machine and tugged my sleeve when the electric train materialised silently. In a carriage full of laughing students, we glided past beautiful wine-growing country heading south.

Charlie clattered north in a carriage jam-packed with tired, pinch-faced civilians and wounded soldiers who shrank down in their seats when burly military policemen, clearly not afraid of a knife and fork, and Gestapo officers, preened as if ready for a photo shoot, came strutting through checking papers. My bus to Stuttgart whirred over wide, smooth roads through open, undulating farmland tamed into submission many centuries ago. In every direction terracotta-tiled rooftops of villages, clock towers of towns, and power-station chimneys ringed the horizon. Small wonder escaped POWs were seldom on the run for long. In readiness for hiring a manual-drive car in Berlin, I gave up on the scenery and googled the German Road Code. It began with this preamble:

> The basic premise of German traffic law is the 'doctrine of confidence' which in effect says motorists must be alert, obey the law and drive defensively at all times so that all motorists and other road users (including pedestrians) can have confidence in each other.

I studied the rules which followed, and it all seemed perfectly straightforward. I read them again in the departure hall while waiting for my boarding call and could feel my confidence ebbing. I read them twice more during the flight to Berlin just to be on the safe side, and by the time we landed at Tegel Airport my confidence was completely shot.

It came rushing back to me that I hadn't driven a manual

car in twenty years and hadn't driven on the right-hand side of the road for forty. I had a black felt-tip pen in my bag and I contemplated writing a large R on the back of my right hand, but I thought the good people at the Eurocars counter would find this disconcerting. The silver-haired woman at the desk could not have been kinder and another nice woman escorting me to my tiny VW converted the GPS to English and programmed in my destination.

I had hoped for a brief twilight, but by the time I lurched out into early evening rush-hour traffic, night had fallen like an anvil. I stalled several times before the first set of lights and was saturated in sweat by the time I reached the second. Aided by a comforting voice and a continuous blue arrow on a small luminous screen, I eventually ended up on a four-lane autobahn heading in the right direction — south-west to Leipzig. I knew my lights were on full beam, but for the life of me I couldn't find the dip switch. Changing gear with my right hand was discombobulating and every time I indicated that I was changing lanes I found I had engaged the windscreen wipers instead, which only added to my stress.

Shortly after this, I became aware of a warm vaguely ferrous-tasting fluid seeping through my moustache and beard and trickling down my neck. My nose was bleeding. There is bleeding and there is bleeding, as this passage from Jim Henderson describing the death of a mate attests: 'A belching groan from Webbo, and back he falls from his seat on the gun, his face looking as if someone had stood back and splattered him in the mug with a brush of red paint.'

I had nothing on that scale, just a microscopic rupture in my nasal epithelium, and still my self-pity was off the charts. I didn't dare stop until a car ahead of me pulled over onto the shoulder flashing its hazard lights. Assuming it was an unmarked traffic cop, I pulled in behind it, fearing the worst. A man built like a hammer-thrower from the days when East German drug cheats dominated world track and field exploded out of his vehicle and came rushing at me bellowing and shaking a massive clenched fist at my full-beam headlights. I lowered my window when he drew alongside and greeted him with a foppish politeness. 'Terribly sorry, dear boy. Rental. I'm afraid I can't find the dip switch.'

Catching sight of blood smeared over my face and hands, he recoiled. It suddenly occurred to me that I resembled a vampire making house calls. Taking a deep breath, he lunged into my car and with a meaty paw flicked something on my dashboard then retracted his arm as if he'd been electrocuted. 'Where is it again, exactly?' I asked, craning at the dark controls, looking for the switch in question. There was no reply. He was already running back to his car.

Most of the blood had coagulated by the time I pulled off the autobahn into a brightly lit service station where forecourt attendants pointed wordlessly to the toilets. It took ages to clean my face and hands. The blood on my shirt and trousers would have to wait. When I finally reached my Leipzig hotel, which had the comforting ambience of a Tudor pub in the Cotswolds, the staff could not have been more welcoming and charming. 'You need a beer,' said the manager. I really needed a blood transfusion, but local beer would do. I downed a crystal bucket of dark ale and went straight to bed and tumbled into an even darker abyss.

Wanting to return my rental before the traffic got heavy, I rose at first light and headed into the centre of Leipzig. Either the city founders were exceptionally forward thinking or vast tracts of Leipzig got flattened during the war and were never rebuilt. Bouncing over suspension-challenging streets, I passed vast sprawling parks and stands of oak above which suddenly reared a gargantuan granite and sandstone structure that took my breath away. The sheer towering immensity of it and the unlikely setting was truly startling. It would have looked more at home in Monument Valley, Arizona. It was the Monument to the Battle of the

Nations. The architect who designed it was inspired by Egyptian sculpture, and the design of the German war memorial on Egypt's Alamein coast, which I would visit in a few days, was inspired by the Battle of the Nations memorial. An architectural wheel turning full circle.

The stone monolith commemorated the defeat of Napoleon's Grande Armée in Leipzig in October 1813. On these fields, over three brutal days half a million soldiers recruited from all over Europe fought to a bloody standstill with no clear winner. At the close of play over 100,000 had been killed or wounded, and a slim majority of the corpses belonged to Napoleon's army — using the military equivalent of the Duckworth–Lewis system used to determine winners in abandoned cricket matches, the combined Austrian, Prussian, Russian and Swedish armies were duly declared the victors. For centuries wars have blazed back and forth across Europe, from the English Channel to the Urals, so it's hardly surprising that Modena and Weinsberg haven't gone overboard about drab POW camps camped briefly in their towns.

§

Not content with the largest war memorial in Europe, Leipzig Hauptbahnhof is Europe's largest railway station. Confronted with nineteen platforms, I had some anxious moments until a reeling, beetroot-faced man reeking of ketone bodies and cigarette smoke, as lots of people do in former East Germany first thing in the morning, kindly guided me to the train bound for Colditz — part of the way at least. The line that took Charlie all the way is no longer fully operational. We pulled out of the huge station into vast shunting yards where grey-green pylons holding aloft overhead wires spread out like a petrified forest. Every signal box was sprayed with graffiti, every warehouse had smashed windows, rubbish was strewn between the tracks. Eventually, light industry graveyards lining the rails transitioned into blocks of cream and muddy brown tenements with backyards filled with potato and pumpkin patches, climbing beans, compost bins and hens. If England was a nation of shopkeepers, as Napoleon taunted, then Germany was a nation of veggie growers.

Leipzig petered out and we entered unkempt country, which made a pleasant change from the overgroomed landscape of the day before. Bare, skeletal trees housed rook's nests the size of wicker clothesbaskets as if an artist sketching this scene caught the nib of his pen in the paper and splattered blobs of ink. The thickets became dense woods then mature plantation forest. The plantation floor, a thick eiderdown of orange leaves, was punctuated regularly with neatly sawn stacks of firewood. During the war it was over 400 miles from these dark woods to the border of a country *not* occupied by Nazi Germany, but it felt as though a POW on the loose stood more of a chance starting from here. I found myself wondering if Charlie made his insane leap of faith out of the toilet window of a speeding train in this neck of the woods.

Not from my carriage anyway. The immaculately clean toilet cubicle was wheelchair friendly but not POW friendly. It had no windows. En route to Colditz Charlie asked to go to the lavatory. The tall, elderly and not unkind guard with a proboscis the colour of methylated spirits, possibly from heavy schnapps consumption, which it closely resembles, the man Charlie dubbed 'Blue Nose', escorted him there and stood outside in the swaying corridor while Charlie answered a call of nature. It wasn't the call of nature Blue Nose was expecting, but rather Charlie's deep-seated need to roam free. Smashing the windowpane, Charlie wrapped his greatcoat around his kit bag and threw the bundle into the freezing rushing wind, the pitch-black void offering no clues as to what lay beyond.

Looking at the pines flashing past my carriage, I remembered the shocking story of two Wairarapa boys who after enlisting in very short order found themselves boarding a train in Carterton heading for Waiouru military camp in the central volcanic plateau. North of Masterton, leaning out of a window in high spirits, they waved to girls in a rear carriage. Rather than returning their waves, the girls may have been desperately trying to warn them. Keith King, who had also just signed up, was seated ahead of them looking back: 'As we passed one of the bridges — I can still hear the sound today — clop! clop! as their heads hit the side of a bridge. They took the bodies off in Eketahuna.' Their war was over before it started. Imagine delivering that telegram to their parents. Imagine receiving it.

That tragedy happened in broad daylight. Charlie was attempting to squeeze through a narrow window in a coal-black night. His injured arm was a hindrance. His emaciation after two and a half years of incarceration helped, but he still stuck fast at one point. Blue Nose pounding on the locked door with his rifle butt and raising the alarm in a loud voice provided the necessary incentive. There was no hoping for the best. Charlie launched himself head-first into the dark, fearing the worst. He landed with a smack onto sleepers, stone chips and the steel rails of an adjacent track and was knocked unconscious.

Out for the count and with no one counting, he had no idea how long he lay there in a crumpled heap. He came round to utter silence apart from his own wincing when he moved. He had a splitting headache and an aching body but no broken bones as far as he could tell. Charlie knew that railway stations were seldom few and far between in Germany. If it hadn't already done so, the train would be pulling into one soon. Blue Nose might have already alerted the authorities. Soldiers might already be looking for him. He had to find somewhere to hide before sunrise. There was no master plan apart from travelling south and west by night and hiding out during the day. With no map, no compass and only a rudimentary grasp of German, a language that he'd had plenty of time to pick up but refused to learn on principle, the odds were stacked heavily against him.

He should have felt fearful and overwhelmed; instead he was suffused with a careless rapture. He was a free man. That trumped everything. Walking back the way the train had come, Charlie was relieved to find his kit bag and greatcoat. He was grateful for its weight and warmth. His teeth stopped chattering. The sky was lightening. He quickened his pace. A plantation up ahead looked promising. Checking the dull gleam of rail stretching back behind him, Charlie cursed under his breath when he spotted a distant figure following him in the gloom. There was something familiar in the silhouette. Blue Nose? Surely not. More to the point, had this person seen him?

When the figure drew near, Charlie scrambled down the gravel embankment and sprinted into the plantation. Fruit trees or pine? He couldn't tell. He appreciated the Teutonic precision of the layout and ran unimpeded to the middle. Crawling into a thicket, he scraped leaves over himself for additional camouflage and warmth. Working as a shepherd on high-country sheep stations, Charlie never minded sleeping rough and was soon dead to the world. Then again, sharing a boarding-school dormitory from the age of nine helped him wake instantly with all senses on full alert when his ears picked up something was amiss — in this instance something more ominous than a student prank.

Peering out of his hiding place in the hazy dawn, he saw armed figures in the distance taking lanes at right angles to each other like castles on a chessboard, leaving Charlie no option but to move diagonally like a bishop. He took off on a crouching run only to find soldiers closing in from all sides. There was a shout when they saw him. He ran wildly hither and yon, bullets ripping bark off trees behind him and shredding foliage just above his head. Too close for comfort. He wasn't going to surrender submissively with his arms high in the air, so he sat on the ground and waited nonchalantly for them to arrive. They stalked him cautiously. When they were confident he offered no threat, they dashed forward and searched him roughly. Had they found any German food on him he would have been shot for pillaging. Blue Nose arrived soon after this, beaming like a proud father greeting a prodigal son.

When Hollywood eventually makes a movie about Charlie, the plantation will be an apple orchard, Blue Nose will arrive first and frantically search Charlie's bag for apples. Finding two, he will stuff one of them in his mouth and start scoffing, frantically taking alternate bites out of each apple, as the other soldiers rush up. 'Has the bastard taken food out of German mothers' and German children's mouths?' screams one of the soldiers, cocking his rifle. '*Nein! Nein!*' shouts Blue Nose, his mouth full.

After his recapture, Charlie was handcuffed to one of the escort guards. When they entered a railway station cafeteria for soup and bread, they were denied service because of the strict dress code — Allied uniforms were *verboten*. Charlie was taken outside and handcuffed to an iron stanchion on the platform while they wined and dined, more like paupers than kings it must be said, but filling their bellies nevertheless. Charlie meanwhile was getting his belly kicked and stomped. While he was chained up like a dog, waiting passengers swore and spat at him. Then young Luftwaffe thugs waded in, booting him repeatedly when he was helpless and couldn't defend himself, until Blue Nose heard the commotion and came running.

My train journey to Colditz ended at Grimma Station. It lived up to its name. The building which dates from before the war would have been handsome once. It sat under a dishwater-grey sky with its walls daubed with graffiti, its windows bricked over, its arched doors bolted shut. Was this the platform where Charlie was left bruised and bleeding? I don't know, but I'd like to think Blue Nose was suitably shamefaced when he emerged and found Charlie barely able to hobble aboard their train for the last leg to Colditz. My head swimming with these thoughts, I walked around the corner of Grimma Station into a deserted square and hopped aboard the 619 to Colditz, an electric bus not much bigger than a Mr Whippy van. Curiously, the driver examined my return ticket as painstakingly as a North Korean border guard.

Blue Nose handed Charlie over at the Colditz front gate on 14 October 1944. To enter the castle, you cross a dry moat to the main gate built into the thick walls and proceed down an arched tunnel past what used to be the German officers' mess. This opens onto a long causeway. Down below on the left, plump geese waddle in the backyards of houses pressed close to the ramparts. On the right is a large courtyard enclosed on three sides by four floors of what used to be the guards' quarters.

Stepping through a door set in large portico doors, you enter another arched passageway and walk past what used to be the guard house and solitary confinement cells. Near the end of the war, Colditz overflowed with new arrivals as other camps were emptied ahead of the Russian advance. Running out of sleeping room, straw was spread on the chapel floor. POWs began deliberately infringing the rules just to get some peace and quiet in solitary. The Germans stopped issuing solitary confinement sentences when it dawned on them that it wasn't considered punishment.

An approach yard leads to a smaller inner courtyard — the prisoners' yard. High walls on all four sides cast long shadows most of the day except at high noon in high summer when hardy souls sunbathed on the sloping cobbles. In

MAJOR WILLAM ANDERSON/COLDITZ PRISONER'S ART GALLERY, COLDITZ MUSEUM

Allied POWs playing rugby on the sloping cobbles of Colditz Castle's inner courtyard.

winter the same hardy souls played rugby in the primeval gloom which rendered prisoners' quarters permanently cold, musty and damp.

Charlie walked into the inner courtyard on his own. Like every stranger arriving unannounced, he was regarded with suspicion, especially as weeks before a British officer had been identified as a traitor in their midst. In a previous camp the officer had been allowed a girlfriend by the Germans, then blackmailed and sent to Colditz to act as a stool pigeon. When the Germans discovered the whereabouts of a tunnel, it was widely accepted that this plant had tipped them off. The Senior British Officer, Lieutenant Colonel Willie Todd, told the commandant that a trial would be held and he would be murdered if he wasn't removed within twenty-four hours.

Dr Fred Moody, a Kiwi, was deputised to check out the newcomer. The consultation was brief and unconventional

Allied POWs exercising in Colditz Castle's inner courtyard, midwinter.

— a shouted conversation through a bathroom window while Charlie showered. Moody knew about Charlie's daring feats and shouted out, 'Hi ya Kiwi.' Charlie snarled that his arm was rooted, blaming 'Fucking Wops!' It was proof enough for Moody. Had I been Charlie I would have held a slide evening, mentioned my VC at every opportunity and hinted broadly that a second one was as good as in the bag. Charlie of course never mentioned his VC and changed the subject if anyone else did.

Charlie arrived at the start of a harsh winter. I arrived in early spring as the first blossoms were appearing. There was still a chill in the air so the heaters were on full blast in the castle's museum and souvenir shop. Also warm was the welcome of Anne Marie, the delightful curator. When I told her I was researching a book about Charlie, she was thrilled. She remembered a picture of him they used to have hanging on the walls. It was in storage somewhere. She was going to hunt it out and hang it up again. She remembered Charlie's daughters paying a visit. She thought they were lovely. She began bringing me every book they had that mentioned Charlie, opening them at the appropriate page and stacking them on the table beside me while I scribbled furiously. When other visitors entered, she ushered me into an adjacent reading room where I would have more peace and quiet. Would I like coffee and something to eat? Having skipped breakfast, I said yes. She returned with a large steaming mug and sizeable wicker basket filled to the brim with an assortment of chocolate-coated shortbread biscuits.

Anne Marie was a tall woman of Wagnerian proportions. A trident in her hands and a helmet with horns on her head would not have looked out of place. When she announced that she had to go the toilet, I knew this could take some time. She asked if I would mind terribly if she locked me in for security reasons. I didn't and so for the best part of forty minutes I was a prisoner in Colditz. I didn't panic. I kept my wits about me. I made a mental note of the spoon in my coffee cup saucer. Had she failed to return I had the means at my disposal and an implacable resolve to tunnel my way out.

In its heyday more than 300 attempts were made to escape from Colditz via secretly dug tunnels and other means, but only between thirty and thirty-six officers were successful (sources differ in the tally), often with the help of rope ladders and mock German uniforms. For a time after the war the

East German Government used the building as a psychiatric hospital, then, in 1994, after unification, such was the cost of restoration and upkeep of hundreds of rooms and 9 hectares of sprawling grounds, Saxony authorities offered it up for sale or lease. Today it is home to a youth hostel and museum and a popular tourist destination for tour parties of a certain age, mostly from Great Britain.

Anne Marie came back with a present. A large, glossy Colditz calendar containing twelve images of the castle ranging from medieval woodcuts to Second World War photographs all extensively annotated. I would love to have known what they said, but it was all in German and the calendar was for 2018 — well out of date, but it's the thought that counts. I purchased two books, *Colditz: the German story* by Reinhold Eggers, the prison's former head of security, and the highly informative and richly illustrated *Collecting Colditz and its Secrets* by Michael Booker. Colditz is a media genre in its own right. Over forty books have been written about it, two movies filmed and two television series made. Board games and video games exist where teams playing prisoners can test their ingenuity and daring against teams playing Germans.

Conscious that the last bus back to Grimma left at four, I hastily packed my books and notes and set off to visit other parts of the castle open to the public. Across the courtyard, a small gallery hung copies of prisoners' art that sparked an immediate connection with a painting I had seen less than forty-eight hours earlier at a van Gogh exhibition in London, *Prisoners Exercising*. Eyes downcast, inmates trudge in an endless circle of torment while above them brick walls glow in the bilious light of a sun we can't see and they don't dare acknowledge. It has a bleak beauty and shimmering resonance. Van Gogh painted it in 1890 when he was a patient in the Asylum of Saint-Rémy.

The simple watercolours that Brigadier William Anderson

of the Royal Engineers painted while he was a prisoner in Colditz have the same power and authenticity as van Gogh's heartfelt masterpiece. They lack the Dutch master's extraordinary glorious, unexpected colours for one very good reason. Anderson painted what he saw: for four years all he saw were the walls of Schloss Colditz — fifty shades of grey.

Despite its drabness, Colditz was as exclusive as the Ritz during the war. Not everyone could stay there. Only after *Oberkommando der Wehrmacht* (OKW), the German High Command, had consulted with security services and a formal recommendation had been made to the commandant, who had the final say, were orders issued for the transfer and admission of a prisoner to Colditz. Your grades as a troublemaker had to be good. Charlie's were outstanding. He qualified as an 'Escapee'. Which is self-explanatory. He also qualified in another category: 'Enemies of the Third Reich'. These were insubordinate POWs who forgot their place, men constantly provoking and insulting their captors.

Wing Commander Douglas Bader, the famous tin-legged Battle of Britain hero, was an inveterate goon baiter before and after arriving at Colditz, which was supposed to teach him a lesson. Self-aggrandising, loud and highly opinionated, Bader got on everyone's nerves, friend and foe alike, which was only fair — his mangled stumps were getting on his. In constant pain, he had to be carried up flights of stairs to his room and needed help bathing, which must have been galling for a proud, vain man. After the war he surprised everyone when he reached out to his former jailers, something Charlie never did. For quite a while after hostilities ceased, Charlie was even hostile to German tractors, ploughs, drills and harrows. This abated when he saw how well they worked on neighbouring farms.

Conditions at Colditz had been deteriorating well before Charlie arrived. Food supplies were perilously low. A pitiful 1300 calories a day per prisoner was all the Germans could rustle up. Fuel for stoves was almost non-existent. Under heavy guard, prisoners were allowed into the woods to collect firewood. Red Cross parcels were no longer getting through due to damage to rail lines from Switzerland. Life was not much better for ordinary Germans who suspected but dared not whisper too loudly that the war was lost. A grim fatalism gripped the populace apart from true believers who became even more fanatical and unpredictable in their criminal lunacy.

Captain Eggers, the head of security, a former school-teacher who wanted all prisoners to sit up straight and face the front but was never a Nazi, pinned a notice on the camp bulletin board that was more polite request than threat:

To all Prisoners of War!
The escape from prison camps is no longer
a sport! In plain English: Stay in the camps
where you will be safe! The days when we could
practise the rules of sportsmanship
are over. All police and military guards have
been given the most strict orders to shoot on
sight all suspected persons.

The notice was quickly taken down by the Germans. The Senior British Officer, Willie Todd, quite possibly after private conversations with Eggers, clearly felt the same way and made an extraordinary announcement on parade that included a coda worthy of Monty Python: 'It is no longer an adventure to get out of this camp. Anyone escaping will get home too late to take part in the war anyway. Furthermore, *I disapprove of kicking a man when he's down . . .*'

This parade took place just a few days before Charlie showed up. Given that he had just been given a good kicking when he was down, he would not have taken these instructions kindly. As it was, he settled in quietly. In his best-selling memoir *Colditz: the full story*, Major Pat Reid wrote that

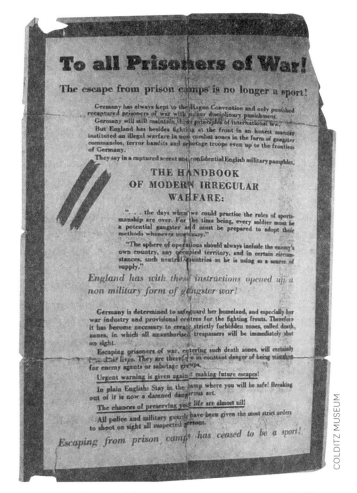

Warning notice to Colditz POWs, posted by camp authorities near the end of the war. The rules have changed.

Charlie's lack of swagger was the perfect antidote to some of the other larger personalities, particularly Douglas Bader, that turned up at Colditz: 'Upham made light of his extraordinary bravery and it was his quiet defiance and Antipodean wit which endeared him to his fellow prisoners.'

In *Colditz: the definitive story*, Henry Chancellor's description of Charlie is similar: 'He hated Germans and all things German. He was a solitary man of immense valour, modest to an extreme.'

In *Detour: the story of Oflag IVC*, a collection of prose pieces, charcoal portraits and cartoons by Colditz prisoners, published by Falcon Press in 1946 with the express purpose of raising money for the Red Cross, there is this description of Charlie: 'An Officer and a Gentleman — determination and singleness of purpose personified, loyal, constructive, quiet, unassuming and friendly.'

Dick Howe, another famous Colditz inmate and best-selling author, was more cautious in his description: 'Charlie

Charcoal sketch of Charlie drawn by another Colditz POW.

DETOUR: THE STORY OF OFLAG IVC

was a difficult man to get to know and when you did get to know him his main topic of conversation was New Zealand.'

Colonel Todd told Sandford that he found Charlie very quiet and reserved. When they circled the cobbles, they talked about sheep farming and the merits of different breeds of sheepdog: 'Conditions at Colditz were somewhat trying and people were apt to lose their sense of proportion, but Charles Upham always remained level-headed and sensible. He was the type of man one instinctively likes.'

Charlie may have appeared level-headed to Todd, but the man Fred Moody described to Sandford was at the end of his tether, his heart broken and his spirit crushed. Writing in general terms to spare his subject, Sandford said that many POWs in Colditz lost their resilience and energy and had to fight for their very souls to remain balanced and undismayed. On three occasions during roll calls, which every prisoner hated, Charlie lost this balance and his behaviour tipped over into crazed recklessness. Hauptmann Pupcke, an officer and a gentleman with a sense of humour, was regarded fondly by many prisoners. But maths was not his strong suit, which infuriated Charlie who frequently blurted out under his breath in a stage whisper even guards could hear: 'This fucking counting business makes me bloody angry, and here's old fuck-up Jack coming!'

During one roll call the British contingent were chatting and reading, but standing more or less at attention, when fuck-up Jack noticed Charlie slouching and sucking on his pipe in defiance of his order banning smoking. Pupcke marched up to Charlie, demanding that he stand up straight and remove the pipe. 'Go fuck yourself!' Pupcke blinked rapidly, looking sideways at a junior officer. 'What did he say?' The interpreter prudently lost the remarks in translation. Told to stand to attention, Charlie remained slouching, pipe in mouth, hands in pockets. 'Please don't cause any trouble, Charlie,' whispered a worried Moody. Pupcke began shouting

POWs assembling unhappily for roll call.

DETOUR: THE STORY OF OFLAG IVC

at Charlie, who stared calmly back at him. Pupcke eventually gave up, shrugged, broke into a bemused smile and wondered out loud: 'Perhaps there is something wrong with him . . .' The count resumed with Charlie nonchalantly puffing his pipe.

Years later, Charlie admitted there was some truth in Pupcke's suggestion. What happened on a midnight roll call would tend to confirm it. Prisoners were roused by siren from their beds when their jittery captors suspected an escape had been made. Grumbling and stamping their feet, they assembled in the freezing courtyard, where they were asked to show their identity discs. Everyone complied sourly apart from Charlie who refused point-blank to show his. Having refused to show it, Charlie then refused to hand it over — instead hurling it at the inspecting officer's feet. It skidded on the cobbles inches from his polished jackboots. Charlie doubled down on this disobedience by ignoring requests to pick it up, suggesting that the German could pick it up himself. The inspecting officer drew his Luger, cocked it and pressed the barrel firmly into Charlie's abdomen, hissing, 'Pick it up!' His blue eyes ablaze with fury, Charlie waited for what seemed like an eternity but was probably only a few seconds before complying. Again, nothing more was said or done.

On another roll call the head of security, Eggers, was doing the count, with Charlie in the front row sucking on a cigarette and quietly reading a book. Eggers screamed at him to take the cigarette out of his mouth. Charlie looked up in a bored way and took no notice. Eggers stepped up and with an open hand slapped Charlie hard across the mouth to dislodge the cigarette. The physical insult snapped something in Charlie and he launched himself at Eggers in a rage.

Other prisoners watching this are convinced that had it not been for the quick action of people standing on either side of him, Charlie would have killed Eggers. He was forcibly pulled back, which saved Charlie's life as well. A Canadian POW commented later: 'Charlie's face looked like a bayonet charge!' A shaken Eggers decided the count was close enough and dismissed the parade. In his biography, Eggers makes no mention of this incident. Either he felt it was of no great moment, which I doubt, or he feared the face-slap would present him in a bad light.

In each of these confrontations, Charlie seemed to be playing Russian roulette with a bullet in every chamber. Did he have a death wish, as some suggest? Was he depressed beyond caring, or were they all finely calibrated acts of defiance? It beggars belief that he wasn't shot on the spot. Nor was he frog-marched off to the punishment cells. Others were court-martialled for less. Could there be a simple explanation for Charlie's charmed run in Colditz? Something that had nothing to do with good luck or divine providence?

Michael Booker's book provides one possible explanation. He writes that German sources indicate that, along with Douglas Bader, Charlie belonged in a shadow second group of select prisoners known as the *Prominente* — celebrities or notables. Charlie was worth more to the Germans alive than dead. There is no way of proving this now. All documentation of that kind was burnt deliberately just hours before the castle was liberated. The official *Prominente*, twenty-one in number, included senior Polish generals, senior French generals, a nephew of the King of England, a nephew of the Queen Mother, Churchill's nephew — Giles Romilly, who had no rank or serial number (he was a war correspondent captured in Norway in 1940 while on assignment for the *Daily Express*), the son of the American Ambassador to Great Britain, the son of the Viceroy of India and the sons of various lords and top military brass. If the *Prominente* were not celebrities themselves, they had famous relatives. Most of the British *Prominente* were registered in *Burke's Peerage* at birth and featured in Debrett's *Peerage*. The label 'ace soldier of the British Empire' would have made the German selectors sit up and take note when they were drawing up the 'B list' of *Prominente*.

Charlie recalled an elderly French general who hated the Germans, who hated him: 'He was very sick. The Germans said they were taking him away to hospital. We were very suspicious. The moment he was outside the gate there was a shot. They said he was trying to escape. Well, the old fellow could hardly walk.'

The guards at Colditz watched the *Prominente* like hawks — as if their lives depended on it, which they did. A firing squad or the Russian Front, which amounted to much the same thing only at a much lower temperature, lay in store for the commandant or Eggers should anything happen to any of the notable prisoners, or should any of them escape. To lessen the chance of such a catastrophe, they were housed in separate quarters, had their own guard detail, and they were checked every two hours during the night.

They were hostages to be traded in exchange for top Nazis if the war went badly, bargaining chips should Hitler need a last throw of the dice. Hitler instructed SS Commander Heinrich Himmler to begin collecting them as early as 1941 when his forces were winning everywhere, so you have to give the monster his due: this showed considerable foresight. Himmler stored them in Colditz for safekeeping. If the Nazis ran out of the first batch, they had Charlie, Douglas Bader and others on the reserves bench.

Did Charlie know he was a member of this second group, and did that knowledge give him licence to push his luck? I doubt it. The thought would have appalled him had he known. If anything, Charlie thought the opposite and considered himself a marked man. In a 1989 profile in the Christchurch *Press*, Charlie told Gay McDonald about one Colditz guard who had it in for him:

> There was one particular rotten little SS bloke in black. He was a corporal in the Death Head Hussars. I told him one day [it should be called] 'Schwarze Liste' (German for Black List). He told me he would do me in before he left. He'd find a reason. He hated me like poison.

With the Allies demanding unconditional surrender, Hitler left it too late to play the hostage card. Having outlived their usefulness, the *Prominente* were surplus to requirements. SS General Gottlob Berger was summoned to the ruined German capital for a final meeting in the War Room with an almost catatonic Hitler and a frenzied, highly vocal Goebbels. Berger's last direct order from the Führer was that the *Prominente* were to be shot. They would be added to Germany's mounting funeral pyre. Describing the scene later, Berger says he decided silently then and there to disobey the order. Germany was utterly destroyed and would fall in a matter of weeks, if not days. Berger hoped Hitler would have other things on his mind. Goebbels somehow read Berger's mind and started shrieking that the order be carried out to the letter: 'When the whole German people is weeping the English Royal Family should not be laughing!'

§

On 11 April 1945 Captain Eggers received a secret order from German High Command that on receipt of the code word 'Heidenröslein' ('Heather Rose'), the *Prominente* were to be removed from Colditz and transferred to Oflag 4A some 50 miles away at Königstein. Two buses arrived and were parked for two days in the outer courtyard where everyone could see them. Tension and speculation mounted in the prisoners' quarters. Late in the afternoon on the second day a secret code word came through along with orders that the *Prominente* were to be moved within two hours of its receipt. Eggers and the commandant, Oberst Prawitt, feared anarchy and bloodshed if the *Prominente* were marched off in front of the other prisoners. In the ensuing chaos some of them were bound to vanish into a hiding place or simply disguise themselves and melt in among the 2000 Allied officers. If they stuck to the two-hour ruling, the operation would surely fail. Eggers recalled his anguish in his memoir: 'And then what? A visit perhaps from an SS detachment. Shooting? The *Prominente* were too hot for us to hold. At all costs we must take this chance of getting them off our hands.'

They must have been sorely tempted to toss the physically menacing Charlie and verbally abusive Douglas Bader into the mix as part of the job lot. After the last roll call that evening when the courtyard was cleared and all prisoners were safely locked in their quarters or in the straw-floored chapel, the Senior British Officer Willie Todd was informed of the move and immediately requested a meeting with Commandant Prawitt, where he argued strenuously that it was madness to send two busloads of prisoners through the ever-narrowing corridor between American and Russian forces at night. Todd demanded that the commandant and Eggers ignore the order. Prawitt refused, and he declined to say where they were being taken. Told bluntly that they would both answer to the Allies with their heads if any of the *Prominente* were shot, Prawitt quickly had a change of heart, disclosing the destination and volunteering the services of the hapless Eggers to travel with them and return with a note of safe passage from the *Prominente* themselves confirming they had arrived unharmed.

At 1.30 a.m., laden with all manner of kit and containers, the *Prominente* and their orderlies, including two additional Maori soldiers, walked to the revving buses. When the British *Prominente*, who were allowed two orderlies apiece, had realised they were short on their entitlement, word went out upstairs for volunteers and these likely lads put their hands up for a trip into the unknown. Eggers was still marvelling at this as they passed over the castle bridge and out of the Schloss heading south-east for Dresden. The bombed and burnt-out city was a horrifying sight, leaving the British *Prominente* gasping, but not the Poles who had witnessed the Nazi destruction of Warsaw.

Consumed with his own fate, Eggers was silent. Hitler would deal to him and his family if any of the *Prominente* escaped and the Allies would shoot him for war crimes if any of them were victims of reprisal killings or died accidentally en route. As they drove through the horror scene, Eggers prayed that Dresden would be spared further raids that night. At Königstein he was hugely relieved to hand over his charges. On receipt of a note of safe passage, Eggers headed straight back to Colditz and was even more relieved to hand this chit over to Todd.

The western horizon lit up like bonfire night every night now, and the air filled with the percussive thump of battle as the American First Army fought their way into Leipzig. Jailers and inmates knew the end was nigh. On the morning of Saturday, 14 April, Eggers received a phone call with the code letters 'ZR' which stood for *Zerstorung–Raumung* (destroy-evacuate). Eggers and his staff began burning files in the boilerhouse. Amid the demented, marathon conflagration, Eggers caught sight of Hitler's speeches printed in miniature type from the government stationery office. He couldn't resist one last peek: 'The Soviets will not take one square foot of East Prussian territory.' Eggers noted with a grim laugh that Russian troops were just 20 miles to the east, and American troops 15 miles to the west.

Willie Todd flatly refused to evacuate his men. They were staying put. The German garrison consisted of 200 middle-aged men armed with German and French rifles with fifteen rounds of ammunition apiece, ten machine guns of four different makes and some grenades. For transport all they had at their disposal was an antique motor vehicle barely working and two horse-drawn carts. Commandant Prawitt and Eggers bowed to the inevitable. Signing a hastily drawn-up surrender document, they handed the keys to the castle to Todd. The SS unit in charge of 500 Hungarian Jews working at a china factory at the foot of the hill had to be denied any clue of the capitulation lest it trigger a retaliatory raid and wholesale massacre, so Colditz guards manned their posts and patrolled the battlements as per normal, except with empty magazines. All other weapons and munitions were placed in the hands of their former prisoners.

§

Prisoners' personal files in the commandant's office files escaped the boiler-room bonfire. After the guards surrendered, Charlie uplifted his:

> I had a file about four inches thick. It was quite funny to get someone to translate their description of you. 'This is a dangerous character who is to be carefully guarded. He has an incorrigible hatred of the German people.' That was true. I couldn't stand the sight of them.

Along with his files, Charlie also helped himself to the paperweight on the commandant's desk. He eventually tired of lugging the heavy file around and abandoned it, which is a great shame — it would make fascinating reading today. Ken Sandford would have made a meal of it. If the print were too small, the paperweight would have come into play. Made of clear glass the size of half a tennis ball, it served as a reading magnifier. Charlie brought the paperweight back to New Zealand with him. His daughters found it ideal for finding and removing thistles in their legs.

I had heard about this paperweight for years — it has taken on something of a mythical status. If it existed, Charlie's story about a file four inches thick was also more likely to be true. I met people, not just Charlie's daughters, who swear the glass paperweight exists, but none were sure of its exact whereabouts. Then someone, I can't remember who, possibly Charlie's daughter Caroline, tipped me off — it resides in a small glass case in the Army Museum at Waiouru alongside an armband that civilian workers in POW camps had to wear, which was embossed with a Nazi eagle clutching a swastika in its talons.

It was a thrill to finally clap eyes on the paperweight. An even bigger thrill was seeing a private collection of Charlie

Upham memorabilia including his Lamsdorf identity disc, pale green with verdigris, which hangs on brown twine in a glass cabinet in a private museum in rural Canterbury. I saw it with my brother-in-law Grant O'Fee, who came with me on a research trip. Grant is a military history buff with a particular passion for the Second New Zealand Division's campaigns in Greece, Crete, North Africa and Italy. He has read everything written by Winston Churchill and can quote whole passages verbatim, whether you want him to or not. He was formerly commander of the Nelson and Blenheim Police District. A crack shot, he once headed the Armed Offenders Squad and led a UN peacekeeping mission in East Timor. His police district included Westport and Hokitika where most of Charlie's men came from, hard bastards who called their commanding officer 'Boss' and had Charlie's blessing to give saluting a swerve.

I value Grant's insights into how men under command and men in command behave when placed in harm's way. As a cartoonist I live daily with the fear of paper cuts, but it's not the same. After visiting Charlie's old haunts at Conway Flat, we paid our respects to his statue in the small town of Amberley in North Canterbury, where, so as not to cause offence in this delicate age, Charlie is throwing a pair of binoculars at the enemy rather than a grenade. Grant of course immediately spotted, and was delighted, that the sculptor had given Charlie a pistol holster with a six-round ammunition clip on the side, as he wore this type in preference to the standard issue.

That done, we headed further south. The sun was sinking behind the Southern Alps when we reached our final destination inland and south-west of Christchurch. The drive took far longer than anticipated, largely because the fuel gauge on Grant's electric hybrid measured zero, forcing him to nurse his Mitsubishi Outlander at a snail's pace for the first hour or so. It's not a good idea to go looking for rural properties after dark. If they have a number, you need the eyes of a field owl or night-vision goggles to spot it.

We eventually identified the right gated mansion and pressed the intercom button at the high fence and electronic gates. Security was tight for reasons which soon became obvious. The widow of a close friend of Charlie's had kindly agreed to let us view her late partner's wondrous and priceless collection of vintage guns and other weapons. Lovingly and beautifully curated, the collection fills a room bigger than a squash court. Charlie's stuff includes the satchel that he carried grenades in, his knife with a knuckle-duster handle, his Lamsdorf identity tag, his ration book and a battle report written after one fiery action. In astonishingly small, almost dainty writing, Charlie lists his platoon members in alphabetical order, detailing their fate — wounded, missing in action, killed, and so on — its very neatness intensifying its grim purpose.

Only fifty prints were ever made of Peter McIntyre's famous painting *The Breakout from Minqar Qa'im*. One hangs on the wall. It has been signed by Charlie and the artist. There is also a replica of one of Charlie's VCs. I took lots of photos on my cellphone. The Palace gives you two spares like car dealers give you two sets of keys when you purchase a new vehicle. It was extraordinarily light in my hand for something that weighed so heavily on Charlie. I have to fight the urge to show the photos to strangers on planes.

Shortly after the war, at the height of Upham-mania in New Zealand, a little boy approached Charlie shyly at a function with a request that would have gotten a brusque response if it had been from an adult.

'Please, sir, can I have a look at your Victoria Cross?'

'I don't have it on me, sorry.'

'What does it look like?'

'Well, if you had a penny and you hammered it with a hammer, it would look like that.'

Chapter 17

'Another VC! Oh, poor Charles'

15 April 1945 dawned strangely silent with a breath of spring in the air.

For the first time in living memory Sunday church bells didn't toll in Colditz village. The stillness didn't last. Mid-morning, American tanks were spotted emerging from the woods on the opposite side of the Mulde River and artillery pieces hidden in the trees opened up a furious barrage; shells falling short of the castle set ablaze houses in the township. Gunners adjusted their sights and shells crashed into the guardroom and third floor of the castle, sending Allied officers scrambling downstairs, but not before unfurling French flags and a giant Union Jack from upper windows — which brought the firing to an abrupt halt.

Supported by tanks and mortar fire, US riflemen swarming across the bridge into the village were surprised by the dogged ferocity of the resistance. There were snipers in every window. SS fanatics fought like people with nothing left to lose. Hitler Youth did the same. One small boy barely in his teens, in an ill-fitting uniform way too big for him, stepped into the open and shot a popular sergeant in the head and was mown down in return. His punctured body lay on the road for two days until his mother asked for it back. The

Americans consented and a horse-drawn hearse straight out of a Hammer House of Horror film clip-clopped over the cobbles to retrieve him.

Less than a year on from the Normandy landings, the Americans, many of them just out of their teens themselves, had become hardened, grizzled veterans. At first hand they had seen the horrors in extermination camps liberated en route to Colditz. Armed to the teeth, filthy and unshaven, they were in no mood to be civil when they burst into the castle, shocking the British with their rough handling and belligerence towards the Germans. They offered to take care of any guards who had treated them badly. Much to the Germans' relief, British POWs hastily assured them that there was no need.

The Germans were exceedingly fortunate that Charlie wasn't part of this conversation. He did have a score to settle, but wisely the SS corporal in question had made himself scarce. The rest of the Colditz garrison were marched off to holding pens across town and a convivial calm settled over the Schloss, only to be broken by the arrival of a tall, leggy, beautiful redhead in a khaki uniform trailing a team of cameramen — legendary *International News* war correspondent Lee Carson — screaming blue murder at not being present at the initial surrender and capture of Colditz as promised for an exclusive story. She had seen the dead boy on the road. She vowed to have an investigation; shooting children was a war crime. The Yank commanders tried desperately to mollify her. Douglas Bader, fighter-ace, war hero and living headline, selflessly tottered forward with stories about himself. They left happily together, and the crisis was averted.

Foraging parties were sent from the castle into Colditz village to find food and bring back anything useful. Some POWs looted fine porcelain, jewellery, cameras and binoculars. A Frenchman manged to have sex with a Polish maid working in the Colditz hotel. Charlie, who had ulterior motives, confined himself to purloining utilitarian eating utensils and stowing them in a backpack.

On the second day, six open-topped American army trucks rolled into the outer courtyard to collect 250 British and Commonwealth officers. SS troops and bands of Hitler Youth, hearts dark with anger, were still at large, roaming the countryside, thirsting for some revenge, so the convoy drove non-stop, fast and furious some 75 miles west to Kölleda airfield, a badly bombed former Luftwaffe base. They swung through gates guarded by Yank sentries wearing top hats and past Yank troops playing baseball and wearing top hats. Everyone was wearing top hats. The *Prominente* would have loved it. Charlie's father would have loved it — the Uphams wore top hats at family weddings and christenings. A nearby millinery factory had just been liberated.

The following afternoon they boarded a fleet of Dakotas and flew to England, touching down at RAF Westcott airfield in Buckinghamshire in the middle of the night, where they were greeted warmly by glorious, exotic creatures, pretty girls in uniform with strange squeaky voices, their faces green and their lips black under yellow hangar lights. After being sprayed with disinfectant, the former POWs were handed cigarettes, served cups of tea and offered newspapers, which were full of stories about Douglas Bader's triumphant return.

§

Charlie wasn't with the returnees in England. He had filed out of Colditz with everyone else, passing under the portico one last time, but while they were clambering excitedly onto waiting lorries he slipped away quietly down a narrow flight of steps leading to the town square. They were the same steps I climbed on a sleepy Sunday morning when there wasn't a soul to be seen and the village was hushed and still, unlike Charlie's morning. Then, the square was teeming with fuming, outraged Americans — they had just discovered the last brutal act of barbarism, a final savage massacre committed by the SS garrison.

Charlie: 'There was this big brick works there full of Russian women, and there was this concentration camp of Hungarian Jews just down below us. There were only three left alive. We found them under the heaps of corpses . . .'

This further confirmed to Charlie that his personal war against Nazi Germany wasn't over. He had unfinished business and if he wasn't quick the war would finish first. He strolled into the Americans' forward command post and asked if he could augment his meagre supplies with one of their combat jackets, a pistol, holster, rubber-soled boots, steel helmet, Tommy gun and some grenades and go into battle with them. They consented to this unusual request and he spent four convivial days with American forces in the Colditz area.

When his absence was noticed in England, he was ordered to return forthwith. He made his way back across the ruins of Germany via Buchenwald Concentration Camp and was sickened by what he saw. In London he applied to join the Occupation Force with the express intention of tracking down Nazi criminals. On the application form, he sought police duties. The application was denied. There was a rule against taking on former POWs.

Well after the war, prompted by Molly, Charlie would concede that he had met some nice Germans. For a long time after the war when he met Germans of a certain age on planes and trains, he asked them if they knew about the concentration camps. If they denied all knowledge, he called them bloody liars to their face.

Charlie: 'Everyone knew. Even the children. There was a concentration camp outside every city — they could see the chimneys smoking!'

When Berger's masters in Berlin discovered that he hadn't executed the *Prominente* as instructed, alternative arrangements to dispatch them had to be made. Berger intercepted a message from SS Group Leader Martin Bormann to Ernst Kaltenbrunner, chief of the Reich Main Security Office in Munich, instructing him to assemble a firing squad. As soon as the *Prominente* truck convoy arrived in the Bavarian capital, they were to be 'made sure of for all time'. And while they were at it, they should shoot Gottlob Berger as well. With his fate now intertwined with theirs, Berger intercepted the convoy, provided them with an armed escort and arranged safe passage to American lines. After the war he came before a US military tribunal charged with war crimes, atrocities against civilians and ill-treatment of prisoners of war. A noose beckoned, but his saving of the *Prominente* was not forgotten. He was sentenced to twenty-five years' imprisonment, which was later quietly commuted to ten. Hitler was right all along — famous hostages have their uses.

§

It was official policy to send all liberated and escaped POWs back home as soon as possible. They had done their bit and were prudently deemed unfit for further service — a liability to themselves and those who served with them. Charlie's chum from Modena, Bob Wood, was sent back to Wellington, where he poured on the charm and lobbied furiously with the Defence Department to be allowed to rejoin the New Zealand Division, eventually getting his wish. He was back in Italy serving as an intelligence officer as the Americans were closing in on Colditz and Charlie was scheming to join in the war's closing act. Hearing that the Hotel Danieli in Venice had been secured by General Freyberg for rest and recreation purposes for Kiwi servicemen, Bob and a Maori mate hitchhiked there in pouring rain and somehow scored a palatial suite overlooking the Grand Canal, despite arriving at the front desk completely sodden. Bob made himself at home, sipping champagne and enjoying room service in a monogrammed bathrobe while his clothes were dry-cleaned and pressed.

Ten glorious days without leave came to an end when the New Zealand Division was ordered at short notice to move north-east on the double and secure the Italian port of Trieste, which was located invitingly on a thin strip of coast between Slovenia and the Adriatic Sea. Tito's ragged Communist forces of horse-drawn baggage cars and obsolete tanks were desperate to claim the city and port for Yugoslavia. For several days, the New Zealand Division and Tito's vagabond militia faced off in the streets in a tense stalemate. Trieste could easily have become a divided city like Berlin — one half in the Communist Bloc and the other half part of the West.

Numerically, it was no contest. Tito had many more troops at his disposal. They slept rough in woods and parks on the fringes of the city. Galloping into a New Zealand camp one night brandishing their rifles aloft like an Apache war party, they demanded a drum of petrol. 'Horses thirsty, are they?' drawled one of the Kiwis. They got the joke and rode off into the night in fits of laughter. Peter McIntyre recounts another occasion when one of Tito's clapped-out Honey tanks clanked up to a New Zealand machine-gun post at a downtown intersection and trained its gun on the crew. Rather than withdraw, the New Zealanders called up one of their own tanks — a big, stonking, brand-new American Sherman tank. The Yugoslav tank quickly turned tail and fled as fast as it could go, which was pitifully slow with the Sherman bearing down on it effortlessly. Rounding a corner at speed, the Yugoslav tank snapped a tread and slewed to a halt. The crew clambered out, desperate to repair it. The Sherman parked right behind, and the New Zealand crew emerged and casually lent a hand. The Yugoslavs lost heart around this time and withdrew completely from Trieste. Round one in the Cold War that would eventually settle over Europe was won by the Kiwis.

In a straight line, 450 kilometres due west from Trieste, lies the southern tip of beautiful Lake Como. Glorious forested peaks soar above neoclassical villas and pink palaces lining deep jade-green waters. Forty-eight hours before Hitler committed suicide, a German convoy raced up its western arm hell-bent on reaching the Swiss border. The Allied forces weren't far behind. It would be a close-run thing. They were stopped by a roadblock in the town of Dongo manned by a large band of heavily armed Communist partisans. The partisans consented to their continued passage provided they handed over any senior Italian Fascists in their party. The Germans quickly agreed. A small, shrunken, dazed and confused, barely recognisable Mussolini and his mistress, Claretta Petacci, were pushed out of a car. The Germans were waved through and the once all-powerful dictator and his lover were taken to a nearby farmhouse and kept overnight. The next morning, they were driven a short distance and executed on the side of the road. Vain to the end, Mussolini asked quietly to be shot in the heart and was duly dispatched with seven bullets to the chest from a sub-machine gun.

Eighteen months earlier, Mussolini had his son-in-law, Count Galeazzo Ciano, arrested by forces still loyal to his collapsed regime for the role he played in its demise. Ciano had no illusion about his fate and wrote in his diary:

> Within a few days a sham tribunal will make public a sentence which has already been decided by Mussolini under the influence of that circle of prostitutes and white slavers which for some years have plagued Italian political life and brought our country to the brink of the abyss. I accept calmly what is to be my infamous destiny.

His wife, the Countess Edda Ciano, hoping to use her husband's incendiary war diary as a bargaining chip with her father, wrapped five journals in cloth, wound the fabric around her waist as a belt, and made her way on foot to the Swiss border where officials assumed she was a simple peasant heavy with child and let her through. Her desperate gambit failed. Terrified of being thought weak by Hitler, Mussolini refused to commute the death sentence. The ice water that Count Ciano implied would flow freely in his veins froze completely on the way to his place of execution outside the gates of Verona, rendering him immobile. He collapsed and sagged to the ground and had to be carried the rest of the way and tied into a chair. Blindfolded, he managed to cry, 'Long live Italy!' before being shot.

While the war in Europe was still raging, the existence of Count Ciano's war diaries came to the attention of US Intelligence. Strapped for cash and thirsting for revenge, Edda bargained hard before agreeing to them being copied onto microfilm and translated into English. They were serialised in the *Chicago Daily News* and later published in England and America.

As I was about to depart Sawtell for the long drive back to Sydney international airport, Bob Wood gave me a parting gift of Count Ciano's diaries.

§

Returning POWs were given twenty-eight days' leave and a free rail pass for the United Kingdom. All Charlie wanted was to be with Molly, who had returned to England to do more nursing. He was horrified to learn she was where he'd just come from — defeated Germany — working with the Red Cross Auxiliary in transit camps for displaced people. 'Come out of there,' he wrote. 'It's dangerous!' Molly managed to wangle a weekend's leave in London to catch up with her fiancé, whose demure letters to her did not match the fiery person newspapers and radio had been describing. He was much thinner, greyer and quieter than she remembered, but still her Charlie. They made plans for their future and she flew back to Germany to complete her nursing tour — both counting down the days until they could be together full-time.

It was good catching up with his old mates from Greece, Crete and North Africa, but Charlie couldn't wait to escape the hustle and bustle of London. His oldest sister, married and settled in Hampshire, was startled one morning by a gaunt face peering in her kitchen window — her baby brother. He loved the peace and quiet of the countryside and playing with her children. The idyll was brought to an end by a letter from London with the Royal Coat of Arms stamped on the envelope:

Central Chancery of the Orders of Knighthood
St. James' Palace S. W. 1

CONFIDENTIAL
Capt. C. H. Upham
New Zealand Military Forces

Sir,
The King will hold an Investiture at Buckingham Palace on Friday the 11th of May 1945 at which your attendance is requested.

It is requested that you should be at the Palace not later than 10:15 o'clock a.m. Doors open at 9:45 a.m.

DRESS:
Service dress; morning dress; civil defence uniform or dark lounge suit.

This letter should be produced by you on entering the Palace as no further card of admission will be issued. I am desired to inform you that you may be accompanied

by two relations or friends to witness the Investiture
but I regret that owing to the limited accommodation
available for spectators it is not possible for this number
to be increased. The spectators' tickets may be obtained
on application to this office and I have to ask you
therefore to return it to me immediately.

I am your obedient servant

It was more command than request. Molly returned from
Germany and, joined by his sister, they got there nice and
early. Waiting in an antechamber with another New Zealand
infantryman, Jack Hinton, who was about to receive a VC
for his heroic deeds in Greece, they had nerves to settle
and time to kill so they ducked out for a quick pint. Hearing
Kiwi accents, barmen refused to let them pay and kept the
beers coming. As a consequence, the medal pinning was less
stressful than it might otherwise have been; chests bursting
with pride had to compete with bladders bursting with beer.
The king informed Charlie that he had been mentioned in
dispatches for his escape attempts and asked what he had
been doing since arriving in London. 'Mostly eating, sir,'
replied Charlie.

Leaving the palace through the great front gates, arm in arm
with his fiancée and sister, Charlie strolled past the towering
memorial to the monarch whose cross he was now wearing.
For her part, gazing straight ahead, scrupulously avoiding
eye contact with the engorged scrotums protruding from the
hindquarters of the massive bronze lions at her feet, Queen
Victoria stares sternly down the grand Mall to Admiralty Arch.
Crossing the roundabout and entering Green Park, Charlie
forgot to salute an approaching brigadier, who drew himself
up to his full height and muttered darkly about impudent
colonials. Then he caught sight of the talismanic deep crimson
on Charlie's tunic, and with head snapping back and eyes
popping, he stood stiffly to attention and saluted Charlie

before wheeling away in awe and embarrassment — which only added to Charlie's discomfort. He hated this sort of thing.

Charlie and Molly married in Barton on Sea, Hampshire on 20 June 1945 and honeymooned on the Isle of Wight, in the New Forest and Scotland, where friends and relatives lent them cars.

> Dear Pum
> July 2 45
> I hope you are very well, also David, Mary and young Bob. I hope Brian is coming back soon. Molly & I are having a super time here together. This heather I picked on the east side near Invergordon. We are now over on the west side. Molly sends her love.
> Love from Chas.

And . . .

> We came up to Inverness to-day. It is a long way in a train. We left London at 7.20pm & did not arrive here till 10.30 the next morning. We are staying at the Caledonian Hotel for 3 days. The country here is very like NZ. I had roast venison for dinner for the first time since I left Island Hills about 8 or 9 years ago.
> Love to you all
> Uncle Charles

Back in London they rented a small flat and kept out of sight. When Charlie went to book passages home for them both an officious navy shipping clerk advised him that spouses were not allowed to accompany their husbands and that Molly would need to travel separately on a civilian vessel. While waiting for a berth on another ship, Molly visited the Fernleaf Club in London, a home away from home for homesick Kiwis, where Lady Freyberg asked her where Charlie was. 'Off the coast of Africa, I imagine,' replied Molly. 'He hasn't sailed without you?' Lady Freyberg was aghast when she heard the details. Something had to be done. General Freyberg issued instructions that Molly was to be flown home as soon as a flight could be arranged. Molly refused the offer. Like her husband, she didn't want special treatment.

While he was on the water, unbeknown to him, Charlie received special treatment of sorts when his old boss, Douglas McFarlane, rang his mother to tell her that he was selling Rafa Downs, the property her son had worked on before the war and always admired. He was cutting it into three blocks, retaining one and selling the other two. He wanted Charlie to have the right of first refusal on one of them.

Charlie's boat berthed in Wellington on Sunday, 2 September 1945. Pleading fictitious duties as an adjutant and needing to catch the steamer for Lyttelton, Charlie gave reporters the slip and disappeared into the dockside crowd without his name being announced. His name was announced through loudspeakers when he arrived in Lyttelton but was largely unrecognised — something that would change overnight in three weeks — and he was able to move anonymously to his waiting family and head off to Gloucester Street. Mrs Upham was taken aback by her son's appearance. He was terribly thin and his teeth were in bad condition. In the living room, he rummaged around in his kit bag, brought out his VC and a blue scarf and handed them to her. After more rummaging, he brought out a meerschaum pipe for his father. When his mother asked about his teeth, he rummaged around again and produced a single plate with two teeth.

Before the war Charlie's smile was already something of an endangered species and after the war it became extinct — publicly at least, certainly when anyone pulled out a camera. A trawl through Internet picture libraries and family albums throws up images of Charlie that are uniform in their solemnity and reserve. I have seen only one photo of him where his grin is so wide a small gap in his front teeth is revealed. This rarity I suspect was the result of embarrassment about his teeth, and after the war the look complemented his darker view of humanity and of the world. In this rare smiling photo, Charlie has a 'rescue me' look on his face, a look all the more startling for being so out of character. The explanation lies to his right in the supplicatory presence of Field Marshal Bernard Law Montgomery, 1st Viscount Montgomery of Alamein. The famous beret crowns his hawklike features and his left breast is carpeted in military ribbon. Charlie is dapper and handsome in a pinstriped three-piece suit and tie with no decorations. It was taken in a Christchurch bar when Montgomery was visiting in July 1947. Aglow with awe, Monty is fawning over quite possibly the only man on the planet he admired more than himself.

Without asking first, Mrs Upham, as only a mother can, committed her son on his return to weeks of sitting perfectly still, in full dress uniform, in the upstairs studio of accomplished Christchurch painter Archibald Nicoll for portraits commissioned by Christ's College and Lincoln College. Charlie had to turn up day after day clean-shaven and with his hair neatly combed. It was torture. One bonus was that he was already kitted and spruced up for the civic reception that Christchurch City insisted on holding for him when he had been home barely a week. On stage he shifted uncomfortably and stared at the floor in embarrassment as speaker after speaker paid tribute. When it was his turn, he rose to thunderous applause. He was hesitant at first, insisting that the honour being paid him was really due the division as a whole. He was only one man in the division. There were thousands of better soldiers than him. This made the crowd adore him even more. He finished with a flourish: 'Before this war, the world's riches were pretty badly distributed. If we are going to make all this worthwhile, we have to get rid of the want and misery in other parts of the world.'

§

Back in London, Molly ran into Howard Kippenberger in the street just after he'd come from Buckingham Palace.

'I had sherry with the king today, Molly. I think I ought to warn you. I think Charles might be getting another VC.'

Molly gulped. 'Another VC! Oh, poor Charles. We'll just have to take to the bush I think.'

Three years earlier, after Minqar Qaim, Jim Burrows and Kippenberger agreed that Charlie deserved another Victoria Cross. Smack on the heels of the breakout came the night attack on Ruweisat Ridge, where Charlie's courage was again off the charts and warranted another Victoria Cross. But nothing like that had ever happened before. *Two* Victoria Crosses for a combat soldier was without precedent — let alone *three*. It was unheard of. General Inglis decided the two separate battles should be regarded as a single event. The separate citations were woven together and the sworn statements and collateral proof dispatched as a single recommendation to London where they gathered dust in a cabinet. Gone, but not forgotten by General Inglis, it was his firm view that there was no statute of limitations on awards for courage. Sandford writes that Inglis approached Freyberg at the close of hostilities:

> Charlie's back. He's sick, pretty worn out but he'll be alright in time. He's got a mention in despatches for his escape attempts. But what about that award for him? It's lying in the War Office — never looked at since Alamein.

Freyberg got onto it. He went to the Army Council, the files were dusted off and the recommendation reconsidered 'in the cooler light of history', as Sandford put it. The same conclusion was reached. Charlie deserved a Bar to his VC, and a briefing paper was prepared for the king's consideration.

This is what it said:

From Jun 27 to Jul 15th 1942 Capt Upham performed five acts of conspicuous gallantry. He was with his company during all the fighting that took place during this period, though he was wounded on three different occasions on the night of Jun 27/28; on the night of Jul 14/15 and again on the afternoon of Jul 15. On the first two occasions he rejoined his company as soon as wounds were dressed and after the third occasion, when he could no longer walk, he was taken prisoner of war. He showed fine leadership at all times and under his command his company earned a remarkable reputation in attack. Capt Upham's complete indifference to danger and his personal bravery has become a byword in the whole of the New Zealand N.Z.E.F.

Jun 27: During the afternoon when the Germans attacked the New Zealand positions at Minqar Qaim the enemy made several attempts to clear a path for their tanks through a minefield. One forward section post of Capt Upham's Coy was occupying an important position on the edge of the minefield, and it was very heavily shelled and machine-gunned. Capt Upham walked forward over the ground that had no cover of any sort and which was swept by enemy fire, stayed with the section for a short period and came away only when he had assured himself that it could no longer carry on and hold its ground.

Night Jun 27/28: During the night when the N.Z. Div broke through the Germans at Minqar Qaim, Capt Upham led his men in inspiring fashion and his Coy overcame several enemy posts. The attack took place in very bright moonlight and at one stage a truck full of German soldiers was seen moving slowly through the soft sand. Capt Upham and a Corporal ran forward together, and in spite of heavy Tommy-gun fire from the Germans they reached the side of the truck and with hand grenades wiped out the entire truck load and left the truck in flames. Not one German left the burning vehicle. Capt Upham was slightly wounded in both arms from the explosions of his own grenades. He did not report to get his wounds treated until the following night when the Div was back in new positions, and he rejoined his Coy.

Night July 14/15: During Attack on El Ruweisat Ridge Capt Upham's Coy, part of the reserve battalion during the six-mile advance, was about two miles behind the leading battalions. Wireless communications had broken down and Capt Upham was instructed to send forward an officer and a jeep to contact the forward battalions and bring back information. He went himself instead and after being fired on by an enemy post procured a Spandau gun and set it up in the car. He had several further encounters with enemy posts, but by operating the gun himself while the driver of the jeep drove through anything in their path, he contacted the forward troops and brought back the necessary information.

Just before dawn, when the reserve battalions and the anti-tank guns were almost onto their objectives very heavy fire was encountered from the strongly defended enemy locality. There were four machine-gun posts and about five tanks. Capt Upham's Coy was the leading company and he quickly directed the attack on the nearest M.G.s, which were using tracer bullets. He personally led the attack on one post which was silenced and the enemy bayoneted. During the attack Capt Upham was shot in the elbow by machine-gun bullets and his arm broken. He stayed with his men until the objective was captured and until positions were consolidated. He then reported to the R.A.P. and then with his arm in splints, went back to his Coy and stayed with it all day under the most trying conditions of heavy enemy artillery and mortar fire. The enemy made a strong counter-attack late in the afternoon, and Capt Upham was again wounded by mortar fire. He was no longer able to walk. Captain Upham was taken prisoner of war on 15 Jul 42.

After reading this summary and conferring with his advisors, King George VI asked to speak to Freyberg. The general was en route to Italy, so an army dispatch rider was sent to find Major General Kippenberger. Having been grievously injured in a minefield explosion and fitted with artificial lower limbs, Kippenberger was easily recognisable shuffling along the Strand with his cane. The rider pulled alongside and informed him that the king wished to see him. The two men talked in the king's private study.

'Tell me, Kippenberger,' said the king, 'what do you think of Upham yourself? Does he deserve another VC?' Kippenberger replied slowly and carefully, weighing every word with great deliberation: 'I was his Brigadier in North Africa, sir. He did so many brave things, in my respectful opinion, Captain Upham won the VC several times over.'

'Thank you very much, Major General,' replied the king, giving nothing away. The Bar to Charlie's VC was announced in a special edition of the *London Gazette* on 27 September 1945.

§

The first hint Charlie had of his new VC came in the form of footsteps pounding up the stairs to the artist's loft in Christchurch, New Zealand and a breathless telegram boy bursting in to hand him a cable. Charlie thanked him, took a quick look, put it wordlessly in his breast pocket and resumed the pose that Nicoll firmly insisted on. But not quite. After an hour or so, Nicoll put down his brushes. 'Is everything okay, Charlie? Your expression has changed.' Before Charlie could reply, there was more thudding on the stairs and a reporter from the *Star-Sun* rushed in. 'Is it true? Is the news flash true?' For a few brief moments Charlie bristled with defiance then sagged despondently and silently handed over the telegram to him. It was from the Minister of Defence in Wellington:

> I have learnt with very great pleasure that you have been awarded a Bar to the Victoria Cross for most conspicuous bravery and devotion to duty in action. The Prime Minister desires me to convey to you on behalf of the New Zealand Government his heartiest congratulations . . .

The smell of oil paint was joined by the roar of a crowd. That dusk pupils from his old school poured across the road to perform a haka at Upham's front gate while Charlie and his mother looked on from the porch, fighting back tears. The boys sang the school song and called for three cheers. As reporters began arriving, Charlie locked himself in a toilet at the rear of the house. He could hear his mother telling people that he was unavailable. Charlie looked at the small window and contemplated squeezing through it — he was back on that bloody train to Colditz again.

The clamour was worse the next day and worse still the day after that. Charlie's father made slow progress to work along Christchurch pavements with people wanting to shake *his* hand. The phone rang non-stop with old mates and reporters wanting a quick word. Congratulatory cards and letters from the length and breadth of New Zealand and abroad piled up on tables, sideboards and sofas. He got a personal telegram from Prime Minister Peter Fraser:

> On behalf of the government I wish to congratulate you most warmly on the signal honour bestowed upon you by His Majesty the King. All people of New Zealand rejoice at the honour which has been added to your name . . .

Not all people were rejoicing. Charlie wasn't for a start. He couldn't believe it was happening and he was angry that he had been singled out for special mention and attention. When coverage in the papers showed no sign of letting up, Charlie went round to a friend's house, probably so his parents wouldn't hear him lose his rag, and roundly abused the editor of the *Star-Sun* over the phone: 'You print any more of that stupid guff about me and I'll come round and break your neck!'

In London the *Daily Mail* tracked down Molly. She explained that she was waiting for a passage back to New Zealand. She had no idea her husband had done anything special in the desert. He never said anything and got very annoyed whenever she asked him about his war experiences. Back in Christchurch, it became too much for Charlie. Just as Molly predicted, he went bush for two weeks and couldn't be found. Sandford makes reference to a seaside haven at Diamond Harbour with no roads, no phones and no rural delivery. It sounds suspiciously like Quail Island in the middle of Lyttelton Harbour to me. A leper colony was the last place anyone would look. While in isolation and completely undisturbed, Charlie finally had time to write a long letter of condolence to the father of an old friend who was killed in Greece. It is not a standard 'sorry to hear about your sad loss' note but rather a comprehensive explanation of his son's role in the Allied forces' retreat on Greece and a thoughtful tribute to his courage.

> Sunday, 7th October 1945
> Dear Mr Bellringer,
> Thank you for your letter. I found out when I was in England that Trevor had died, but up until when I was made a POW in Italy, '42, I hoped he would turn up. I was an old friend of Trevor's at school and afterwards, and when he went freelancing in England we used to write. I was in Egypt when he and his 7 Anti-Tank Coy. landed and I went down and we had a yarn.

A rare shot of Charlie smiling, showing hitherto unsighted gap in his front teeth. Pictured with an even rarer shot of Field Marshal Bernard Law Montgomery, 1st Viscount Montgomery of Alamein, KG, GCB, DSO, PC, DL admiring someone he admired more than himself — Charlie. Taken in Christchurch, 1947.

Charlie with a man he had the highest regard for, his former commander in chief, Governor General Sir Bernard Freyberg VC. Taken in 1949 at a war memorial ceremony at Lincoln College, Charlie's alma mater.

Charlie and Molly with their brand-new twins, Virginia and Amanda, photographed outside their brand-new house at Parnassus, on their Conway Flat farm south of Kaikoura, North Canterbury.

The Upham girls at the front gate at Conway Flat. The distinctive letterbox was stolen within days of Charlie and Molly leaving the farm for the very last time.

Charlie loved horses and couldn't bear the thought of them being destroyed
at the end of long and loyal service, so he turned his farm into a sanctuary for
unwanted nags.

Charlie and Molly during celebrations of the centenary of the Victoria Cross in London, June 1956.

Proud father of the radiant bride at Caroline's wedding.

Molly and Charlie — last days on the farm before moving to Christchurch.

The beach below Charlie's farm seen through a gap in the cliffs carved by a river.

Commonwealth war graves at Suda Bay, Crete, with snow-capped Lefka Ori mountains in the background.

Cemetery Hill, near Galatas on the Chania coast, Crete, looking south, with the monument to Allied soldiers falling into disrepair.

Above: Forward German position on the El Alamein battlefield. This is the closest Rommel's forces got to Cairo, which is 260 kilometres to the south-east. Another plum target, the ancient port city of Alexandria, is less than half that distance in a straight run, due east along the coast. **Below:** Further east, Montgomery's line in the sand — the Forward Allied position marking the beginning of the minefields between the two great armies who were within shouting distance of each other. Both historic markers are slowly vanishing under the rubble of motorway construction.

Above: The author at an Italian war memorial on the Alamein coast.
Below: At the pyramids.

Above: The distinctive hill behind Weinsberg that the author used as a guide to the former campsite. **Below:** All that's left of the once-sprawling campsite is this small nondescript hut at the end of a dead-end street, backing onto a stream and vineyards. With barred windows, it houses a small museum dedicated to the former POW camp — visits by appointment only.

TOM SCOTT

Above: Brenner Pass, a beautiful alpine pass between Italy and Austria where Hitler and Mussolini famously met several times to discuss Italy's role in Hitler's dark and bloody opera.
Right: The inner courtyard at Colditz Castle on a quiet Sunday morning, March 2019.

TOM SCOTT

Caroline's Andy Warhol-inspired 'Chanel No.5' print, in pride of place in her Gisborne home.

Charlie's coffin being carried into Christ Church Cathedral, 28 November 1994, having just been borne on a gun carriage at a slow march through city streets lined with mourners.

Graveside at the Upham family funeral plot.

Charlie's final resting place — St Paul's Anglican Church Cemetery, Papanui, Christchurch.

Charles Hazlitt Upham, VC & Bar.

The next time I saw him was at the Servia Pass where he was with the 6th Field Arty attached to the 4th Bde. I was in 20 Bttn. 4th Bde. When we pulled out from there, I and my crew helped Trevor's lot drag their guns out of the mud onto the road, we were being heavily shelled. The infantry that the Germans put across the river were all either killed or captured by the 19th Battn. We would never have been beaten out of that position at Servia, but the enemy broke around on each flank and we were lucky not to be cut off. We got out and passed through the 5th Bde. people behind us and that is where Trevor and his guns held off the enemy when they came up and so let the 5th Bde. get clear.

You will wonder why Trevor and his crew were left there. I will try and give you an idea how we fought a retreating battle; it is the hardest sort to fight and in most cases the wounded are left behind, also lots of material. That is how I became a POW later. This is how the campaign went.

The Germans, after a few days, broke right through the Yugoslav army which was not ready or equipped for modern war and came down on to Greece. At the border they were held up by some Aussie infantry, English artillery and N.Z. Machine Gunners and the Greeks. They broke through and were held up again by Aussies and Greeks at Kozane. The Greek army was ill-equipped and had no motor or horse transport. When the Germans broke through in tanks, the Greeks could not retreat and form a line elsewhere. Also the Greeks were fighting a large Italian Army in Albania. We, in the N.Z. Div. and the Aussies and a Bde. of Tommies were strung out along roughly where the Aliakmon River runs across Greece. At this stage the Germans were coming down in three or more columns. We easily held them at our places in the Servia region but they broke through the Greeks on either side. There was only one road to get out, called the British road as we had built it from Athens to Salonika in the last war. It was the only real road in Greece, the railway was bombed out of commission.

The idea was one group would hold the Germans up and blow the road up and cause the Germans who outnumbered us tremendously to deploy. At night we would pull out south and pass through another lot of our chaps and they would hold off the Germans in their turn while we got into a position some 50–80 miles behind them — they would pull out in the night and pass through us and do the same. In this way, by travelling mostly at night, we managed to get 75% of the Greek Expeditionary Force of two Divisions out. We had no tanks, no aeroplanes and no anti-aircraft guns at this stage whereas the Germans had thousands.

While all this was going on, the Divisional Cavalry in armoured cars and the anti-tank regiments with 2 lb guns on trucks would always be the actual rearguards and drove back last, always just in front of the Germans, shooting up any of them that try to come on too fast ahead of their main Force. This was a very perilous job, as the Germans advance first with aeroplanes and then with tanks — the only time they used infantry we easily defeated them at Servia. The only anti-tank gun we had were 2 lb guns and they were not good enough to stop a German tank except at very close range. That meant they had to wait until the tanks were right on them and whilst shooting at one tank the other tanks got sitting shots at the gun and crew. They had more tanks than we had guns. We used our 25 lb field artillery as anti-tank guns as well. Both lots of guns knocked out German tanks and that is why the bulk of the force got out.

Now the reason why Trevor's guns who were up with the 4th Bde at Servia did not go through the 5th Bde at

Bralos Pass must have been the scarcity of anti-tank
guns, normally they would have come back with us to
Thermopylae and then again to Thebes.

As you can see, this fighting against a very much
heavier and better armed force was very different to the
fighting at the end of the war when the boot was on the
other foot and we were on top and chasing the Germans.
A rearguard is the hardest fighting there is, much more
difficult than advance. After the Greek campaign General
Sir Maitland Wilson, who was in charge in Greece, said,
'We did not know of another Division that could have
done as we did.' Those German divisions we and the
Aussies fought were the same ones that advanced later
right across Russia to Stalingrad and were later beaten to
a pulp there.

It was because Trevor and people like him stood to
their guns to the last, that the N.Z. and Aussies and
Tommys got away (or 75% did) otherwise there would
not have been a N.Z. Division and there would not have
been a Suez Canal or anything else afterwards. I cannot
understand why Trevor's great work there and his mates
was not recognised, the man in charge of them who
knew all about it was most likely killed himself soon
afterwards. I'm sorry to say there were many and always
will be many such cases. It is always the best men who
were killed, the last to leave in a retreat and the first to
advance in advance. It is because people like your Trevor
got killed that we are now living in peace and plenty. My
brother-in-law was killed in Italy and no officer wrote
to my sister or said how it happened or anything, it
is always possible that the only ones who knew were
themselves killed or made POW.

I hope I have helped you picture what happened.
You see, it was the anti-tank boys with their little 2 lb
guns and the Divisional Cavalry in their armoured cars

who kept us always in touch with advance guard of the
Germans and held them up to let the other forces get
away on ahead. Later in the desert and Italy, the Division
got better long-range and harder hitting guns and they
could knock out the German tanks with much less loss to
themselves.

I knew quite a few of Trevor's mates in the 7th Anti-
Tank Regt. and they all thought such a lot of him. He
was a real soldier, it is unfortunate for the world that in
every army those are the people who get killed, maimed
and overrun; the ones who stand their ground. I hope
this long letter is of some use to you, Mr. Bellringer, in
understanding how things were there. Trevor was one
of my real friends at school and was often round at our
house where I am . . .

I am yours very sincerely,
Charles Upham, ex. N. Z. E. F.

Charlie came out of seclusion a few days after writing this
letter, for a state luncheon held in Parliament Buildings in
honour of all the New Zealand winners of the VC. Politicians
from both sides of the House made fulsome speeches and
proposed toasts. Charlie replied on behalf of the recipients. He
began by insisting that he was the representative of 100,000
others whose exploits were as fitting of reward as his:

'One thing I would ask is, when these men come back,
people who are in a position to do so should show them
thanks in a practical way. There will be among them
men who are maimed, still suffering from wounds, ill, or
mentally ill. They will need homes, furniture and jobs.
Please show them your practical help and your greatest
patience . . .'

Perhaps unwittingly, perhaps not, Charlie was making a

plea in mitigation for himself as well. He returned south to the fresh hell of the mayor of Christchurch, backed by the editor of *The Press*, launching a campaign to raise £10,000 to buy him a farm as a present from the grateful people of Canterbury. The idea appalled him. As Charlie told a mate: 'What would be the good of having a farm and having every bastard going past saying I put a hundred quid into that farm.'

He wrote to the mayor:

> I am deeply conscious of the honour intended to be bestowed upon me and I shall always carry with me the knowledge in my heart that the people of Canterbury wish to pay me such a wonderful tribute. The military honours bestowed on me are property of the men of my unit as well as myself. Under no circumstance could I consent to any material gain for myself that I, in conjunction with 100,000 more, rendered to the Empire in her hour of need. Could I suggest, sir, that the fund which you all so generously proposed to give me be used to alleviate genuine distress among children of those men who gave their all for us, and to help brighten the lives of those men who because of some war disability are unable to lead a full life in the community . . .

The fundraising continued on that basis. Over £10,000 was quickly subscribed. The money went into a Charles Upham Scholarship Fund to award study grants to the children of servicemen attending Lincoln College or Canterbury University.

But Charlie did finally get his farm.

Chapter 18

'I don't want to be treated different to any other bastard'

Charlie paid for a farm himself with the help of a government rehabilitation loan.

Contrary to rumour and scuttlebutt, which persists in some quarters to this day, there was no under-the-counter deal, no rigged draw with Charlie's number on every marble, and Charlie's name was not pulled from a hat where every slip of paper had 'Upham' written on it.

Phil Bennett from the Land Settlement Board, the body who assessed and approved Charlie's eligibility for a rehabilitation loan (made available to all returning servicemen except Maori, to New Zealand's eternal shame), emphasised this point in detailed communications with Sandford. Following up on McFarlane's phone call about his plans for Rafa Downs, while his son was still at sea, Upham senior contacted the Land Settlement Board in Wellington expressing an interest in one of the blocks. When Charlie arrived home, Bennett rang him at the height of the giddy, flamboyant talk of buying him a farm wherever he wished free of all cost as a national gift, and as a consequence Charlie was blunt and uncooperative.

He softened when told a subdivision of Rafa Downs was 'for sale' and 'would not be' a gift.

Bennett:

> It was necessary for him to come to Wellington. He was still very much incognito and out of circulation. I could not get him to leave Christchurch until I had assured him of complete secrecy and no publicity. We arranged for him to be flown up one afternoon. There was a spare seat on an Air Force flight. He was met at Rongotai and brought to the Waterloo Hotel where I was waiting in the foyer. I asked him if there was anything he wanted me to do. I have met many hundreds of lads and quite a number have been difficult, but never have I felt anyone put the aggressiveness of his whole personality into a question as he turned to face me full on and barked out, 'There is only one bloody thing I want.' 'What's that?' I asked. 'I don't want to be treated different to any other bastard.' I stepped back at pace. I looked him up and down from his toes to his head, and with a tenseness that tried to match his aggressiveness, said, 'And why the bloody hell should you be?' When we got back to tin tacks re Rafa Downs we found a roading problem that ruled the place out for ordinary settlement and I suggested to the P.M. and L.S.B., [Land Settlement Board] and Rehab endorsed it, that the State undertake the roading in recognition of C's deeds and it not be loaded onto the land in any way. P.M's only condition was that a good job be done. This, as far as I know, was the country's 'thank you'.

So, at the age of thirty-seven in 1945, Charlie became the proud purchaser and owner of a 385-hectare block of land that had previously been part of Rafa Downs. Charles and Molly would name it Lansdowne in memory of an ancestral holding. At a meeting of departmental heads, the prime minister reminded everyone that the vehicle access they were going to bulldoze through needed to be designated a public road or Charlie would baulk at the proposal. Other farmers would use it as well. They were just bringing forward work that would have been done in the future in any event. As stipulated by the prime minister, a good job was done by the Ministry of Works employees, but not at the rate Charlie wanted: 'If that bloody road is not finished in three bloody days, I'm going to break some necks.'

The road gang were scared stiff of him. Likewise, surveyors marking out his property were given a hurry-up and sprinted up hill and down dale, through gorse, manuka, kanuka, marshy swamp and swollen creeks lugging heavy tripods and theodolites. Charlie wanted lots done in readiness for Molly's return.

December finally came round. Charlie took the overnight ferry to Wellington. He was on the dock, almost certainly clutching red roses, when the *Mooltan* tied up and Molly waved to him from the deck. They moved to their partially broken-in half-wild, half-tame block of land at the end of the half-finished road, living with the McFarlanes while foundations were being laid and plans finalised for their new house by an architect who had been a POW with Charlie. The blueprints included an extra-large living room because of his post-capture aversion to confined spaces. With the house built on a plateau above the coast, the lounge and kitchen would take full advantage of sweeping vistas of the majestic Seaward Kaikoura mountains to the north.

There was a huge amount of work to be done to get his property into working order. Conway Flat was a raw and wild place back then. The last eight miles of the road were loose, rutted shingle. There was no bridge over the Conway River. It had to be forded, always a challenge after heavy rain inland. And the rain was often heavy inland. In winter everyone was blocked in for weeks on end.

They had to wait years for a bridge to be built and for power to reach them. Living off the grid, they had a small petrol-driven generator for lighting and powering their radios. Kerosene fridges worked well enough until they flared up, blackening the contents and tainting everything with an unpleasant smell and off-putting taste. When the phone was eventually put in it was a party line, with a crank handle. People could eavesdrop on each other's calls, but not easily — the line was dreadful. Charlie objected strenuously to the cost of telephone poles and rigged up his own using manuka poles along his section of roadway.

All the properties stepped up in bush-clad terraces to the jagged summit of the Hundalee Hills, where wild pigs and deer proliferated. Charlie said: 'Going there after the war was like being pioneers. The land was in infancy. A farm had to be carved out of the scrub.'

Through back-breaking toil they slowly prevailed, clearing manuka, kanuka and fern, except in deep gorges and ravines where it persists to this day, along with virgin bush not burnt off by the first settlers or destroyed in lightning strikes or ignited by flaming meteorites. After ploughing and discing the rich soil, they sowed pasture. It was heart-breaking when wild pigs came down from the ranges and rooted up whole paddocks and more heart-breaking still when they came down and feasted on newborn lambs.

His neighbour's teenage sons, the Wilding brothers, Frank and Peter, accompanied Charlie on many a pig hunt. At the back of beyond at a place called Arkansas Ridge, one afternoon Charlie's dogs bailed up a monster boar, and one of the party fired off a .303 round, wounding the big tusker, which hurtled angrily into dense scrub, chased on foot by Charlie. They could hear man and boar madly thrashing about, one cursing vividly and the other squealing loudly. The Wilding boys caught glimpses of the whirling mêlée and thought Charlie's number was up. The boar had one huge, curled tusk caught in

Charlie's belt, narrowly missing goring him in the abdomen, and was tossing Charlie about like toilet paper stuck on the sole of a shoe. The precise details are lost in the mists of time, but somehow the boar was shot in the skull at point-blank range, quite possibly with the US Army pistol that Charlie had brought back from Colditz. Charlie survived with just a few cuts and bruises and with intestines and vital organs intact.

One dawn in December 1946, by the light of a hurricane lantern with no glass bulb, Charlie was pouring petrol from a can into his Morris Oxford. Petrol spilled, fumes ignited and within seconds dry grass was on fire. Attempting to put it out with a sack, Charlie set his strides on fire. It was too far to run and plunge into the sea. He rolled on the ground to put himself out. A neighbour ran to tell Molly that her husband was on fire and swearing graphically. Charlie said it was nothing and next morning drove to Christchurch as planned. He had a meeting with the builder who reported later that Charlie never let on that he was in agony. Late in the day he went to Christchurch Hospital emergency rooms, dropped his tweeds and was immediately rushed into surgery. He spent two months in Christchurch and Burwood hospitals getting skin grafts. For several months after that, he was an outpatient, which required regular trips into the city.

Charlie needed a driver. Frank Wilding stepped in. As a result, the two became close friends. 'It was about five hours to Christchurch in those days,' said Frank. In the neighbourhood there were two returned servicemen needing skin grafts — the other one an old army mate of Charlie's — and Frank drove them regularly to Christchurch Hospital to get the wounds seen to and dressings changed.

'I remember Charles had a terrible injury as a result of the war — one arm was completely useless. He had to support his arm and it would do odd things. He got round it though; it certainly didn't impede his ability to farm.'

But he did need driving to hospital, and then, of course, he had to go to lots of official functions, although he hated leaving his family, and he detested all the fuss.

> 'He did enjoy meeting his old friends, and the two returned soldiers certainly needed a driver then, especially coming home after a few whiskies. At first I addressed him formally as he was "Mr Upham", and then as I grew older and came to know him he became just "Charles" and, eventually, "Charlie" to me.'

They were the closest of mates until the end of Charlie's days. Frank has passed away now too. I was lucky to meet him in time.

§

Charlie's daughter Amanda put me onto Frank. I spoke to him briefly on the phone, then booked the next available flight to Blenheim. It was pitch-black and the rain was horizontal when I clambered into my Hilux for the short drive from my house on the edge of Wellington's town belt to the airport. It's a heavy vehicle with a truck chassis considered dangerous in road accidents because it crumples other cars. It's favoured by ISIS *and* American military contractors conducting Black Ops in Iraq and Syria because it *never* stalls at the lights. It's the truck Jeremy Clarkson couldn't kill on *Top Gear*. But it was no match for the winds buffeting the capital. Several times I feared being flipped over or blown off the road on the Lyall Bay foreshore.

My flight to Blenheim was delayed forty minutes while they cleared clumps of seaweed whipped out of the ocean and dumped on the runway. In the dark, with lashing rain and strobing orange lights of airport rescue vehicles, it looked as if miniature Highland cattle were sleeping on the tarmac. Once in the air, our turboprop climbed vertically like the Space Shuttle. Magically, the weather improved the instant we were clear of Cook Strait.

My brother-in-law Grant accompanied me. We drove down the ruggedly beautiful Marlborough coast in bright sunshine. First stop was Rafa Downs, a secret strip of wild North Canterbury coastline only reachable through the Conway River gorge. We had lunch on the lawn of Frank and Jo Wilding's property, looking back at the brutal beauty of the Seaward Kaikouras plunging into the dark Pacific. Frank, stooped but still massive and powerful well into his eighties, was as sharp as the blades in his small sawmill sheltering in the Garden of Eden at the rear of his house where avocados, grapes and oranges defied the climate. He spoke with an easy grace and the comic timing of a born raconteur.

Frank had been a student at Charlie's old schools, boarding at Waihi and Christ's College, where boys and staff gathered around radios to listen to Charlie's VC broadcast from the Western Desert. Frank had followed the war closely. The whole school did. Once a week in assembly there were casualty reports of former pupils. Old boys' deaths were acknowledged with prayers and a minute's silence.

Frank spent school holidays back at Conway Flat. The air force used one of their big paddocks as a refuelling depot for light aircraft en route from Blenheim air base in Marlborough to Wigram air base just out of Christchurch.

It was before the road was put in. When it was time to send stock to the saleyards or the freezing works, his father and Doug McFarlane mustered sheep and drove herds of cattle along the beach below the high cliffs along the grey-sand and gravel shore running beside the ocean to the main road.

Early in 1946, Frank left school when he was sixteen to work full-time on the family farm, Te Mana. He felt very proud of driving Charlie and the other returned soldier to

Christchurch in an old Ford Mercury. While doctors monitored their recovery and nurses changed their dressings, Frank went to the pictures. One trip home they stopped to buy fish and chips. The owner, a Yugoslav, wouldn't sell Frank a pack of cigarettes because of his age. Charlie lost his temper and called the owner 'a fucking Nazi'. Frank smiled fondly at the memory. 'Jeez, Charlie was impressive in full rage. He could get momentarily very violent.'

Frank went off message momentarily to tell the story of Charlie attempting to emasculate a notoriously wild bull with a knife. Locked in a pen in Charlie's yards, the bull took a dim view of the castration procedure and lashed out with his hind limbs, splintering timber and sending Charlie flying. Frank happened to be passing, saw the demolition in progress, and stopped to help Charlie complete the castration. But even outnumbered, the bull wasn't having a bar of it. 'Fuck it!' said Charlie. 'I'll shoot the bastard.'

Charlie didn't shoot the Yugoslav. They hopped back in the Ford Mercury and all lit up cigarettes. Charlie had already calmed down. Leaning back in his seat, he ventured that the Yugoslav was just being a prick. The rest of the trip passed without incident in convivial silence.

The towering teenager and the diminutive war hero with the itchy trigger finger became close friends. Frank happily became Charlie's designated driver long after his wounds had healed. When Charlie had RSA functions to attend or civic duties to perform far afield, Frank would do the honours and drive Charlie there and back, which meant Charlie could relax and have a drink or two and not worry about driving inebriated.

Frank said Charlie would sometimes talk about the war on these long trips, but only if he was in the mood and never when prompted. He could be hilarious and at other times his tales were harrowing and shocking. Like the time in North Africa when Charlie and his boys overran enemy lines. Germans in slit trenches surrendered en masse. The New Zealanders were in a hurry and told them to keep their hands up and kept on running. They hadn't gone far when the Germans started shooting them in the back, very badly as luck would have it, then the Germans ran to their parked trucks and high-tailed it into the desert. Two nights later on patrol along the Libyan coast, the Kiwis came across a two-storey house with colonnaded balconies surrounding an inner courtyard where the trucks they recognised from forty-eight hours earlier were parked, with German soldiers fast asleep in the back. They crept close and hurled grenades. Trucks and half-tracks burst into flames. Ammunition and petrol tanks started exploding. Men started screaming. A German officer dashed out onto the balcony cursing and damning the New Zealanders. Racing upstairs, Charlie's men grabbed him by his arms and legs and tossed him over the balustrade into the fireball. For good reason, this story did not make it into *Mark of the Lion*.

With palpable love and affection, Frank described a tough, blunt, irascible but honourable man with a strong sense of duty — well read and curious about the world, with well-considered, crisply enunciated views on the issues of the day. 'His advice, if you asked for it, was so well thought out that he was a really wonderful person to have in your life.' Frank had many fond memories of him.

'Once we took the harvester down the beach behind the crawler to do some harvesting for him. The tractors and headers were my father's. My brother Peter and I were being paid by my father and wouldn't accept anything from Charles, so he gave me a pistol. When he had been released from Colditz it was by the Americans, and he advanced with them into Germany for several days. Of course, he needed to be armed, so they gave him a .32 Colt pistol, which he in turn gave to me for doing this harvesting work. At my age at the time it was wonderful to have — I was about seventeen or eighteen, I suppose, and I was very impressed. I gave it to his son-in-law in the end. No one is quite sure where it is now and there are conflicting stories about its origin. When it surfaces it might have a serial number that will help put the matter beyond doubt.'

When Charlie Upham and Miles Handyside bought their respective properties, both places were overrun with wild cattle. Frank remembers it well. 'They allowed us to go out and shoot them and, as kids, we'd go out and shoot some beef.'

Charlie became a local identity, and he opened the refurbished community tennis courts by carefully pouring a bottle of champagne on them after laying out the nets for the first time. According to Frank,

'Charles did a lot of things here, such as opening the hall . . . he was like the patron of it all. He was very interested in helping returned service people and helping the locals. He always used to go to the hall and play Father Christmas.'

He also got roped in to presenting awards at school prize-givings, cups at sports days, ribbons at Agricultural & Pastoral shows, was the guest of honour and kissed all the girls on the cheek at debutante balls all over Marlborough and dressed as Santa and handed out presents at Conway Flat School Christmas parties. Charlie was so busy in fact that Frank became concerned his old friend hadn't seen enough of his sons-in-law. The Wildings invited Charles up to their family bach, which Frank had built close to the water's edge at Torrent Bay, in the Abel Tasman National Park.

'I arranged for the two sons-in-law to come at the same time. I remember Molly saying Charles wasn't very well.

When we left, she told me not to give him any whisky —
to give him a sherry. Charles gave her an odd look. We
got up to Torrent Bay and I said, "Charles, would you like
a sherry?", and he just looked at me until I poured him a
whisky! That time gave him an opportunity to talk to his
sons-in-law . . . he really did enjoy talking to people.'

Frank and Jo wanted me to know that there was another side
to their old friend that was less volatile, more easy-going,
amusing and readily amused, curious and knowledgeable
about all manner of subjects. True, he liked a good argument
and debated issues vigorously, loud and long, but without
the fury that previously chilled friend and foe alike. He loved
yarning about the old days, especially about his time on
Molesworth Station before the war. He particularly enjoyed
reminiscing about the horses and dogs he had owned.
Animals and his family brought out the soft, gentle side of
his nature. In reality he was far removed from the tough,
uncompromising man that many believed him to be.

Frank explained that, above all, Charlie could be absurdly
kind and generous to a fault. Like his namesake, Lyttelton's
Little Doctor, Charlie was a soft touch for anyone with a horse
they wanted to get rid of. Friends, neighbours and complete
strangers from further afield took advantage of Charlie's
unwillingness to turn away a horse in need of a home. Ex-
racehorses, ex-trotters, ex-stockhorses and busted-arse hacks
and nags of every stripe in every stage of decline ended up
ending their days on Charlie's farm — the equine equivalent of
his uncle's leper colony.

Quite by chance he accumulated some good stock as well,
the odd thoroughbred, mares still able to breed and a virile
stallion or two. Eventually, he had an unmanageable horse
herd eating him out of house and home at Lansdowne. Most
of them were worthless old hacks of no value apart from
dog tucker or glue, but Charlie would only put a horse down

if it was an act of mercy, and even then with the utmost reluctance. I once asked Amanda if she ever saw her father cry. She replied that it was very rare, and only when he had to shoot a favourite dog — to put it out of its misery if it was suffering in some way, and tears would stream down his face.

In the late 1950s, Charlie heard that a big block of land was up for sale, 16 kilometres up the main highway north towards Kaikoura, called Rocky Peaks. Charlie rode up to take a good look and liked what he saw — hill country that had once been a part of the huge Kahukura Run. He thought it ideal to graze the overflow from his ever-expanding flock of half-bred wethers and also as a possible sanctuary for his ever-expanding horse herd.

His offer for the block was accepted. He turned his wethers out to graze on Rocky Peaks and relocated his horse sanctuary up there as well. Somewhat fancifully, Charlie thought that if he introduced a good stallion and let nature take its course, over time he might breed a superior sturdy, hill-country hack that he could sell for good money. It wasn't all the introduced superior stallion's doing, but very soon Charlie had over a hundred feral horses running in separate mobs, each ruled by a dominant stallion.

Dreams of sales of a superior breed of farm hack did not eventuate. Even so, Charlie often rode out to Rocky Peaks to check on them. His daughter Virginia Mackenzie believed he took a great deal of comfort and joy from just simply looking over the fence, sucking on his pipe and watching his spirited horses roaming free, unfettered, untamed and unbowed.

The 1980s were tough times for farming, the new Labour Government changed the rules, pulling the plug on farming privileges, axing subsidies, and then meat and wool prices slumped. It was not a good time to put property on the market, especially Rocky Peaks, because it came with protected tenants — 150 wild horses, that much like their North Island counterparts, the wild Kaimanawa horses of the Central Plateau and Desert Road, had evolved into small, sturdy, aggressive animals perfectly acclimatised to harsh hill country.

In 1985 when the adjoining property, the last chunk of the original Okarahia Downs Station, came on the market it was snapped up by Richard Watherston, a young man who, like Charlie, had mustered in Otago and in South and Mid Canterbury and, like Charlie, had worked as a contract fencer.

According to Frank, Charlie said to Richard one day, 'I'm selling the farm and I've decided you will buy it because I know you will look after the horses.'

Once the two parties had agreed on a fair price the deal was sealed with a handshake with one stipulation — Richard had to adopt Charlie's horses and become patron of Charlie's equine rest home. Richard agreed. He would keep as many horses as he could for as long as he could. He became the new owner of a lush property, the last of Charlie's wethers, plus 150 wild horses, much to the envy of other locals who coveted the prime land but never got a look-in.

Never look a gift horse in the mouth, not 150 wild ones anyway, but Richard couldn't fail to notice alpha stallions fighting viciously for control over the harems of mares. These were brutal encounters, full of kicking and biting. Several times he saw horrific fights that ended in stallions killing one another. Even if a battle didn't end in death, it almost always ended with one stallion badly injured, limping and bleeding. A dominant stallion would also kill or drive off any rising colt that he considered a threat to his leadership of his herd. It could be dangerous for Richard entering Rocky Peaks' paddocks riding a mare. Several times he had to drive off aggressive stallions with his shepherd's crook.

As well as vicious competition they were capable of extraordinary cooperation. He once witnessed a bunch of wild horses burst out of one paddock into another with better pasture by forming a battering ram and galloping in a tight bunch, twenty strong, headlong straight at the fence and through sheer weight of numbers ripping it asunder and trampling it underfoot. The first horses, flipping over top wires, landed awkwardly and were cut and dazed, the rest, an unstoppable tidal wave of pounding horse flesh, swept through the 30-metre-wide gap. How Charlie would have loved to have seen that — the perfect re-enactment of the breakout from Minqar Qaim.

In October 2000 Charlie's three daughters, enjoying a reunion in the South Island, called in at Okarahia Downs to enquire about the wild horses. Richard happily drove them out to Rocky Peaks. The herd had been culled for practical reasons, but Charlie's daughters took comfort in seeing many of their dad's beloved horses running wild and free as he would have wanted.

§

Frank says that Upham had no time for real estate agents and preferred to do things his own way. When Charlie finally decided to sell Lansdowne, he naturally approached Frank.

> 'We were his next-door neighbours then and he said one day, "I'm going to sell but I want to keep the house, so the logical person to buy is you because you won't need the house." And I told him it suited me down to the ground. We bought the land and, later, when he and Molly sold the house, I was once again asked if I would like to buy it because he didn't want to be dealing with "bloody real estate agents". So that's how it happened, and in November 1993 we purchased the house.'

At the time, Charlie and Molly were looking to buy a flat in Christchurch.

Frank's son, Tim, recounts how every Saturday Frank used to collect the newspaper from the drop-off at the entrance to Conway Flat and take it to Charlie, every Saturday, every week without fail.

Tim also remembers nights around the table listening to yarns:

> 'I always regret not having had a tape recorder with Charlie because when we were small, we used to hear all these incredible war stories while sitting around the dining-room table. Dad would feed Charlie up with a couple of whiskies, and some of the most amazing stories used to come out. The two of them used to go up to Torrent Bay together a bit, and I guess like everyone when they get a bit older, they sort of loosened up and told wonderful stories.'

In respect of Charlie's medals, Frank feels that the Upham girls did the right thing in selling them. 'Charles treated his Victoria Crosses as something he had that would set up his girls for life. He never talked about them; he always said that other people deserved them more.'

Clearly, Charlie made a huge impression on those who lived side by side with him after the war. As Frank says,

> 'He was absolutely trustworthy, and expected everyone else to be. If people were interested in him, he was interested in them. He had one of the best brains I've ever come across. I don't think he ever regretted anything he did in the war — he did a job that had to be done. He mellowed over time. I remember him giving me a frightful ticking off because I bought a German tractor, and then, of course, I got my own back when he bought a Japanese car — a Datsun!'

Listener columnist Denis Welch knew nothing about the softening of Charlie's fabled Axis Powers motor vehicle prohibition when he attended the formal opening in April 1990 of the Atatürk memorial on the ridge above Tarakena Bay on Wellington's wild south coast, built overlooking Cook Strait because of its uncanny resemblance to the landscape of the Gallipoli Peninsula. Charlie was one of the VIPs attending the ceremony. Afterwards as everyone headed down the path to the car park, Charlie, eagle-eyed as always, must have noted Denis taking shorthand, deduced that he was a reporter and asked him if he had a car. Denis confirmed that he did, and Charlie asked if he and his old mates could cadge a ride to the airport.

Denis, who drove a rusting Toyota at the time, started quietly shitting himself. The old diggers had been on the turps for most of the day. Full bladders needed to be emptied. Into spinifex and flax as it happens and not over Denis's car which he feared, so Denis was hugely relieved as well. Everyone squeezed in and the short, nerve-wracking journey in a Japanese car was completed with no one commenting on the country of manufacture.

§

It was exhilarating and a privilege to hear the stories about what Charlie did and who he was. When I asked what Charlie's most defining characteristics were, Frank listed honesty, loyalty and integrity — which didn't surprise. He added kindness and generosity — which I wasn't expecting. Charlie was a kind man, albeit with a quick temper if he thought something was wrong, unjust or just plain daft and stupid. They all commented on his piercing gaze, which you had to meet head on if you were to gain his respect. They also noted his physical toughness. His left arm was next to useless after the war, but he didn't shy away from hard physical labour and he drove his open-topped Land Rover in all sorts of weather. Charlie also had a good sense of humour. Frank recounted some yarns just as Charlie had told them to him. They were wry, self-deprecating, deftly observed and hugely entertaining.

The Wildings took Grant and me further up the coast road to the old Upham homestead. It was a modest bungalow because after the war there were strict limits on the size of the house you could build with a rehab loan. As they earned his trust, Charlie opened up to Frank and Richard about his war experiences. He told them shocking stories that never made it into the pages of *Mark of the Lion*, which is probably no bad thing.

We discussed at some length Charlie's emotional state near the end of the war. They believe he was very depressed but doubt that he was suicidal. They were adamant he never had a death wish. They insisted he loved life too much for that. They are horrified by theories postulated that he was merely a killing machine. He was certainly very efficient at killing Germans. As he told Frank and Richard, he just did what had to be done. War was brutal and sometimes necessary — and sometimes it was necessary for good men to do brutal things. What set him apart was he did these things better than everyone else.

I enquired into the urban legend that Charlie shot at Japanese squid boats fishing off the coast. This legend has some basis in fact, even if it has grown somewhat over the years. Apparently, one afternoon Charlie turned up at Frank's place sheepishly admitting he may have overstepped the mark. Elaborating, he said that driving home earlier that day — a rare day when the Pacific lived up to its name and was calm and still — Charlie spotted a squid boat bobbing just beyond the breakers and some fishermen having a picnic on the shingle shore below the cliffs of his property. Fetching his .303, he put a single shot through the wheelhouse of their boat. The driftwood bonfire was abandoned and they rowed frenziedly back to their boat and hoisted anchor.

The squid-boat captain later contacted the Japanese

Embassy in Wellington, who contacted the Christchurch police, who contacted the police at Amberley, who sent a senior sergeant out to have a quiet word with Charlie and take temporary possession of his Winchester rifle.

That story dovetailed neatly with a similar one that the multiple award-winning and multiple Oscar-nominated production designer and art director Dan Hennah shared with me. Many years ago, he was the skipper of a deep-sea trawler working out of the port of Nelson. In the mid-80s, after a break on dry land, Dan was back in the wheelhouse of his boat checking charts in preparation for another voyage to their favourite fishing grounds off South Westland, when two of his hardest, toughest, roughest deckhands joined him for a natter and a smoke. Dan asked casually how their Easter shore leave went and they went pale and like the Ancient Mariner they had a ghastly tale burning within that needed to be told.

They had been deer stalking in the Hundalee Range above Conway Flat and ventured too low. They were sneaking stealthily through tussock and straggly shrub below the bush-line when one of them felt a rifle barrel prod him in the small of his back and heard a cold voice snarl, 'You bastards are trespassing! This is my land!' The deckhand spun around and found himself staring into the coldest blue eyes he'd ever seen belonging to a small, white-haired old man, whose icy calm made the encounter all the more chilling. 'Hands up. Drop your guns!' Disarming their weapons, he told them to bugger off and never come back. They had no problem with that last stipulation — nothing would induce them to return. Both men had never been so terrified in their lives and felt even worse later when they worked out that they had run foul of Charlie Upham VC & Bar.

Chapter 19

'Boy, she knows her horses, that girl'

Given their father's great love of horses, it was only natural that the Upham daughters — the twins Amanda and Virginia, and later Caroline — learned to ride almost *in utero* and competed in gymkhanas growing up.

As a young teen, Caroline was riding her horse along the beach one day, cantering through shallows, when the gelding got jittery and her dogs started yapping and yelping. She turned around to check on the fuss and saw a large orca perched up on the sudsy, draining gravel and sand, having launched itself out of the foaming, churning water. It caught its breath before heaving itself back into the ocean.

Years later, National Geographic film crews and David Attenborough's BBC Wildlife teams shot chilling footage of 'killer whales', hunting in packs to tip seals off ice floes and snatch sea lions off lonely shores.

With or without the spectre of lurking orca, the sea below the cliffs of the Upham farm, while beautiful, is uninviting. The undertow and rips look too fierce, the surf too bruising and the water too cold. Charlie would only allow the twins to swim in the sea if they were roped to the shore. He would drive a stake deep into the sand, tie one end of a long, strong rope to it and secure the other end around their waists and watch over them carefully as they waded into the surf to be tossed about like socks in a tumble dryer.

A safer solution to the long, scorching North Canterbury summers came in the form of Charlie's swimming pool — an open-topped steel tube that Charlie had made for them from an old milk tanker tank, sliced horizontally like a baguette with the two halves welded together, end to end, to make it longer. It is still there, cantilevered drunkenly out over the small woody creek running beside the house paddock. Supplied from upstream, leaf tannin and other organic compounds discoloured the water to the point where it resembled strong woolshed tea. To give it a more refreshing and tropical aesthetic, Molly used Hansells blue food colouring and little cotton satchels of Reckitt's washing blue to rectify the situation, which meant the girls ended the summers with a pronounced blue rinse each, something that didn't seem to dent their popularity. If anything, it put them ahead of the curve. They predated punk by fifteen years.

They were always ahead of the curve. In 1966 Charlie and Molly came back from a trip to Australia with a copy of the Beatles' *A Hard Day's Night*, which wasn't yet available in New Zealand, and it got a thrashing on the gramophone in Caroline's bedroom. When the Beatles performed two shows in Christchurch's Majestic Theatre later that year, Amanda and Virginia were shouted tickets to one of the shows by their parents and took the bus up from their Timaru boarding school, returning to Craighead Diocesan later that night. Aged thirteen, Caroline was deemed too young to attend the concert.

§

Miles Handyside's son, Dennis, farmed in the southern Wairarapa. I drove over the Rimutakas on a grey and mournful Sunday and talked to him in his modern, light and airy, architecturally arresting home nestled snugly into rolling vineyard country south of Martinborough, filled with his wife's stunning artwork and his beautifully hand-carved wooden bowls. He went to the same one-classroom, twenty-six-pupil primary school in Conway Flat as the Upham girls, who, he said, were a lot of fun. His wife went to the same boarding school as the Upham twins, Craighead Diocesan in Timaru, and remembers them as stunning, lively, exotic and attractive girls. Even without their father's famous name, they stood out in the crowd.

Lively, headstrong and fearless like their father, the girls were good at sport, especially swimming and athletics. Doe-eyed, lithe and pencil slim, they were picture-perfect amalgams of sixties' fashion icons, film stars, pop singers and models like Jean Shrimpton, Charlotte Rampling, Jane Asher and Twiggy, and were never short of suitors and admirers. When puberty struck them, Charlie must have spent many a sleepless night longing for Weinsberg's high double-boundary perimeter fencing with fierce dogs, watchtowers and searchlights placed at regular intervals.

§

Conway Flat used to be called 'Gong Alley' because most of the husbands were highly decorated returned servicemen. In those early days living off the grid, with no phone and never enough money, it was tough going for everyone, but they were all in the same boat. They chipped in and helped each other. Being isolated, they had to make their own fun, and they did, heaps of it. Women shared secrets and baby clothes, the men shared farm equipment, lent each other a hand in myriad ways, large and small, and became good mates. So what happened between Miles and Charlie — who got on well with everyone else but not each other? Where had the bad blood come from?

Much like his father, I suspect, Dennis Handyside struck

me as a sensible, composed, measured man. He knew about tensions between his father and Charlie. He accepted that every man of that generation came back from war damaged to some degree, including his father, who never smoked, never drank and never spoke badly about Charlie, though he might have had good cause on occasion. Apparently, his mother, Betty, had no time for Charlie and made her feelings plain. Mrs Handyside attributed strange nocturnal scraping sounds along the weatherboard cladding of their house to Charlie stalking their property in the dead of night and running a broom or rake along exterior walls.

Frank Wilding said the feud began early on with a sheep-drafting incident. Charlie and Miles preferred different breeds. When a mixed load arrived by truck and trailer at a common stockyard, they had to be separated. Operating the drafting gate at the head of the race leading to different holding pens, Miles was too vigorous in shutting the gate and snapped the neck of one of Charlie's ewes, killing it instantly.

Charlie was ropeable. Miles apologised profusely and offered Charlie one of his sheep by way of recompense and replacement, which should have been the end of the matter. But no, like a child that has dropped an ice cream on the ground, Charlie didn't want *any* old replacement — he wanted *that* ice cream. Nothing else would do. For quite some time, nothing would satisfy Charlie but the dead sheep brought back to life.

Then there was the time one of Charlie's ewes strayed onto Miles's property. As soon as he spotted the trespasser, again with possibly too much vigour, Miles marked it with copious quantities of identifying raddle, heaving it back over the boundary fence when he got the chance. A few weeks later when one of Miles's ewes ventured into one of Charlie's paddocks, it was returned smeared in so much different-coloured raddle it looked like it had come straight from the Holi festival of colours in the Punjab or an explosion in a paint factory.

Charlie was a good farmer and prided himself on his fine wool clip. It always fetched top dollar and he was very protective of his flock.

Miles wasn't the only former soldier that Charlie clashed with over sheep. He had a run-in with another neighbour, Derek Anderson, quite possibly as a consequence of the crackly phone line. One evening Charlie rang Derek to inform him that he would be shifting sheep from his top farm the next day and asked whether Derek had any plans to use the road. Derek didn't and assured Charlie that the road was his.

The Met office said it would be a scorcher and they were right. To the north, wearing a shawl of fresh spring snow, the Seaward Kaikouras rose purple and blue into a clear, cloudless sky. Closer to home, tablelands cleaved with ravines dense with black beech, kanuka and manuka stepped down in ancient marine terraces to cliffs running along a savage misted shore. Massive breakers rolling in from a cobalt Pacific smacked into banks of grey shingle and were sucked away, leaving cobwebs of foam. Memories of this landscape were all that kept Charlie from completely unravelling in the dark years behind wire.

It was early and the day was already heating up. Two hundred ewes panting in their winter fleeces trotted ahead of him, kicking up dust along a gravel road lined with poplar, wattle and macrocarpa. Birds sang, bees droned, flies buzzed, butterflies floated, cicadas clacked back and forth in rhyme, trees whispered and sighed in the breeze, lupin seeds snapped, crackled and popped in the heat. Charlie stood in his open-topped Land Rover. With his buggered left arm, he shook a rattle made from tin-can lids threaded onto wire. Rolled-up sleeves revealed angry white scars on tanned skin. He put fingers into his mouth and whistled to his darting, quicksilver dogs.

Charlie was in no hurry. Controlling the steering with his knees, he spread loose Park Drive tobacco along a slip of Zig-Zag paper, licked the top edge, rolled it into a tube and reached for matches. There was an ocean breeze on his face. Warm sun on his shoulders eased the ache in old wounds. He drew smoke into his lungs and exhaled contentedly. You wouldn't want to be dead for quids. Approaching Hundalee, Charlie's expression curdled as swiftly as a pH change in a laboratory beaker in third-form chemistry. 'FOR FUCK'S SAKE, DEREK!' Coming up the road towards him was another mob of bleating sheep being driven by Derek. 'Bloody hell! I told the prick!'

On competing trajectories, the two flocks were about to smash into each other. Slamming on the brakes, Charlie leapt from his vehicle and waded frantically through his mob to get to the front and head them off. This served only to scatter them in panic. Hooves clattered, wires pinged, dags rattled, pellets of dung sprayed from rear ends and rolled down the road. Sheep bleated, dogs barked and Charlie cursed. 'SHUT THE FUCK UP, YA FILTHY MONGRELS! GET IN BEHIND!'

The mobs met in a swirling whirlpool of wool, ammonia and dust. Charlie emerged from the mêlée most unhappy.

'I FUCKING TOLD YOU, Derek, I fucking told you!'

'Sorry, Charlie, I forgot it was today.'

This set Charlie off even more. He charged at Derek, his eyes blazing with fury, and jabbed a finger firmly into his chest.

'I HAVE KILLED BETTER MEN THAN YOU!'

Derek was a good man, even finding his equal would have been a tall order and taken some doing but given the sheer number of men Charlie had killed, statistically this was not an outlandish claim. It was almost certainly true, and they both knew it. Derek did the only thing a sane man could do under the circumstances — he went white. 'Jesus Christ, Charlie. You're putting the wind up me now!'

§

On 4 January 1994, the Cheviot community south of Conway Flat gathered to farewell Charlie and Molly from the district. When he spoke, Charlie had wistful words of advice. 'Don't wait too long before you leave. I'm cracking up. I should have left years ago.' He said his love of the district was one of the reasons he had stayed as long as he had. It was foolish of him. He could no longer walk around the farm that he had nurtured for forty-seven years. He fell in love with this country before the war when as part of a gang of eight he mustered from Glyn Wye to Lake Sumner, Charlie told his audience. It was a perfect life for a young man, but that life was coming to an end.

Charles Upham died on 22 November 1994 at the Bishopspark retirement village, seven months after shifting to Christchurch. He was afforded a full military funeral in Christ Church Cathedral, with a memorial service also held in London. Draped in flags and ferns, his coffin was adorned with red roses, and a lemon squeezer hat and a ceremonial sword were mounted on a catafalque atop a gun carriage towed at a slow march to the slow throb of a drum behind an open-topped Land Rover, with gleaming new shovels and picks fastened to its side. It was led by a lone, solemn soldier bearing Charlie's medals on a red-tasselled cushion. The procession moved through hushed streets where more than 5000 people stood in respectful silence, heads bowed as the cortège moved past.

Soldiers of the 2nd/1st Battalion escorted the coffin into the cathedral and mourners overflowed into the square. The service was broadcast by loudspeaker to an overflow crowd of 2000 outside. 'The 20th are here to remember a friend,' said Canon Ivor Hopkins, the original battalion padre. He said he had selected a particularly appropriate line from Rudyard Kipling's poem 'If—' to capture the essence of the 20th's most highly decorated soldier: 'If you can talk with crowds and keep your virtue, Or walk with Kings — nor lose the common touch . . .' That's how Charlie was he said, smiling, the congregation smiling with him.

Hitting a sour note, one man who had yelled obscenities and gave the Nazi salute as the cortège passed down Rolleston Avenue was arrested. Appearing in court three months later, an unemployed man, Christopher Boulter, whose conduct was called disgraceful by the judge, was fined $350. In his own defence, Boulter said he could not condone the glory and the hype that went with blocking city streets for a killing machine.

In the wake of his death, tributes for Charlie poured in from all over the globe, none more succinct than the one paid by his friend and fellow VC winner Jack Hinton of Christchurch, who said simply, 'Charlie had a ton of guts. Charlie called a spade a spade and he wouldn't ask anyone to do anything he would not do himself.' In England glowing obituaries were published in *The Times* and *Daily Telegraph*. New Zealand newspapers devoted pages and pages to heartfelt eulogies and lavish tributes, some even printing in full the original citations accompanying the awarding of his VCs — which made stirring reading and still beggared belief.

§

Charlie would not have been pleased with all the attention, an overly theatrical end for someone who'd spent his life shunning the limelight. His disdain for honours of any sort was legendary. Contrary to what *Mark of the Lion* said, and some Christ's College pamphlets and a number of newspaper and magazine tributes claimed after his death, Charlie was never knighted, but not through lack of trying by the powers that be. With her voice tinged with regret, Amanda hinted to me that her father turned down the honour on several occasions — when perhaps he shouldn't have. Amanda said her mum would have quite liked being Lady Upham. I got the distinct impression during these conversations that Amanda wouldn't have minded being Lady Upham's daughter either, but Charlie didn't want a bar of it.

Strict protocols and procedures are followed when awarding titles. To avoid embarrassment on the day, recipients are always sounded out well in advance and asked if they will accept the honour. I imagine the conversations went something like this:

It is dusk in London and dawn in New Zealand. The new day down under is an orange glow lighting up the rim of the dark Pacific. A rooster crows. Phones ring. Dogs bark. A number of farmers on Conway Flat in dressing gowns totter down halls and into kitchens to pick up receivers. 'G'day!' 'Hello?', 'Yeah?' A lofty, patrician English voice wants to speak to Charles Upham. One by one they get off the party line, leaving just Charlie. Maybe one or two nosey parkers linger and are responsible for the enduring rumour. Charlie stands in the hallway in his slippers and pyjamas, rubbing his stiff left shoulder. 'Speaking. This is Upham. What can I do for you?'

'You are Charles Hazlitt Upham? Formerly Captain Upham?'

'Oath. Last time I looked.'

'Sorry?'

'Correct . . .'

'This is her Majesty's Private Secretary, Sir William Heseltine, ringing from Buckingham Palace in London, here. If Her Majesty, Queen Elizabeth, were of a mind to offer you a knighthood in the New Year's Honours' list, what would your response be?'

'Fuck off!'

'Terribly sorry. It's a dreadful line. Didn't catch that. Could you repeat that for me, please?'

'NO THANKS! That's very kind or her. Thank Her Majesty for me, but no thanks. What sort of day is it over there? It's been crook here, pissing down . . .'

The truth, as it nearly always is, is more mundane. In a *Sunday Star-Times* interview in 1994 with Matt Conway, Molly said that in 1946 the then Governor General, Sir Bernard Freyberg, appealed to her personally to persuade Charlie to allow his name to go forward to be considered for a knighthood. 'He was against it. He didn't want anything other soldiers didn't get. The Freybergs weren't at all pleased. It was a private affair best forgotten.'

Caroline reckons turning down a knighthood would have been an easy decision for her father: 'He didn't want to be different. He never did . . .'

If Her Majesty felt strongly about awarding Charlie a knighthood, she had numerous opportunities over the years to ask Charlie in person to accept one. Every royal tour to New Zealand included Charlie in civic receptions or state banquets, and he and Queen Elizabeth were often seen together locked in animated conversation. Pressed later about these exchanges, Charlie would only say admiringly, 'Boy, she knows her horses, that girl.'

An earlier example of his reluctance to put himself in the spotlight was his decision not to attend the Victory Parade in London in June 1946, only consenting when Prime Minister Peter Fraser rang and asked him personally. Charlie's BOAC Lancastrian was the first plane to land at London's new airport — Heathrow. He refused to attend a reception arranged for him by the New Zealand Government, and the *Daily Sketch* of 1 June 1946 wrote a short piece headlined: 'Shy Double V.C. Upham Slipped into London — Declined Reception'.

When a reporter recognised him walking through Lowndes Square, he wouldn't talk about himself, except to say that he had to rejoin the army to take part in the parade. Offered a flash, up-market hotel to stay in, Charlie opted to sleep under canvas with the other soldiers in a tent city in a London park.

'They gave me the full works, medical, attestation,

everything, but don't think I went through all that for the Victory Parade. I wanted to see some old pals. Don't say I'm staying in the army. I'm not. I'm getting back to the farm just as soon as this is over.'

Another brush with officialdom came in November 1947 when Charlie received a bulky package, not from rural delivery as such — that was another luxury denied them for a few more years. Locals took it in turns to buy newspapers and collect mail from the general store at Hundalee and drop them off along the road on the way home. The package was from the Department of Internal Affairs on behalf of Major General H.K. Kippenberger, Editor-in-Chief of the War History Branch. They were collecting the experiences of New Zealand prisoners of war via a lengthy questionnaire. Because of Kippenberger's involvement Charlie couldn't refuse.

The yellowing pages with his impatient replies in blue-black ink are held in storage in Archives New Zealand in Wellington. Even allowing for the fact that he'd probably spent a gruelling day wielding a slasher with one good arm in broiling sun, his answers are remarkably short and curt. He hasn't devoted a lot of time to this and there is a lot he isn't saying, which in itself tells you heaps. Other POWs' answers that I perused in the folder were voluble and lengthy. Most clearly saw it as a rare opportunity to get things off their chest, pour their hearts out and dispense some home truths. Charlie's brevity contrasts sharply with their answers and with his own chatty letters home from Egypt early in the war, and even more so with the marathon letter of condolence he sent to Mr Bellringer.

Being a prisoner of war changed Charlie, which he only partially concedes in the answer to one question. While his tone may have changed in this questionnaire, the economy of language and blunt directness is unmistakeably his voice:

SURNAME: UPHAM

CHRISTIAN NAMES: CHARLES HAZLITT

Civilian occupation: Land Valuation Rural Staff

Regimental Number: 8077 Rank: Capt. Unit: 20 Inf BN

CAPTURE: -

1) *What was the place of your capture?* Ruweisat Ridge

2) *On what date were you captured?* 15th July '42

3) *What were the circumstances of your capture?*
We had made a night attack & advanced some distance.
We were only a salient & were surrounded & being cut
off. We were not reinforced & were overrun by a tank
attack the evening following the attack we made.

4) *Were you ever given any instructions in the event of
capture (e.g. regarding escape)? If so, what?*
Yes. We had always been told the easiest time to escape
is soon after capture.

5) *Did you before capture know anything of the
provisions of the Geneva Convention regarding
treatment of prisoners of war?*
No. I was not interested, but could have found out.

6) *What happened immediately after your capture?*
I was wounded & was given morphine by a German M.O.
The men were parked in the centre of a tank laager.
The whole area was under shell fire by our guns, there
was quite a lot of confusion, the enemy were being
continuously reinforced.

7) *Were you interrogated? If so, what procedure did the
enemy follow?*
No. I told the others with me to say nothing at all & I
would ask for food & water for us.

8) *How were our wounded treated immediately after
capture?*
The German casualties were very heavy & they had no
bandages etc but gave morphine to the most wounded &

promised us attention when they had fixed up their own men.

9) *How long after capture and by what means was your captivity notified to our authorities or to your relatives?*

I don't know, I think the Rome Radio broadcasted news of me in a few weeks.

10) *How did you move from your place of capture to a transit camp?*

We were taken the next day to a casualty dressing station & then that evening back to an area staffed by Italians & the next day to a hospital area in Matruh.

11) *What were the circumstances of your life in transit camps (quarters, food, treatment in general; mention location or number of camps)?*

Life in the so-called hospital at Matruh was very bad, life on the hospital ship to Regia Calabria was good, our train to Caserta was good. In Caserta hospital it was not good, on train to other hospital near Bologna was good, life in this hospital was good. Train to Modena good. Life in Modena was good. Transit to Germany was not good. Life in Stalag 8A was good & Oflag at Weinsberg was good. Journey to Colditz good. Life in Colditz was only fair, & was very bad at odd times.

Life in Camps

12) *What permanent camps were you in (approx. dates)?*

Modena, Italy Jan '43 till capitulation of Italy. Stalag 8A some days. A French camp for some days. Weinsberg about a year. About the same time in Colditz in Saxony.

a) *How often did the representative of the International Red Cross or of the Protecting Power visit the camps you were in? Was he able to accomplish anything so far as you know?*

I believe they made periodic visits to camps & hospitals & must have accomplished a great deal as our camps were quite different from those housing Russian prisoners.

b) *How were your living quarters with regard to buildings, space, light, heat, washing and sanitary conveniences, vermin etc?*

In Italy (at Modena) it was concrete & very airy & good being an ex Italian O.C.T.U. In Germany were usually in wooden huts sometimes very overcrowded. Colditz was an old medieval castle. Sanitary conveniences were usually not sufficient according to our standards, & on trains no chance of using anything often for a matter of days. Vermin were well controlled usually & cleanliness encouraged.

c) *How much and often did you receive Red Cross food?*

We were supposed to get one a week. Sometimes we got them once a fortnight, sometimes once a month. In Caserta we got none. At Castel San Pedro almost none, at end of war none.

d) *What were your lowest, highest, and average rations from the enemy (with approx. dates)?*

Best rations were at Modena in Italy where we had Red Cross parcels & bought a lot of fruit & vegetables from the Italians. The rations in North African camps were very poor as were rations at end of war.

e) *Were you able to supplement this in any way?*

In Modena in Italy we bought for (POW currency) a large amount of fruit & vegetables. In the Oflags in Germany it was difficult to supplement rations.

f) *What cooking and mealing arrangements were there at your camps?*

In Italy good stoves, in Weinsberg good stoves. Elsewhere mostly by blower handmade paper burning stoves.

g) *What clothing did you receive from the enemy? Were Red Cross supplies adequate?*

We got no clothing at all from enemy, but usually adequate supplies from Red Cross.

h) *How did you manage for tobacco supplies?*
The longest I was without any at all was just on six
months. At other times I was well off & often was short,
but usually had a little.

j) *Where and when did you find the best provision for
recreation (e.g. books, games, art, theatre, music, sport,
handicrafts, gardening)?*
In Modena in Italy we had room enough for basketball
etc, most other camps there was not enough space to
play games, ground was usually paved or very uneven.
At Colditz there was no area at all.

k) *Did you make any use of educational classes in any
camp? What type proved of most value? Did you sit any
examination?*
I did not specialize in anything but attended many
lectures & certainly gained a tremendous amount of
general knowledge.

l) *How did you fare for letters and parcels received?*
In Italy, I did not get any letters for the first 11 months
& no parcels at all. In Germany I received about 2/3 of
letters sent & 1/4 of parcels sent.

m) *Do you remember any good or bad points regarding
the prisoners' own administration in any of the camps?
How did it cope with the enemy authorities?*
The camps were usually run well from the Prisoners side,
the senior officer usually doing all that he could to make
the enemy keep to the Geneva Convention.

n) *What in your experience did the enemy regard as
breaches of discipline?*
Almost anything, but they put up with much more
annoyance from the prisoners than one would expect.

o) *What punishments inflicted by the enemy did you, or
others that you know of, experience?*
I saw men tied up to the barb wire with feet off the
ground in North Africa and left all night. Some were

beaten up. In Italy & Germany punishments consisted of long spells in the cells on short notices.

p) *What arrangements were made about pay? Were you ever able to use camp money outside a camp?*
Pay was a farce in all the camps I was in. In Italy the Italians charged us rent for the camps etc.

q) *What service were you able to get from camp canteens?*
In Italy we could buy wine. In Germany the only thing was inferior toothpaste and watery beer.

r) *Do you remember any outstanding cases of trading or black-marketing in camps?*
In the Oflags, no, but in the Stalags it was easy to exchange Red Cross stuff for bread etc.

s) *Do you remember any rackets that went on in the POW camps?*
Not in the camps I was in, but I heard of many in other camps.

t) *What facilities did you experience for medical treatment (camp and hospital)?*
We always had medical officers, also prisoners in our camps, sometimes they had access to facilities, sometimes they could do almost nothing.

u) *What facilities did you experience for dental treatment?*
The same as for 't' facilities & dental equipment was sometimes non-existent.

v) *Were you exposed at any time to danger from (action?) of the Allied forces (Navy, Army, Air Force)? What happened?*
When first captured, some of us were killed by bombing.

w) *Did, in your experience, protected personnel (medical, padres etc.) receive any special consideration?*
Yes, they experienced very special consideration often to the detriment of the other prisoners.

Ill treatment, Propaganda etc.

13) *Were you made to work? If so, what kind of work and under what conditions (pay, quarters, etc.)?*
No.

14) *How did you find enemy civilians?*
I had nothing to do with them, but what I saw of them both Italian & German they seemed to be much more accustomed to being rigidly controlled than anyone would believe.

15) *Do you know of any cases of sabotage carried out by prisoners of war?*
Many.

16) *When you were moved any distance by the enemy, under what conditions did you travel (train, ship, marches)?*
From Matruh to Regio Calabria in hospital ship was very good, as I was only prisoner amongst enemy officers. From Regio to Caserta by train good. From Caserta to Castel San Pedro by train good. From Castel San Pedro to Modena by train good. From Modena by train to Stalag 8A poor. From Stalag 8A by train to French camp poor. From French camp to Weinsberg by train poor. From Weinsberg to Colditz good. When a small party travelled it was usually good, when a large party travelled it was usually poor.

17) *Were there ever any special security measures taken by the enemy to guard against escapes etc.?*
Often they threatened to shoot 10 men or anyone who escaped etc. I was manacled on trains twice.

18) *Did you witness any examples of ill-treatment? What took place?*
Yes. In North Africa I saw men shockingly treated. I saw Russian prisoners starved to death in Germany.

19) *Do you know of any attempts to force prisoners to labour on military works?*
Yes, to unload ammo ships.

20) *Do you know of any cases of collective punishment or reprisals, etc?*
Yes. Collective punishments are almost the only way of enforcing discipline in a camp.

21) *Can you recall any examples of the use of propaganda for prisoners of war?*
Yes. It was always there, was very poor.

22) *Were you ever allowed out for walks on parole?*
I went for no walks.

23) *Do you know of any variation in treatment: -*
a. *According to the period of war?*
When the war was going against the enemy the guards were much more human, when they thought they were winning they were much more arrogant & nasty.
b. *According to nationality?*
Yes. British prisoners were treated best, Americans next best & Russians the worst.

24) *What in general is your opinion of the treatment received while in enemy hands? (Compare Italy and Germany if in both countries)*
The low-grade Italian is only a savage, but the Italians were usually soft hearted, the Germans usually correct. The German SS men usually savages.

Morale, Escapes, etc.

25) *In prison camps what thoughts most occupied your mind, and what mental states were most prevalent?*
When first captured acute despair. Those people soon became accustomed to prison life & there were always some characters who kept the others going. We were always planning escapes & their chances of success.

26) *What do you consider helped to maintain morale in prison camps?*
News, Red Cross parcels & mail from home. Success of our forces etc.

27) *Did you receive news through a secret radio or otherwise?*
Yes, we had a secret radio at Colditz. Elsewhere we always had news of some sort, it was often false.
28) *Was any information sent out from your camp to the Allied authorities?*
Escaping prisoners took our information.
29) *Were any instructions or material originating from the Allied authorities received in your camp?*
Yes, we had instructions to remain in our camps in Italy, this was the cause of so many of us having no chance to get away before the Germans took us over.
30) *Do you know of any photographs illustrating any phase of captivity taken by the enemy or others and where they are likely to be found? Similarly do you know of any drawings?*
Nothing of any importance.
31) *Were you able to accomplish anything with your guards by means of bribery or threats?*
Yes. There was always guards who were friendly, or temporarily short of a smoke when we had some.
32) *Do you know of any successful escapes? What was the general attitude to escape?*
Yes, many successful escapes. The general attitude to escapes was to escape if the chances were anything like any good. Older men couldn't make the effort and were not interested.

Liberation.
33) *Did the enemy attitude or treatment change in any way before liberation?*
Yes. At end of war, many of the rottenest of the Germans became the sweetest.
34) *How were you liberated?*
By the 61st? Division of Gen Hodges 1st? US Army.

35) *How did you fare immediately after liberation?*
Very well indeed.

36) *Where were you evacuated to, and by what route?*
England (by US army trucks to Weimen, then US Air Force planes to England).

37) *What aspect of the reception facilities in England did you find most helpful?*
Being able to get away from the general atmosphere of being in a camp of any sort.

38) *What physical effects did you find, and do now find, that captivity had upon you? Did you have medical treatment on your return?*
I had effects of malnutrition & treatment for it.

39) *Have you suffered from any physical ailments since your return?*
NO.

40) *What mental effects did you notice at the end of your captivity, and do you still notice them?*
Most prisoners have become more philosophical than ordinary people.

41) *How do you feel towards the people of the country in which you were held prisoner?*
I look down on the Italians in the South as barbarians. Those in the North are normal. The Germans are mostly blockheads, with a streak of intense savagery.

42) *What did you find was your attitude to normal civilian life after your return? Did you return to your former occupation? If not, what did you take up?*
I took up farming as I had done that in the past. After being a prisoner, selfishness in an individual is held to be a serious crime. Some normal aspects of civilian life disgusted us at first.

43) *Could you say that you have gained any benefit or learned anything from your captivity? If so, what?*
Yes. I think most prisoners are more thoughtful of others,

much less given to self-seeking. Many are lethargic &
not so capable of the effort to strive to get on, & many
become very easy going & even lazy.

The above is, so far as I can recollect, a true record of my
experience at the times and places mentioned.

Signature CH Upham
Date 29 November 1947

In 1950 Howard Kippenberger rang Charlie to ask another
favour. The Greek Government was unveiling a memorial
dedicated to the sacrifice of New Zealand soldiers in Crete —
the one I visited on Cemetery Hill that has fallen into bleak
disrepair. Kip was going. He wanted Charlie to come with him.
Charlie said he couldn't. It was smack in the middle of shearing.
Anticipating that excuse, Kip was prepared and waiting. He said
he'd already made arrangements for someone to come in and
shear Charlie's sheep for him. Somewhat reluctantly Charlie
went and of course loved it, returning with mementos he hung
in pride of place on the walls — just as in Galatas homes I saw
greenstone tikis and souvenir tea-towels printed with iconic
New Zealand images such as Mt Cook, Milford Sound, Rotorua
geysers, Hawke's Bay hillsides dotted with rice-grain sheep
and the like hanging on living-room walls.

The someone that Kippenberger had spoken to about
shearing Charlie's sheep was Miles Handyside. Miles agreed
immediately to the request but warned Kip that Charlie
mustn't be told it was him. It had to be kept secret. Why? The
Wilding boys knew.

Chapter 20

'The medals are too big really'

Amanda Upham, in a Radio New Zealand interview, said that, until their early teenage years, neither she nor her sisters had any idea their father was anything more than an average bloke.

He was a very unassuming man: 'We didn't realise he was a well-known soldier till we went to boarding school and we were shown the magazine with his photographs. We were very embarrassed but very proud of course.' The fact her father was a war hero who had won two Victoria Crosses was never mentioned at home.

Caroline first became aware that other people regarded her father as someone special and out of the ordinary when she accompanied him as a seven-year-old to the air force base in Blenheim, where people made a fuss of him and he gave a speech in return. They sat in the front row and people brought her glasses of Coca-Cola, a huge treat. After half a dozen glasses of Coke, she would have been wide awake, chatting nineteen to the dozen to her newly discovered famous dad on the long drive home.

As they grew up, of course, Charlie's deeds and fame became part of his daughters' lives. They lived in the shadow of a famous figure, something sometimes endured rather than enjoyed, especially as they may have often felt Charlie belonged to the nation rather than just being a loving dad and husband. This was never more the case than with the controversy surrounding his medals.

Before his medals were donated to the Army Memorial Museum in Waiouru for the purpose of display, Charlie kept his VCs buried in a drawer in his small apartment in Christchurch. They were rarely worn and seldom without Charlie complaining: 'The medals are too big really, they spoil your suit by dragging down on it, and the car seat belt is inclined to pull them off. They wouldn't be such a nuisance if they were smaller.' This reluctance was not a late-blossoming phenomenon. As early as 1956, at a London reception with Admiral Lord Louis Mountbatten, 1st Earl Mountbatten of Burma, Charlie was asked by His Lordship why he wasn't wearing his VCs. Charlie rummaged around the loose change jangling in his pocket and produced them, proclaiming, 'My wife made me bring them.'

Among the files Caroline Upham lent me is a copy of a signed August 1997 Deposit Agreement between Caroline and the Registrar of the Queen Elizabeth II Army Memorial Museum at Waiouru (now known as the National Army Museum) for a long-term loan for display purposes of item 28.1997 559 — a small pocketknife. The two-page, ten-clause agreement states in Clause 4 that no charges are payable by either party. Clause 3 asserts that the museum will take good care of the deposit and maintain it in good repair and insure it against fire, theft and water damage.

Two years earlier, in the Christchurch *Press* of 20 July 1995, there is a photograph of Molly handing Charlie's small clothes rack of medals to General Sir Leonard Thornton, a former Chief of Defence Staff. The accompanying story says they had discussed the fate of Charlie's medals and agreed they should go to the Amy Museum on permanent loan so the public could see them.

I have not sighted that deposit agreement, but I imagine the terms were similar to Caroline's contract for the small pocketknife. My guess is that Clause 5 was the same: It states:

> The depositor has the right at any time within a period of twenty (20) years from the date of the deposit to give two (2) weeks' notice in writing to the museum that they require the museum to return the deposit to them or to reassert their title to the deposit and enter into a new agreement for its custody.

In April 1995 Molly sent a wistful postcard of the Christ Church Cathedral and Arts Centre to Caroline from Bishopspark retirement village. On the back, after wishing everyone a happy Easter, she points out that it would be a first Easter without Charles. 'Last year we went to the Riccarton races, and life isn't the same and <u>never</u> will be . . .' She had firmly underlined 'never'.

In October 1995 at HMNZ Naval Base, Devonport in Auckland, Molly dedicated the navy's newest purchase, the logistic support ship named after her late husband: HMNZ *Charles Upham*. (The ship did not enjoy the illustrious career of its namesake. Stability problems saw it soon withdrawn from service and finally sold in 2001.)

That same month New Zealand Post issued six stamps commemorating famous New Zealanders. Some 90,000 people selected the final half dozen from a list of 221 celebrities in various categories. Charlie made the final six in the 'service, business and development' category. (In 2011 he also appeared in a New Zealand Post stamp series featuring New Zealand's twenty-one Victoria Cross recipients.)

In her later years, Molly missed Charlie terribly. She passed away in August 2000, aged eighty-eight.

§

In April 2006 there was nationwide uproar when the Upham daughters announced they were willing to sell their father's medals to the highest bidder. Defence Minister Phil Goff accused the daughters of ignoring Charlie's wishes by attempting to sell his prestigious medals for a reported $3.3 million. The family defended its attempts to sell the Victoria Crosses, saying the time was right. Virginia was quoted in the Christchurch *Press* saying, 'We have had endless offers over the years, and we are selling them to be fair to all members of the family. If it goes on to the next generation, it will get messy.' She added, 'We are enormously proud of them and it's a personal thing. It's very awkward . . . If we were multi-millionaires, we would buy each other out, but we're unable to do that.' The family had offered the government first option on the medals as a courtesy. 'We thought it appropriate to be fair to the people of New Zealand to offer them to the New Zealand Government.'

Virginia would not disclose the amount the family had asked for the medals, but Phil Goff said the family set a price in an email of $3.3 million to match the sum a private buyer had offered them over a year earlier. The government did not follow through on that suggestion. The sale of Upham's Victoria Cross & Bar to a private buyer would be a huge public loss, Goff said.

> While the decision is one for his family to make it would be hugely disappointing for the medals to be lost from public access. However, the government does not believe it is appropriate for the public to pay the $3.3 million asked for the medals. This would clearly be unfair to the 19 other families who have gifted or lent VCs to New Zealand museums, seeking nothing in return.

When I spoke to Frank Wilding about the medals' sale, he was blunt and unequivocal. His old friend gave the medals to his girls to do with them what they wished — he wouldn't have minded the medals being sold to help them, but he would have hated the publicity and media storm surrounding the sale.

In the end a fairy godmother in the form of the Imperial War Museum in London came forward and purchased the medals and loaned them to New Zealand for 999 years, at which time presumably the debate will erupt all over again.

The heated public argument about where the medals belonged and their monetary value was not lost on a bunch of petty crooks operating out of Palmerston North, just a couple of hours' drive south of the museum. In the early hours of Sunday morning, 2 December 2007, in an operation the police described as well-planned and slick, the thieves gained entry to the first floor of the fortress-like museum via a rear fire escape and made their way to the 'Valour Room' with its locked glass cabinets. There they smashed and grabbed a haul of over ninety-six medals, including nine Victoria Crosses and two George Crosses, evading and circumventing patrols, alarm systems and security cameras.

It was all over in four minutes. In different circumstances in another time and place, Charlie might have admired their skill and daring. The country though was appalled, angered and alarmed. Prime Minister Helen Clark spoke for many when she called the theft deplorable and expressed her fear that the robbery might have been a heist done to order for a reclusive wealthy overseas collector and New Zealand's sacred medals might never be seen again. Border security was stepped up and recognised medal collectors and museums the world over were alerted to the possibility they might be offered stolen goods.

A wealthy overseas medals collector, Lord Michael Anthony Ashcroft, the owner of the world's largest private collection of VCs, who called Charlie's VC & Bar the Holy Grail of war medals, supported by a Nelson businessman, Tom Sturgess, put up a reward of $300,000 for information leading to their return. As a result of a tip-off, three months later in February

2008 police recovered the medals and subsequently charged a career criminal, James Joseph Kapa, with their theft. Kapa was convicted and sentenced to six years in jail for his role in the theft. He was also ordered to repay $100,000 of reward money — which suggests he had wanted two bites of the apple, and tipped the police off about the medals' whereabouts, hoping foolishly it wouldn't lead them to him.

§

In that more trusting, more carefree age, I had my innocence punctured when I saw my very first Second World War movie — the original *Dunkirk* starring John Mills and Richard Attenborough. It was 1961, I was fourteen years old. We were on vacation in Tauranga in midwinter and had an entire holiday park and motor camp to ourselves. It rained the whole time. When the novelty of a dozen toilets, a dozen showers, half a dozen toasters and half a dozen kettles to choose from wore off, and the park was too muddy to play in, even with half a dozen washing machines on standby, Mum walked us, for what seemed like miles, into town in a heavy drizzle to watch the movie. It was electrifying and haunting.

To my fear of water and my fear of abandonment, I was able to add fear of being strafed by Messerschmitts and dive-bombed by Stukas. The next day we drove for miles around endless bush-clad inlets and bays in our sluggish Vauxhall Velox to visit the port of Mount Maunganui. Today, there is a high, curved bridge spanning the harbour at its narrowest point that takes you there in minutes.

I negotiated those same bays recently to get to the Pacific Coast Highway running to Whakatane to visit Charlie's youngest daughter, who lives in Gisborne. I didn't recognise anything from half a century ago. Mind you, such is the rate of growth along this stretch of the Bay of Plenty, if I'd visited there a month earlier, I'd barely recognise anything today. It was a relief to finally leave the industrial parks, bulk barns, boat yards, motor dealerships, busy intersections and new housing divisions and hit the open road.

Approaching the coast, the skies opened up. Heavy rain ricocheting off the tarseal thumped on the underbelly as well as the roof, overwhelming the wipers and reducing me to a blind crawl. Then it stopped. I was driving under a purple sky, alongside a black sea trimmed with white lace when National Radio started playing Moana Maniapoto singing John Lennon's 'Imagine' quite beautifully — easily the equal of the original. While I overnighted in Whakatane, Charlie was uppermost in my thoughts and the line in the song about the world living as one stayed with me the next morning as I drove inland through the beautiful, misty Waioeka Gorge, exclaiming out loud, as I drove, which I don't normally do, 'Wow! Oh man!'

The sun came out when I reached the Waipaoa River heading into Gisborne. For some reason, the row upon neat row of pruned grapevines standing to attention in white plastic puttees reminded me of a war grave cemetery. Like seeing a white horse in a paddock in Ireland or catching a glimpse of Everest on a hill trail in Nepal, or seeing the pyramids as you land in Cairo, it was a sign! A good portent! I was so transfixed I stopped to take a photo.

I was anxious about meeting Caroline. Just arranging a face-to-face interview had been nerve-wracking. In 2006, when Charlie's other daughters, Amanda and Virginia, announced they were selling their father's VCs to the highest bidder, there was a lot of huffing and puffing and public outrage. I chimed in piously with a cartoon saying the VCs came with an exchange card so recipients could swap them for something else if they so wished. 'You drew that cartoon, didn't you?' Caroline reminded me on the phone. I gulped. I knew immediately what she meant and replied limply in the affirmative. To my relief, she laughed at my discomfort.

The subject of the selling of her dad's medals came up

My cartoon for the *Dominion Post*, drawn at the height of the controversy over Charlie's daughters attempting to sell his VCs to the highest bidder.

again near the end of my first visit. Caroline's innocent face clouded over. 'Amanda said it was payback time!'

'Payback time? What did she mean by that?'

It was a rhetorical question so I remained silent. I didn't know for sure, but I could hazard a guess.

Caroline, a vivacious, pretty woman and her still chiselled, if a little grizzled, husband Marty Reynolds live in a beautiful, two-storey colonial home overlooking the lazy Turanganui River as it winds through leafy suburbs in downtown Gisborne. Inside the house is a tasteful riot of eggshell-blues and yolk-yellows — supremely elegant and stylish, gleaming and pristine, as if permanently poised for a *House & Garden* photo shoot.

In Amanda's Auckland home, photos of her dad in uniform and Peter McIntyre's famous painting *The Breakout from Minqar Qa'im* and assorted Second World War memorabilia lined the walls and filled the shelves. Interestingly, she has inherited her father's vocabulary and frankness. There was never any dithering with Amanda. She came straight to the point, spitting out crisp four-letter words like a Bofors gun. It was curiously endearing. I liked her a lot. I imagine she was the most like her father in spirit, candour and temperament. When I asked her if Charlie ever swore in front of his family, she looked at me in shock and horror and snapped, 'No! Never!'

Similarly, Caroline is genuinely baffled by the number of euphemisms journalists employed describing her dad's vocabulary — it was always salty, tangy, spicy, peppery, picturesque, earthy, colourful, rude, ripe, robust, agricultural, high country, would make a drover blush, and so on. The delicate euphemisms continued after his death. At the Service of Thanksgiving for His Life held at the glorious St Martin-in-the-Fields Church in Trafalgar Square, with representatives of the Royal Family present, the Australian former soldier, diplomat and long-time friend of Charlie and Molly, Sir Roden Cutler VC, described his fellow VC winner's vernacular as follows: 'Charlie interlarded his views with a delightfully all-embracing vocabulary which possibly he had absorbed from the New Zealand West Coast miners with whom he had served.'

In truth, the miners had nothing to teach Charlie. After Charlie's high-country days mustering stubborn ewes, they may well have learnt a word or two and picked up some choice phrases from him. Caroline swears that she only ever heard her dad swear once. She wasn't supposed to hear, and he was mortified when he realised she had.

I arrived outside Caroline and Marty's cul-de-sac just as they were about to head off somewhere, but they cancelled their plans and rushed me indoors for a cup of tea. They were welcoming, engaging and delightful company. Within minutes, I felt I had known them all my life. Caroline showed me family photograph albums and other Charlie stuff she had pulled out of storage, while Marty prepared vegetable soup for lunch.

In the living room above the fireplace was a huge Andy

Warhol-style screenprint of a Chanel No.5 Eau de Parfum dispenser, with a yellow label inscribed with black print, on a crimson bottle set against a black background. It's stunning. When I asked if it had any special significance, Caroline informed me that Chanel No.5 was her mother's favourite perfume so every birthday and every Christmas, without fail, all their married life, Charlie purchased Molly a bottle. Brilliant. No traipsing through shopping malls and department stores for Charlie, waiting for something to leap out at him. Every husband should be so lucky. Charlie was lazy *and* smart, while Molly was thrilled. It was pragmatism raised to high art.

After lunch, I asked Marty what it was like meeting Charlie for the first time. He admitted that dating one of Charlie Upham's daughters was daunting in the early days. 'Meeting Charlie for the first time was sheer terror, really.' Marty had been lying on a sofa on a verandah with his arm around Caroline when Charlie turned up. As if to absolve herself of any culpability, still sounding defensive and aggrieved forty years later, Caroline chipped in to say that she was trying to swot at the time. It was a student flat in Christchurch. Marty was studying for a diploma in agriculture and farm management at Lincoln, Charlie's alma mater, which immediately stood him in good stead with his future father-in-law, and Caroline was training to be a nurse like her older sisters.

As it happened, Marty had nothing to fear — Charlie did not rush forward, pistol drawn, hurling grenades. The two men got only really well, then and ever after. Marty says that apart from his own mother and father, Charlie had more influence and impact on him than anyone else in his life.

They had differing opinions on the way forward for farming, argued long and hard about many things, but never with rancour. Charlie loved repeating Churchill's maxim — a man who wasn't a socialist up until the age of thirty had no heart and a man who wasn't a conservative after thirty had no head. Charlie had a novel solution to watersiders and freezing workers going on strike every summer — farmers should respond in kind by stockpiling their wool clip and keeping their stock back a year to deprive the strikers of their livelihood and let them see what it felt like for a change. Charlie was convinced that all the farmers in New Zealand would only have to do this once for freezing workers and watersiders to learn their lesson and never down tools again. Stoppages, strikes, go-slows, working to rule and the like would be a thing of the past.

Charlie ran this radical plan past his good friend and local Member of Parliament Tom Shand, who was Minister of Mines, Works and Labour in the National Government of the day. Shand gently advised Charlie to leave governing the country to politicians and to stick to farming.

Things were decidedly more delicate when Marty and Caroline lived together in London in the mid-70s and Charlie and Molly came to visit them in their flat at Clapham, South London. They were not yet married, and Marty was acutely conscious of Charlie counting the bedrooms and doing the maths in his head. 'Molly and Charlie were quite old-fashioned and Victorian in some of their attitudes and very progressive in others. Caroline and I tested their boundaries.'

Marty made an honest woman of Caroline in October 1974. There is a beautiful picture of Caroline in her white bridal gown taken with her father. She is radiant, half turning and beaming adoringly over her shoulder at her dad who is bursting with pride and joy. He is only sixty-six, still lean, but harsh sun, driving wind and rain, cigarette smoking, bad dentistry, the war and unremitting physical toil have all taken their toll on him — he could easily be her grandfather.

The London sojourn provided proof that Charlie's capacity for physical menace had not aged one jot. One morning Marty had to drive a Kiwi lawyer chum, Robert Dobson, into legal chambers in Kensington to pick up a document. Marty invited

Charlie along for the ride. He accepted readily and squeezed without pause or hesitation into the back of their VW and they headed off into the city. They parked illegally in a no-parking zone while 'Dobby' Dobson, who later became a respected High Court judge in New Zealand, dashed inside. A Cockney flower-seller, his truck parked next spot along, took exception to this breach of the law and approached them, remonstrating loudly and cursing colourfully. Marty explained politely that it was only a fleeting transgression, his friend would be out in a second and they would be on their way forthwith.

Unplacated, the flower-seller raised the decibel and vulgarity level to fever-pitch, prompting Charlie, who had been crouched anonymously in the back seat, to uncoil like a spring and lean over Marty's shoulder and thrust his face out the driver's window very close to the flower-seller's angry red mug and hiss coldly, 'WHY DON'T YOU FUCK OFF!' Marty didn't see Charlie's facial expression or catch his gaze, but assumes they must have been fearsome — the flower-seller immediately dashed back to his lorry, jumped in, turned the keys and pulled out into the traffic without indicating. Charlie meanwhile settled back into his seat, chuckling quietly to himself.

Charlie later appeared in a 1985 episode of the television series *This is Your Life* devoted to him, where a swag of old comrades like Dr Fred Moody, who was in Colditz with him, Denver Fountaine and Dave Kirk who witnessed first-hand Charlie's feats on Crete, and Brigadier 'Gentleman Jim' Burrows who saw him in action in the Western Desert all attested to Charlie's prowess as a soldier and skill as a leader of men — an officer who cared deeply about soldiers under his command. Burrows said he was 'the kindest man you'd meet in a long day's march'. Allan Shand, who had hired him as a shepherd and musterer straight out of Lincoln College before the war, chipped in with, 'He was the kindest man I think I've ever seen to his horses and dogs.'

This is not the impression that Simon Morris, the host of

Radio New Zealand's weekly film review show, *At the Movies*, got after seeing the show. 'Upham was very old but he must have still had something. I don't think I have ever seen so many scared people in my life.'

Simon was exaggerating wildly for effect, but host Bob Parker and the guests did treat Charlie with extraordinary deference and caution. It was obvious at the start that this reserved and modest man didn't really want to be there — the guests knew it and they didn't want to add to his misery, but towards the end of the show the sheer weight of old mates showering him with respect and affection eroded his misgivings and he almost looked as if he was enjoying himself, especially when Molly and his daughters joined him.

The show drew huge ratings and was much lauded. For many New Zealanders seeing Charlie on screen for that length of time as opposed to glimpses of him in news footage taken at some quasi-military event, or in old black-and-white archival newsreels, was like a panda giving birth in captivity — a rare and wondrous event. It was like sighting a mythical creature — a taniwha, unicorn or Loch Ness monster. The legends and folk stories weren't fairy tales — there really was a Captain Charles Upham VC & Bar. He did exist. Ken Sandford hadn't made it all up. He walked among us.

Charlie was fleetingly sighted on screens a decade later as an unwitting participant in a six-part TVNZ mockumentary, *In Search of the Great New Zealand Male*, hosted by comedienne and gifted actress Ginette McDonald, in her iconic Lyn of Tawa persona. Filming at a South Island bull sale, she happened across a short, frail, elderly gent. Bailing him up and thrusting a microphone at him, she hit him with her best adenoidal, shop-assistant drone and the old geezer played along happily:

'You look like an interesting old codger.'

'I *am* an interesting old codger.'

'Are you here for the bulls?'

'No. I'm here for the girls!'

It was Charlie, which a patrician local woman felt obliged to point out haughtily to Ginette when the interview was over. 'I hope you realise that you were talking to Charles Upham, VC and Bar, just now!' Ginette didn't realise this, but Michael McDonald, her brother, producer, director and brilliant co-writer, did, and he provided this vivid account of the encounter:

> It was at Amberley, at a bull sale. Still recovering from a recent stroke, he was slurring his words and stood about five foot three in his brogues. What remained of Charlie Upham VC & Bar were his eyes. Often remarked on by captors and comrades alike as his most arresting and terrifying feature, the eyes in that collapsed 86-year-old face were like two chips of sapphire: extraordinarily intense. Even though Charlie Upham at this stage was a little old man slurring his words, when he fixed those eyes on me, I could sense the danger and the menace still in them. I saw what that German commandant saw as Charlie lay enmeshed in barbed wire, casually lighting a cigarette and staring back at him; I saw what that swaggering Italian officer saw when the seriously wounded Charlie confronted him, demanded his dagger — and got it. Small, frail and old he might have been, but the dangerous man was still there within.

Well into his seventies, Charlie was still utterly fearless and a dangerous man was still within. Frank Wilding was horrified when Charlie told him about some of his encounters with hoons in SUVs doing wheelies and driving at reckless speeds along Conway Flat's deeply rutted metal road, showering precious shingle into the verge and worsening the corrugations. When Charlie heard them blatting past, he would make his way down to the dead-end road, plant himself in the middle with his dogs and shepherd's crook and wait for them to return, as he knew they had to. Careening back, they duly came, blaring their horns and flashing their lights when they saw Charlie blocking their path, forcing them to slew to screeching halts. Heated verbal abuse would be exchanged and Charlie would commonly whack off a wing mirror, and stove in a headlight with his crook for good measure. When they leapt from the car to deal to him, at his command his dogs would surround them snarling, snapping and slobbering inches from their crotches, at which point discretion got the better part of delinquency and they retreated meekly to their vehicles and drove off humbled.

§

Late in the afternoon my visit with Marty and Caroline came to an end and it was my turn to drive off — south to my twin sister's house on the hill overlooking Napier airport and the city. The visit had been a lot of fun and most useful. Bidding each other fond farewells, they said I had to come back and stay longer. I was at home in Wellington a few weeks later when Caroline rang to say that a thorough search of their house and barn had uncovered several suitcases and boxes of Charlie's stuff — photograph albums, newspaper clippings, scrapbooks, cards and letters and the like — that I could borrow if it was any use to me.

Rather than waste precious time on another long road trip, I jumped on a plane. This visit was even more agreeable than the first — we talked too much, drank too much, we visited the recently opened C Company Maori Battalion Memorial House museum, went to bookshops in search of a poetry book by Clive James and Ron Rosenbaum's *Explaining Hitler*, and queued in light rain for excellent coffee at a suburban pop-up café with white plastic seats and heavy tables hewn from fence posts.

I stayed in the guest bedroom downstairs and couldn't help

noticing that instead of locks on the toilet and bathroom doors, cute stuffed animals filled with sand or heavy lead shot were placed by the occupant against the door to alert any would-be intruder that the facility was already in use. Caroline explained that her dad couldn't abide being locked in, any place, anywhere, anytime. She added that at Conway Flat all the doors had been fitted with rubber stoppers, so no doors could be slammed by accident or design, the latter almost unavoidable with three supercharged teenage daughters in the house.

During one of their long conversations, Charlie had admitted to Sandford: 'I was lucky. I never suffered from nerves, but I will jump at a door slamming behind me. The noise of MG fire never used to bother me, but I jump at a car horn now.'

Being easily startled or frightened and always being on guard for danger are symptoms that fit PTSD. Charlie most probably suffered from some form of post-traumatic stress — and who could blame him?

Caroline dropped me off at the airport in a heavy downpour. I wasn't going to trust Charlie's precious Second World War photo albums and scrapbooks to a cargo hold and squeezed as much as I could into my overnight bag and thrust the rest into my R.M. Williams satchel, both bulging suspiciously and weighing a ton. The incoming flight from Wellington was late so I had plenty of time to listen to repeated admonitions from a crackly speaker above my head about strict restrictions on cabin luggage size and weight.

The deluge got worse. When we finally were called to board, I had to negotiate a gauntlet of suspicious Air New Zealand ground staff at the departure gate, smiling warmly while gravity was doing its utmost to dislocate my shoulders. I carried my bags as if they were as light as a feather, mere trifles possibly even filled with helium, all the time thinking guiltily that if our twin-engine turboprop ATR 72 failed to lift off the waterlogged runway and slammed into semi-submerged paddocks at the far end of the tarmac it would be entirely my fault.

No worries; we lifted into the air without incident and broke through rain clouds into bright sunlight. I was sitting, as I hoped, on the right-hand side of the aircraft again, and as I hoped the cloud parted and the Central Plateau loomed up in all its splendour, Lake Taupo reflecting late-afternoon sun like a burnished silver plate, the three volcanoes, the big blunt peanut slab of Ruapehu, the perfect cone of Tongariro and the prolapsed Ngauruhoe, glowing iridescent pink in the last rays of the setting sun. Then, as we droned further south, away out to the west on the distant Tasman shore a dark pyramid rimmed with a glowing edge appeared above the eiderdown of cloud — the not quite perfect cone of Mt Taranaki, looking just as Maori legend says: as if she has had a blazing row with her sisters in the middle of the island and is sulking on her own. I have seen this beautiful vista on several flights and it moves me every time. Looking at Mt Taranaki out on her own, solitary, noble and defiant, reminded me of Charlie, and a Maori proverb came into my mind:

'Mehemea ka tuohu ahau me maunga teitei.'

'If I should bow my head, let it be to a high mountain.'

If Charlie ever bowed his head, it would only have been to a lofty mountain.

I made two trips to see Frank and Jo Wilding as well, staying two nights on my second visit as I had with Caroline and Marty. We drank a lot of Jameson's whiskey around a roaring fire, talking late into the night about Charlie. It gave me confidence to pass Frank a slip of paper with a single sentence on it that I had written trying to sum up Charlie. It read: 'Charlie Upham believed that all human beings were equal and defended this principle with an all-consuming passion, fury and courage on a scale that did the very thing he hated most — it set him apart.'

Frank read it and said quietly, 'That's it, that's him. That's Charlie.' Frank passed it to Jo. 'Yes, that's him,' she smiled.

Epilogue

On my last day in Sawtell, New South Wales, Major Bob Wood decided to take me for a spin into lush, wooded countryside that Charlie would have loved to farm. Bob drove like a man who had lived a long full life with nothing left to prove or lose, and gunned along merrily, paying scant attention to centrelines, verges or stop signs. It was a relief to get to the pretty colonial hamlet of Bellingen where I shouted him lunch. We toasted Charlie in absentia.

Before heading back, Bob wanted to check out a second-hand bookstore. I bought a copy of *Wonders of the Universe* by theoretical physicist Professor Brian Cox and Andrew Cohen, based on the BBC television series of the same name. It was strangely comforting that final night reading about the infinite cosmos, dark matter and dark energy. It shrank the darkness that lurks in the human psyche down to its rightful size. The book reminded me of something that had stuck with me from Tom Stoppard's novel *Lord Malquist and Mr Moon*, which I read when I was floundering in vet school in 1968. The same year Apollo 8 astronaut William Anders took his famous *Earthrise* photo of our moist blue planet suspended in blackness above the dead, dry as a bone, silver-grey surface of the moon. I reached for the novel when I got back to Wellington and searched out the paragraph. Abridged, it reads as follows:

> Nothing is the history of the world viewed from a suitable distance . . . the human struggle takes place on the same scale as insect movements in grass and carnage in the streets is no more than the spider-sucked husk of a fly on a dusty windowsill.

Acknowledgements

I wish to acknowledge the assistance of: Anna Cottrell; Amanda Upham; Caroline Upham and Marty Reynolds; Jim Henderson; Robert and Beth Wynn-Williams; James Wynn-Williams; Bob Wood; Peter Bush; Chris Pugsley; Judge Jane Farish; Ken Longmore; Grant O'Fee; Stelios; Anne Marie; Fati; Amir; Roger Sandford; Dolores and Windsor and the National Army Museum Te Mata Toa, Waiouru; Colonel Karl Cummins; Roseanne Robertson; Liz Halliday; Brian O'Flaherty; Ron Palenski; Dan Hennah.

I am hugely indebted to Vanessa Tedesco, who in 1988 as a sixteen-year-old student at Linwood High School decided to make Dr Upham the topic of her local study project and did a truly remarkable job of piecing his life story together. She wrote to Charlie asking for information about his uncle, saying she was willing to come to Kaikoura to photograph or photocopy anything they had. She got a sweet letter back from Molly saying that Charlie was not well and she was replying on his behalf. She enclosed a newspaper article that might help and told Vanessa that she typed very well.

Books mentioned in the text and some sources I drew upon

Beevor, Antony, *The Second World War*, Weidenfeld & Nicolson, 2012

Booker, Michael, *Collecting Colditz and its Secrets: a unique pictorial record of life behind the walls*, Grub Street Publishing, 2005

Brickhill, Paul, *Reach for the Sky: the story of Douglas Bader*, Collins, 1954

Broad, John E., *Poor People — Poor Us*, H.H. Tombs, 1945

Cameron, Colin, *Breakout: Minqar Qaim, North Africa, 1942*, Willsonscott Publishing, 2006

Campbell-Begg, Dr Richard and Dr Peter Liddle, *For Five Shillings a Day: Personal Histories of World War II*, HarperCollins, 2000

Chancellor, Henry, *Colditz: the definitive story*, Hodder & Stoughton, 2001

Cleland, John, *Fanny Hill, or Memoirs of a Woman of Pleasure*, first published 1749

Davin, Dan, *Official History of New Zealand in the Second World War, Crete*, War History Branch, Department of Internal Affairs, New Zealand, 1953

de la Billière, Sir Peter, *Supreme Courage: heroic stories from 150 years of the Victoria Cross*, Little, Brown, 2004

Deakin, F.W., *The Brutal Friendship: Mussolini, Hitler and the fall of Italian Fascism*, Harper and Row, 1962

Eggers, Reinhold, *Colditz: the German story*, W.W. Norton, 1961

Elworthy, Jack, *Greece Crete Stalag Dachau: a New Zealand soldier's encounters with Hitler's army*, Awa Press, 2014

Gardiner, Noel, *Freyberg's Circus*, Ray Richards/William Collins, 1981

Harper, Glyn, and Colin Richardson, *In the Face of the Enemy: the complete history of the Victoria Cross and New Zealand*, HarperCollins, 2006

Henderson, Jim, *Gunner Inglorious*, H.H. Tombs, 1945

Jones, Norm, *Jonesy*, Craig Printing, 1981

Kingsbury, Benjamin, *The Dark Island: leprosy in New Zealand and the Quail Island colony*, Bridget Williams Books, 2019

Kippenberger, Major-General Sir Howard Karl, *Infantry Brigadier*, Oxford University Press, 1961

Levi, Primo, *If This is a Man*, first published 1947

Marshall, Bruce, *The White Rabbit*, Evans Brothers, 1952

Mayer, S.L. (editor), *The Best of Signal: Hitler's wartime picture magazine*, Hamlyn, 1984

Monteath, Peter, *Battle on 42nd Street: war in Crete and the Anzacs' bloody last stand*, NewSouth Books, 2019

Moorehead, Alan, *African Trilogy*, Hamish Hamilton & Harper, 1945

Mulgan, John, *Report on Experience*, Oxford University Press, 1947

Pringle, D.J.C. and W.A. Glue, *20 Battalion and Armoured Regiment*, Historical Publications Branch, Wellington, 1957

Reid, Major P.R., *Colditz: the full story*, Macmillan, 1984

Riddell, Oliver, *Behind the Hedge: 100 years at Waihi Preparatory School*, Henry Elworthy, 2007

Robertson, Bruce, *For the Duration: 2NZEF officer Bruce Robertson on active duty and 'in the bag'*, Ngaio Press, 2010

Ronson, Jon, *The Psychopath Test: a journey through the madness industry*, Riverhead, 2011

Rosenbaum, Ron, *Explaining Hitler: the search for the origins of his evil*, Random House, 1998

Sandford, Kenneth, *Mark of the Lion*, Hutchinson, 1962

Speer, Albert, *Inside the Third Reich*, Orion Books, 1970, first published 1969

Stoppard, Tom, *Lord Malquist and Mr Moon*, Anthony Blond, 1966

Tedesco, Vanessa, Linwood High School, Local Study Project, 1988

Vonnegut, Kurt, *Slaughterhouse-Five, or The Children's Crusade: a duty-dance with death*, Delacorte, 1969

Wood, Lt. J.E.R. (ed.), *Detour: the story of Oflag IVC*, Falcon Press, 1946

Wright, Matthew, *Freyberg's War: the man, the legend and reality*, Penguin, 2005

Wynn-Williams, R.B., 'Turning Point 42', *New Zealand Memories*, issue 124, February/March 2017